CAMBRIDGE IBERIAN AND
LATIN AMERICAN STUDIES

GENERAL EDITOR:

P. E. RUSSELL, F.B.A.

The limits of illusion:
a critical study of Calderón

The limits of illusion:
a critical study of
Calderón

ANTHONY J. CASCARDI

ASSISTANT PROFESSOR OF SPANISH AND COMPARATIVE LITERATURE
UNIVERSITY OF CALIFORNIA, BERKELEY

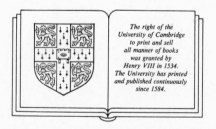

The right of the
University of Cambridge
to print and sell
all manner of books
was granted by
Henry VIII in 1534.
The University has printed
and published continuously
since 1584.

CAMBRIDGE UNIVERSITY PRESS

CAMBRIDGE

LONDON   NEW YORK   NEW ROCHELLE

MELBOURNE   SYDNEY

Published by the Press Syndicate of the University of Cambridge
The Pitt Building, Trumpington Street, Cambridge CB2 1RP
32 East 57th Street, New York, NY 10022, USA
296 Beaconsfield Parade, Middle Park, Melbourne 3206, Australia

© Cambridge University Press 1984

First published 1984

Printed in Great Britain at the University Press, Cambridge

Library of Congress catalogue card number: 83-27305

British Library Cataloguing in Publication Data
Cascardi, Anthony J.
The limits of illusion.—(Cambridge Iberian and
Latin American studies)
1. Calderón de la Barca, Pedro – Criticism
and interpretation
I. Title
862′.3 PQ6312
ISBN 0 521 26281 X

For Trish

Contents

Preface

This book is a critical study of Calderón. My purpose is to see across a broad spectrum of his work a variety of perspectives on the use and the limits of illusion; each chapter takes up one or another reflex of this formal and thematic concern. Because this is a critical study, I have tried throughout to judge Calderón's theatre according to criteria consistent with the premises implicit in it. Any reader is likely to be struck by Calderón's preoccupation with illusion, but that in and of itself says little: it does not, for instance, tell us how we might distinguish Calderón from Shakespeare, Racine, or Corneille, other dramatists whom I will discuss; nor does it point up the contrast between Calderón and Cervantes, who found the play of illusion to be so central to the making of *Don Quixote*. In seeking the distinctive features of Calderón's engagement with the problems of illusion, I have found it essential to take the theatrical aspect of his work into account. In ways I shall explain, this representational feature of his work is of crucial importance in determining the place of illusion in it.

Seen from one angle, Calderón's entire production is his attempt, as a Christian dramatist, to deal with the fact that he must professionally embrace illusion, which morally he would abjure. Thus there is a tension between theatrical form and the themes of illusion, but we can judge his work on how deeply this tension is felt, on how insightful Calderón's poetic perceptions of it are, and on how successfully it is brought to the stage. The theatre, as a form of representation, is a form of illusion, but Calderón finds that this is no reason to reject it. Indeed, as *La vida es sueño* seems to say paradigmatically, some dose of illusion is necessary. The path to personal transcendence, to responsible action, to political prudence, requires passing through, not around, illusion. Theatre thus may serve ethically justifiable ends. As in the allegorical *auto sacramental*, *El gran teatro del mundo*, this thematic concern is given voice through the

ix

guiding conceit of the *theatrum mundi*: the world as a theatre, life as a play. In both *El gran teatro del mundo* and *La vida es sueño* we have evidence of Calderón's ability to think theatrically, to formulate the paradox of illusion in a way that is dependent on the idea of a theatre itself.

As a model for these formal and thematic concerns, and as a canonic statement of the cultural and epistemological functions of theatre, I take Luis Vives' *Fable About Man*, the *Fabula de homine*. Vives' text suggests a definition of theatre as a form of self-imagination (and of self-critique) and raises questions which are directly pertinent to Calderón's work: how can we use the theatre to form an image of ourselves, and thereby to know ourselves, if the process of image-making depends on the making of illusion? How can we know how to act, what course of judgment to follow, if we can only form self-reflective images of ourselves? In Calderón, the moral and social implications of these questions are given a full and nuanced range of treatments. His work is of importance precisely at the juncture where we accept the skeptic's threats that we cannot know for certain who we are or that the world exists at all. Life may be a dream – Segismundo says as much – but, as with the theatre itself, this is no reason to reject it. Instead, we must find ways to incorporate this skeptical position into a moral life-plan. Calderón is aware that the theatre, in its paradoxical place between reality and illusion, has enormous potential for this absorption of skepticism.

Thus one concerted thrust of Calderón's work is to explore the options available to us given the fact that the skeptic may well be right. Philosophically, there are close affinities between Calderón's concerns and those of his contemporary, Descartes, and I shall explore the parallel more fully in my discussion of *La vida es sueño*. In both there is a push to counter the skeptic's threats. But whereas Descartes looks to demarcate the limits of certainty and to establish the foundations of knowledge, Calderón looks to absorb skepticism by the power of Christian ethics. Temperamentally, of course, there are vast differences between Calderón and Descartes as well. Perhaps surprisingly, the worn Scholasticism which Calderón inherited places him in relationship to Spinoza. As I shall discuss, there are problems crucial to Calderón's work – the nature of form, the limitations of space, the ethical ramifications of self-imagining – which find their philosophical complements in Spinoza. Their conclusions are of course vastly different, but more important is Calderón's continual adjustment of his concerns within the parameters set by the idea of a theatre.

The problem of illusion and its limits in Calderón is thus formal and ●
thematic. The formal concern is always present, because Calderón is always conscious of the representational nature of his work. It shows up in vastly different ways, however: in "encyclopedic" works like *El gran teatro del mundo* and *La vida es sueño*, in the social comedies like *La dama duende*, and in the pageant plays like *Eco y Narciso* and *Hado y divisa de Leonido y Marfisa*. And, thematically, "illusion" runs through the relationships of courtly-type love and social convention (*El secreto a voces*), to role-playing (*La dama duende*, *El médico de su honra*), political authority (*En la vida todo es verdad y todo mentira*), the passions (e.g. jealousy in *El mayor monstruo del mundo*), and the powers of the mind, as in *La estatua de Prometeo*. In some of Calderón's most interesting works, there are overt recognitions of the contiguities between theatrical form and the thematics of illusion. In *El mágico prodigioso* and *El mayor monstruo del mundo*, for instance, religious transcendence and jealousy, respectively, relate directly to the theatre as a form of tangible (i.e. spatial and visible) representation. In *Eco y Narciso*, the temptingly seductive illusions of the natural world are themselves the dramatist's work, and this makes for a remarkable poignancy in Calderón's critique of illusion there.

For the most part, these conjunctions of form and theme produce a healthy means of social self-imagining and critique, one which may account for the viability of the *comedia* as a genre over roughly a century, from 1580 until 1681. But in Calderón's final play for the secular stage (*Hado y divisa de Leonido y Marfisa*, the last play I shall discuss) this balance is destroyed. The play is representative of an entire body of work Calderón wrote in his final years, most of which is impressive in theatrical effect but formulaic in structure. The play shows Calderón's technical mastery, his own capacity for illusion, turned to wholly uncritical ends. This is a hard judgment but not, I think, unfair. Moreover it illuminates certain factors which may have contributed to the demise of the *comedia* following the death of Calderón in 1681. Historically, the *comedia* was fashioned to shore up those collective social values which, after 1580 or so, were felt to be seriously in danger; as I shall explain in my discussion of the "illusions of history" below, those values were the ones we would associate with the caste bias of Spanish axiology. The threats came in a variety of different forms, some from within (e.g. the reduction of the castes with the decreed expulsion of the *moriscos* and, earlier, the mandatory conversion of the Jews), others from without (e.g. the increasing capitalistic pressures which were felt as a result of involvement in international trade after the discovery of America). From Calderón's appointment as court dramatist, and the representation of his plays at the new Palace of the Buen Retiro from the 1630s onward, his *comedias* came to express not only the collective values of the Spanish people, but those values as filtered through the royal optic. Politically, this meant that Calderón was expected to congratulate monarchs (Philip IV, Charles II) whom it would be kind to describe as ineffectual. We know that the *comedia* usually conforms to the plot-structure of romance (yet another possible point of comparison with Cervantes' work), and that romance tends strongly toward the positive identification of collective values, but in the case of Calderón's later plays the persistence of romance in the form of the adventure plot weighs heavily against the dramatist's ability to form critical judgments of the society within which his work is inscribed.

In evaluating Calderón's accomplishments, my concern has been to acknowledge the fact that the *comedia* is an eminently public genre, and that its values are highly culture-specific; this has meant that comparison with the work of Lope de Vega and Tirso de Molina, the two dramatists without whom Calderón's *comedias* would have been vastly different, has an important place in my discussions. Still, this has left room for contrastive treatment of the work of the other great European dramatists of the sixteenth and seventeenth centuries: Shakespeare and Marlowe in England, Racine and Corneille in France. These comparative investigations will, I hope, provide the broad base necessary for my claim that Calderón's finest work shows an unmatched awareness of the possibilities offered by theatre for self-criticism and the absorption of illusion.

Since I hope that my concerns with theatrical form and the limits of illusion will prove to be of interest to a readership beyond professional Calderonistas and students of Spanish Golden Age theatre, I have provided translations of all foreign-language passages quoted in the text. Unless noted otherwise, these translations are my own. In them, I try to negotiate the difficult course between idiomatic English and faithfulness to the (usually Spanish verse) originals. If they provide access to this subject for readers who have no Spanish, or who wish to check their comprehension, they will have served their purpose well.

Berkeley, California
1983

Acknowledgments

Writing this book has placed me in debt to numerous individuals and institutions, and it is a pleasure to record my gratitude here. Roughly half of the material here published was submitted, in a different form, at Harvard University, as part of a doctoral dissertation entitled "The Forms of a Theatre." I am particularly grateful to Stephen Gilman, who directed the dissertation, for his unstinting help during the period of its preparation, and to Claudio Guillén, who acted as second reader, for his generous comments on the text. Both were supportive of my decision to leave the dissertation behind and to write the present book. Juan Marichal read a portion of the manuscript, and offered recommendations that have been incorporated into Chapter 9 ("The Illusions of History"). Jack H. Parker read the dissertation, and I am grateful to him and to the University of Toronto for an invitation to participate in the symposium celebrating the Calderón tricentenary in 1981. Chapter 1 was also read during the tricentennial year, as part of the University of San Diego symposium on "Calderón y el Siglo de Oro." I am grateful for the cordial reception given by friends and colleagues there. The final version of the manuscript was read by John E. Keller, who offered encouragement and advice. Chapter 6, *El médico de su honra,* appears here by kind permission of the *Kentucky Romance Quarterly.* The translations from the French have benefited by the expert advice of Deborah Lesko and Cynthia Liebow.

I am especially grateful to the anonymous consultant chosen by the Cambridge University Press for having read the manuscript with diligence, care, and enthusiasm, and for numerous suggestions which have been incorporated into the text. I am indebted to Ms Sarah Stanton, my editor at Cambridge, for her sustaining interest in this project, and to Professor Peter Russell of Oxford, who read the typescript and who invited its inclusion among the Cambridge Iberian and Latin American Studies.

I have benefited at various stages of my work from grants awarded by the Committee on Research of the University of California, Berkeley, from a Faculty Mentor Grant kindly endorsed by Thomas G. Rosenmeyer, and from the assistance of colleagues in the Department of Spanish and Portuguese and the Department of Comparative Literature.

Finally, I must record debts which are too large to be repaid. My parents provided the encouragement and support which made possible not just this book but the studies which preceded it as well. They never lost faith that my efforts would yield a book. My wife Trish, to whom it is dedicated, read each chapter and listened to the argument of the whole on more occasions than I am sure she would care to recall, always without complaint, and she offered numerous suggestions which have substantially improved the text.

To all, my heartfelt thanks.

Note on texts and notes

The notes are principally bibliographical in nature, and give complete references for material referred to in the text. No separate arguments are conducted there. For a full bibliography of the secondary literature on Calderón, readers may consult Jack H. Parker and Arthur M. Fox, *Calderón de la Barca Studies 1951–69* (Toronto: University of Toronto Press, 1971), which while limited in scope is useful as a critical bibliography, and the annual bibliographies published in preceding and subsequent years in the *Bulletin of the Comediantes*.

At present, no satisfactory text of Calderón's complete work exists. Following the practice of most Calderonistas, I cite from the three-volume *Obras completas* (Madrid: Aguilar, 1960–7, and later reprints). References have been checked against the nineteen-volume facsimile of first editions (Farnborough, Hants: Gregg International Publishers Ltd, in association with Tamesis Books, London, 1973), edited by D. W. Cruickshank and J. E. Varey, and against modern scholarly editions where these exist.

I cite Shakespeare from the text of the Cambridge edition, edited by William Aldis Wright (Garden City: Doubleday & Company, 1936). Quotations from the works of Marlowe are taken from *The Plays of Christopher Marlowe*, edited by Leo Kirschbaum (Cleveland: World Publishing Company; New York: Meridian Books, 1962). All other references are given in the notes.

Introduction

Shortly after he met Erasmus in Louvain in 1518, Juan Luis Vives wrote the *Fabula de homine*.[1] Since it is one of the pivotal Humanist texts for the problems of form and theme that I shall be discussing in Calderón, I want to begin by recounting it. What I call the theatrical "idea" in connection with Calderón's *La vida es sueño*, as well as most of what I have to say about the importance of theatrical form in Calderón's development of the thematics of illusion, has immediate roots in the Humanist notion, exemplified in Vives' fable, that all the forms of human self-imagining bear directly and critically on the substance of that self-image. Theatre for Calderón, I shall be arguing, serves this function of self-imagination and critique.

At Juno's birthday feast, the goddess asked Jupiter, her brother and husband, to arrange some entertainment. At Jupiter's command, an amphitheatre appeared – stage and galleries. The divine spectators were seated in the uppermost gallery, in the skies; the earth was placed in the middle, as a platform for the actors. Jupiter was the director of the troupe; they knew tragedies, comedies, satires, farces, and mimes. Juno was greatly pleased. She walked among the gods and asked them which of the actors they considered the finest of the group. In the opinion of prominent critics, man was deemed worthy of highest praise.

Looking carefully at man, the gods who were seated near Jupiter could see some similarities between him and his master. In his wisdom, his prudence, his memory, in many of his talents, man seemed god-like. Peering through his mask, man the actor seemed to partake of Jupiter's immortality. He was gifted with the capacity to transform himself. He could change his costume and his mask. He appeared disguised now as plant, now as animal – lion, wolf, boar, cunning fox, sow, hare, envious dog, ass. He withdrew behind the curtain and, after a brief time, once again appeared as *man*. He went

1

about the cities of the world with his fellow men. He partook of
political and social life. He had authority over others, and was himself
obedient.

Man's metamorphoses pleased the gods. They watched in expectation of further transformations. Finally, man was changed into one
of their own race. A long, loud round of applause followed. The gods
begged Juno to allow man into the gallery, to sit with the onlooking
gods. Peering several times at Jupiter's stall and glancing at the stage,
the gods could barely distinguish Jupiter from his creature. Some
argued that this was not man at all on stage, but a sly and cunning
Jupiter himself.

The gods prevailed upon Jupiter to allow man to be seated among
them, to have him take off his mask and cease to be an actor. Jupiter
complied. He recalled man from the stage. Mercury proclaimed his
glory and saw to it that he was seated in a place of honor among the
gods. There was a great silence as man took his place.

Mercury carried the costumes and mask into the gallery. The gods
inspected them with interest. The head was proud and intensely
thoughtful. The ears were bound with sinuous cartilage; they did not
droop with soft skin nor were they rigid with bone. They were able to
receive sound from all directions. They acted as filters, keeping dust
and gnats from entering the head. There were two eyes, set high in
order to observe all things; they were protected by lashes and eyelids
to guard against tiny insects, dust, bits of straw. The eyes were the
noblest part of the mask; they were the guides of the soul. The costume
was remarkable in its own way. It was divided into legs and arms,
which were long and ended in fingers. Together, the mask and
costume were the most useful garb that could be imagined for man.

The gods praised him greatly. They deemed it unworthy of him to
appear on a stage as an actor and participate in the disreputable
business of the theatre. They saw that his mind was fertile, full of
inventions, that it brought forth towns and houses, that it conceived
useful applications of stone and metal, that it gave names to things.
With language, through writing, man established doctrines, re-
ligions, the worship of gods, the cult of Jupiter himself.

Seeing themselves and Jupiter so well portrayed in man, the gods
looked at the creature as if at a reflection in a mirror. They were
curious to know how he was able to act so many different parts and
assume so many different guises. They hailed man's abilities, drinking
ambrosia and nectar in celebration. The gods drew near man and

tugged at his cloak. They bade him sit down with them. At Jupiter's signal, Mercury led man to the orchestra, to sit among the first rank of gods, to watch with them the games that would follow. Then, at Juno's request, Apollo dimmed the lights and man reclined at table with the gods. He put on his mask and enjoyed a sumptuous feast.

The roots of Vives' fable reach deep. Tracing backward, they touch seminal sacred and secular texts: Genesis, the *Republic*, the *Symposium*. Cicero voiced his praise of man in passages of *De legibus* (I, 8–9) and in *De natura deorum* (II, 60–1). Pico della Mirandola's *De hominis dignitate* and Giannozzo Manetti's praise of human dignity are immediate antecedents. The theatrical simile is anticipated in the writings of the Neo-Platonists (e.g. in Plotinus, *Ennead*, III, 2) and in the Stoics, Marcus Aurelius and Epictetus; the metaphor of human life as a fable ("quomodo fabula sic vita") is a topic of Seneca's *Epistles* (75–6). As a meditation on the problem of self-imagining, Vives' fable fits into the mainstream of Renaissance essays on human knowledge, from Cusa's *De docta ignorantia* to Petrarch's *De sui ipsius et multorum ignorantia*. Ficino and Pomponazzi (especially in *De immortalitate animae*) stand in the immediate background of Vives' text. If the *Fabula de homine* is an ingenious and engaging fable, still it could be said that Vives says nothing particularly new in it. Partly for this reason it is good to keep the *Fabula de homine* in mind when reading Calderón; plays like *La vida es sueño* and *autos* like *El gran teatro del mundo*, which I shall discuss, have also been seen as formulaic in philosophy and as lamentably traditional in thought. But this is because the theatrical form in which that thought is given has largely been ignored. The *Fabula de homine* will stand as a reminder of the "theatrical idea," which assumes even greater importance in Calderón.

Working along these lines, Ernesto Grassi in a recent book has redeemed Vives from any possible charge of complacent conventionality. The *Fabula de homine* can now be seen as one of the most radically original works of the entire Humanist movement, indeed of the Renaissance as a whole. The *Fabula de homine* offers a complete "reversal of the medieval interpretation of metaphysics and a renunciation of the primacy of all speculation about nature, a disowning of every form of a priori or formal thinking."[2] The claim is large. What Vives does is to offer a definition of man in which the very form of the definition becomes part of the definition itself. The piece is, first of all, a fable (literally, an "idea"), such as was supposed to

offer truth under the guise of fiction. Vives makes the fictional form
essential to its philosophical content. He defines man and human
culture in terms of each other, just as man in the fable gives evidence
of himself by the products of his mind. In this double definition, the
theatrical metaphor is more than an embellishment, it is part of the
very substance of Vives' vision of man. Theatre and thought are
bound together because the true object of Vives' meditation is man's
own nature as a reflective animal.

In his "reversal" of medieval metaphysics Vives rejects taking the
objects of contemplation as first principles – unchanging, static, or
eternal. He takes the changing, thinking mind as the object of
thought. This attempt at self-knowledge is possible only to the extent
that the subject–object distinction is not rigid. Whereas Hegel would
later solve this problem by the invention of his dialectic, Vives solved
it by erasing the absolute polarity between viewers and viewed,
containing both terms within a single space. At first, man and gods
are apart. But that separation is gradually blurred. As man ascends to
the gallery, and as the gods see themselves in him, a continuity
emerges between spectators and actors, as between gallery and stage.
No one really knows if man is made in the image of the gods or if the
gods are fashioned in man's image.

The fable is "about man," but it is driven by a question. Vives asks:
Who is man? He knows that this question entails finding out how man
can know himself. He sees that the human mind cannot give direct
evidence of itself. Man cannot know himself immediately. He is
defined as a series of skins, a costume, a mask. Never does Vives say
what the human essence is. He refuses to define man in terms of the
philosopher's *quid*, or implies that when the human mind asks this
question of itself, no satisfactory answer can be found. Instead, he
turns to the question of *use*. He defines human nature through the
products of human culture – cities and towns, human language and
religion, the cult of Jupiter, indeed the whole attempt at human self-
imagining of which his fable is a part. Through the things of human
making, through things fashioned in his image – not directly – man
comes to self-knowledge. Because Vives' aversion to the question of
essences is balanced by a will to interpret nature itself in terms of use,
rational uncertainty, fuel for skeptical thought, is overruled by the
claims of custom and law, domains of the statesman and politician. In
La vida es sueño, Calderón's Segismundo faces the possibility that life is
a dream, the world an illusion; but he succeeds in defining himself in

terms of the social relationships that he orders in his well-made state.

The theatre, like the polis which it mirrors, becomes the principal locus for human self-definition. If man can come to no knowledge of his essence in the images he makes of himself, the image-maker must accept the responsibility of fashioning ethically and socially useful, morally sound products, works good for the improvement of civic life. The burden which falls upon the dramatist as a primary exponent of human culture is exceedingly large. But this is the social standard which Calderón implicitly accepts for himself; it is also his strongest defense against charges of wanton promulgation of illusory forms. His strength as an artist lies in his ability to wage a constant war against the unrestrained use of illusion.

Calderón's best characters all have a large capacity for self-imagining and reflection. Not all have the success of Segismundo. Angela of *La dama duende* can fashion roles; Basilio of *La vida es sueño* can dramatize those around him. They mobilize a theatrical space according to their respective needs. But the primary goal of Calderón's characters is not to find out *who* they are, for most of them find that their self-definition is contextually, situationally, or socially formed. The moral consequences of social relationships, understood theatrically through dramatization and role-playing, the central metaphors of his work, are part of Calderón's broader awareness that man himself is defined in terms of these relationships.

One of Calderón's "versions" of Vives' fable – there are several, and none follows it exactly – is the *auto sacramental El gran teatro del mundo*. Written by 1635, and probably in 1633, the play is roughly contemporaneous with *La vida es sueño*.[3] In thought, plot, and style, it is a fair sample of one large segment of his work: the abstract universality of the theme, the intellectual order and carefully measured order of the poetry and, of course, the theatrical conceit, are typical also of plays like *La vida es sueño* and *En la vida todo es verdad y todo mentira*. Calderón uses the topos of the world as a theatre and life as a play, which by the mid-sixteenth century was common coin. Yet the conceit is carried out with remarkable authority and confidence of design. The poetry itself is an admirable weld of the precision and exuberance such as is characteristic of the finest style of the Baroque.

The "argumento" of the *auto* is familiar and quickly summarized: the stage director, *Mundo* (World), distributes roles and costumes to various characters; these are human types, actors in the "Great

World Theatre" – Rich Man, Peasant, King, Beauty, etc. Each
character is charged with playing his or her role well. The role is a gift,
an endowment which must be used to its full potential. Thus the
costumes and roles disguise a shared dignity and deeper common
worth. Doctrinally, Calderón teaches the same lesson of responsibility
as the Biblical parable of the talents, although in Calderón the
individual moral has a necessary adjunct in the social dimension. Yet
what is most interesting, and to my mind particularly significant,
about the arrangement of roles in this *auto* is that the impresario of the
Great World Theatre, the *Autor* who is responsible for the play-
within-the-play, is not included in it. The *Autor*, who is of course also
the Creator, authorizes the characters' roles and anchors the
perspective from which they will be judged, yet he stands apart from
the characters as they act in the great "theatre of the world." This
may be meant to imply that the characters have the requisite freedom
to choose their actions, even though their roles are assigned. But
beyond this the *Autor* provides a meaningful encasement for the
Great World Theatre; without this, the vision of the world as a play-
within-a-play might well be suggestive of the radical instability of self-
embedding forms such as we see in Gnostic fables. Calderón's
conception of the world as a theatre always implies the existence of
some greater level which comprehends the representation but which
is not itself comprehended by it. The function of the play-within-the-
play as a locus for the realization of human value hinges on this
dependence on the englobing figure of the *Autor*: Calderón imagines a
world which, like a theatre, is not sufficient unto itself and for which
value rests on a higher plane.

There is no reason, however, to restrict the interpretation of this
theatrical conceit to the ostensibly moral dimension of human
actions, to the exclusion of the aesthetic sphere. On the contrary:
there are reasons in this *auto* and other plays to believe that Calderón
would accept judgments of *actual* theatre, and indeed of all aesthetic
objects, along the lines sketched above. The allegorical *Hermosura*
(Beauty) summarizes the conventional, mistaken assumption about
the self-sufficient status and function of the aesthetic object:

> Yo, para esto, Hermosura:
> a ver y ser vista voy.   (III, 212a)[4]

(My role is Beauty: I go to see and to be seen.)

She understands that the beautiful object must be persuasively attractive, but she forgets that she must also lead *away* from herself. She takes herself as autonomous and represents the temptation to mistake the theatrical space for the whole space, to forget the one greater term which encases the representation, and to which the dramatist must be held responsible.

Because the Creator stands apart from the play-within-the-play in Calderón's *auto*, he is easily identified with the dramatist himself. Calderón knows that the artist is in danger of overlooking the limits of the theatre, and he is on constant guard against such abandon; this concern figures prominently in Calderón's pastoral play, *Eco y Narciso*, with its characteristic emphasis on the natural world, as we shall later see. Calderón's constant recognition of the limits of theatrical representation, and of the separation of poet–maker and Creator, would have helped him to avoid the dangerous Spinozistic equation, "Deus sive natura" (roughly, "God equals nature"), inherent in the conflation of the divine realm and the space of human activity. Kenneth Burke derived a tellingly theatrical description of God from Spinoza's formula, a description which would seem to put Spinoza close to Calderón; Spinoza, he said, takes God "as the kind of scene in which . . . an action would be possible; namely, a scene allowing for human freedom."[5] In Calderón's *auto*, the theatrical space of the World Theatre is a place in which the characters try the limits of their freedom, but Calderón avoids the Spinozistic equation which makes it impossible to say whether God is a concept of any wider purview than the space in which human freedom is enacted. Traditionally, and in Calderón, God is of broader bounds than nature; but Spinoza claims they are of identical reach, thus making it impossible to tell whether he deifies nature or whether he naturalizes God. In the first definition in the *Ethics* – that God is self-caused (*causa sui*) – Spinoza resolves the potential antinomies between freedom and necessity, and between action and passion, within an Absolute Space; but this is a directionless space, with no higher plane in which to establish and value the qualities which Calderón so highly esteems: virtuous action, prudent judgment, and forbearance in suffering. The purely "intellectual love of God," to which the human mind is prone, and which Spinozism exaggerates, is fundamentally equivocal and unsatisfactory for Calderón, because in a space where God and Nature are coterminous it is virtually impossible to construct a point of view capable of *transcending* man's position in the play-within-the-play.

In Spinoza's conception, the human vision of the world will change with each man according to his body:

Those who have more frequently looked with admiration upon the stature of men, by the name man will understand an animal of erect stature, while those who have been in the habit of fixing their thoughts on something else, will form another image of man, describing man, for instance, as an animal capable of laughter, a featherless bird, a rational animal, and so on, each person forming universal images of things according to the temperaments of his own body.[6]

In contrast to Vives, where the "perspectivist" idea is expressed, as in Calderón, through the metaphor of the world as a theatre like the mind, Spinoza's perspectivism is guided by the "temperaments" of the human body; in this he is not unlike some of the eighteenth-century rationalists (e.g. Locke), who described the workings of the mind in terms of the physics of ideas. As I shall discuss in connection with Calderón's Herod and Hercules plays (*El mayor monstruo del mundo* and *Los tres mayores prodigios*), Calderón always seeks to overcome the determinism of physical substance, even if he discovers that this is not entirely possible. In a play like *La vida es sueño*, which I will consider at greater length in the following section, something like a Spinozistic perspectivism can be embraced, man and the world can be defined situationally, but only if these relationships are not limited to physical nature; indeed, an important part of Segismundo's achievement consists in learning to overcome his passions (what he calls his "fiera condición," his "beastly nature"). But the suppression of the natural passions also means that some of Calderón's characters will misunderstand the metaphor of intellectual perspective and err in the opposite direction, as is the case with Prometheus of *La estatua de Prometeo* and Gutierre, the surgeon of *El médico de su honra*, who practices his profession as a "science" and who keeps himself at a cool distance from the terrible bloodletting of his wife. Thus Calderón can accept what Kenneth Burke, writing on Spinoza, called the "paradox of substance," but only if this paradoxical definition of substance in terms of relationships is extended to include an element of self-conscious awareness. Burke described the "situational" conception of (human) nature which I have been discussing in Vives and Calderón as a "dramatistic" notion, whereby "a character cannot 'be himself' unless many others among the dramatis personae contribute to this end, so that the very essence of a character's nature is in large measure defined, or determined, by the other characters who assist or oppose him.'"[7] Clearly, this could be said of almost any character in any play, but Burke is not describing a play, or is only incidentally doing so; he is describing a certain conception of nature in terms of a play, and my claim for Calderón is that his own theatrical or "dramatistic" conception is only successfully embodied in self-conscious individuals. What this means in terms of theatrical representation and the dramatist's use of illusion, however, is that the theatrical illusion will have to be *both* dispelled and embraced. I shall be arguing that Calderón's most successful plays owe their virtues, in large measure, to an effective theatrical handling of this delicate thematic paradox.

Calderón's use of perspective is more humanistic than what we find in either Spinoza or Vives. But this has certain paradoxical implications for his own aesthetics. Calderón shows us the use of theatrical space as a locus for cementing social relationships because theatrical space is bounded and limited. It is a space which allows man to define himself in terms of the restrictions which others place on his freedom of action. Calderón does not, like Spinoza, circumscribe God within nature. He posits a more ultimate, transcendent anchor of the human relationships he sets in motion. If his stage mirrors the mind as an arena of action, it always suggests some larger space, some greater limiting – but not itself limited – circumference. Thus his theatre will efface itself, despite the stylistic and technical exuberance that goes into its making; and Calderón will accept the painful proposition that the aesthetic object is insufficient in itself. He will say, with Renaissance thinkers like Giordano Bruno, that beauty itself is, and must necessarily be, elusive:

Whatever species is represented to the intellect and comprehended by the will, the intellect concludes there is another species above it, a greater and still greater one, and consequently it is always impelled toward new motion and abstraction in a certain fashion. For it ever realizes that everything it possesses is a limited thing which for that reason cannot be sufficient in itself, good in itself, or beautiful in itself, because the limited thing is not the universe and is not the absolute entity, but is contracted to this nature, this species or this form represented to the intellect and presented to the soul. As a result, from that beautiful [*sic*] which is comprehended, and therefore limited, and consequently beautiful by participation, the intellect progresses toward that which is truly beautiful without limit or circumspection whatsoever.[8]

The beautiful always stands just *outside* a particular space. Unlike the allegorical Beauty in Calderón's *auto*, who thinks herself self-sufficient, who takes herself as autonomous, the ideally beautiful object must lead away from itself, like Rosaura of *La vida es sueño*, emblematic of beauty in the sublunary world.

Given these restrictions, there is a pronounced vein of self-constraint in Calderón's work. He recognizes the need to limit illusion because he understands that the forms of representation are not ultimate and must not be taken as such. Yet as a dramatist Calderón was by trade a maker of illusory worlds, representational spaces, many of them impressively brilliant in stylistic and technical effect. The result is a wide-ranging tension between form and theme in his work. As the following chapters will explore in greater detail, "illusion" in Calderón's work nearly always involves, as a formal principle, the idea of a theatre; but thematically the matter reaches to questions of social responsibility and role, of authority, of politics, and of collective concerns which are mirrored publicly. The tension between form and theme is not always resolved in favor of "reality" at the expense of "illusion"; the choices are not that simple. Some of Calderón's characters are able to relinquish their interest in illusion and to mature by doing so, but for others there are heavy costs involved. In some of his most interesting plays, the route to responsible action in the world in fact passes through illusion and requires its embrace.

I

La vida es sueño: Calderón's idea of a theatre

For the Spanish *comedia* as a genre, *La vida es sueño* represents the most accomplished example of what Francis Fergusson once called the "idea of a theatre," the sustained attempt at self-imagining through representation.[1] Writing in 1949, when literary Modernism was still in force, it may have seemed that the theatrical "idea" was no longer viable. In 1933 Antonin Artaud had written that "An idea of the theatre has been lost. And as long as the theatre limits itself to showing us intimate scenes from the lives of a few puppets, transforming the public into Peeping Toms, it is no wonder the elite abandon it and the great public looks to the movies, the music hall or the circus for violent satisfactions, whose intentions do not deceive them."[2] Whereas *La vida es sueño*, like *Hamlet*, is conscious of itself as a form of theatrical *representation*, dramatists in recent times have turned toward more spectacular forms of theatre, perhaps in order to compete with music-hall comedies, circus spectacles and the movies (as we shall see, Calderón's later plays have a similarly spectacular bent). Brecht for instance tried heedlessly to overturn the entire Aristotelian tradition in drama, replacing mimesis with "epic theatre" and the ''street scene." Beckett gave us characters stuck in garbage cans; Cocteau one side of telephone conversation (*La Voix humaine*). Ionesco's last gasp of an historical drama (*Le Roi se meurt*) is itself a disappearing act. Claudel composed with a lavish opulence throughout many decades, but his work tends toward the dramatic novel or the oratorio more than toward the theatre per se. Lorca's world is tensed and dramatic, but it draws on peasant ballads, and it is not particularly theatrical. In Eliot, the effort to restore theatrical representation to its classical place as privileged reflector of a society, an elevated form of collective imagining, is strained and artificial.

This anti-theatrical prejudice has philosophical roots that reach at least as deep as Plato,[3] but after contemporary philosophy has taken such determined turns away from epistemologies built on the idea of a representation of the world to the mind, the aversion to theatrical representation is all the more worrying. In the modern philosophies which eschew the representational mirrors of the mind, as in the propaedeutics of Dewey, the hermeneutics of Gadamer, or the archaeology of Foucault – in all the contemporary versions of philosophy constructed without Cartesian mental mirrors – the very idea of representation seems suspect. It was this radical questioning of the use of representation in the service of self-imagining that Artaud undertook in his writings on theatre and Western culture, metaphysics and the *mise en scène*, and the "theatre of cruelty." Yet the theatrical "idea" which Fergusson studied, and which has in modern times seemed all but impossible to achieve, if not illicit on philosophical grounds, was nuclear to the theatre of the Spanish Golden Age. Where today it is difficult to conceive of a society dependent on the theatre for reflecting images of itself, since ours looks instead as Artaud said to the movies or the music hall, the society of seventeenth-century Spain was grounded in the theatrical images it made of itself, and the idea of theatrical imagining was philosophically central to some of its most important works. By Calderón's time, the "idea of a theatre" was, in most of its variations, such common coin that the topic was a cliché; Cicero's slogan about comedy, for instance, is already a stock phrase applied to the *comedia* in the *Quixote* (1, 48) and in Lope's *Arte nuevo*. Yet refurbished, magnified, and restored to a place of absolute centrality in both technical and philosophical terms, *La vida es sueño* is the stunning achievement of this theatrical "idea."

Fergusson took Dante's *Divina Commedia* to be the prime example of the theatrical idea, the single most complete representation of an action, that could be found in Western literature. Since Dante's poem, there have been few literary artifacts capable of a similar breadth of statement. Dante had at his command virtually the whole of extant culture; each canto, strophe, and line makes reference to some relevant part thereof. *La vida es sueño* commands a similar breadth of reference and moral pertinence, if confined to a smaller place. Like *Paradise Lost* or the *Comédie humaine*, the play is an encyclopedia, a *summa* of thought and generic response. Calderón demonstrates a capacity for wholeness and order, a force of cohesion, that is remarkable. Admired by Schlegel and Goethe as "catholic," Calderón is not unlike Dante at all. Like the *Commedia*, *La vida es sueño* is a watershed work: after this play, we find *comedias* of comparable authority on only local, intermittent occasions.

Yet at the same time Calderón is temperamentally very unlike Dante. The difference is telling. His play lacks the utter specificity we find in the *Commedia*. Nowhere do we find the names of persons and places which lend anecdotal ballast to Dante's poem. Calderón shuns specific history and individual circumstance; he achieves a wide perspective without the mass of detail and observation that inform Dante, as later they would Balzac, Zola, and Proust.[4] Calderón understands the individual through the universal, each man's story as illuminated by the patterns of collective transcendence. In the space of three acts, he alludes to the three states of mankind: fallen beast, being of temporal illusion, and self-saved man, magnanimous master of himself. He embraces the natural, artistic, and sociopolitical realms. He looks to the philosophical, scientific, aesthetic, and political bases of man's condition.

The crucial difference between Calderón's theatrical idea and Dante's, though, is perhaps more simply stated. The difference is formal, or rather theatrical. As a play, *La vida es sueño* excels in its use of representation in the service of its own critique. Calderón knows that the theatre can be indicted as illicit illusion, as illusory spectacle, that the mirror in which we represent ourselves can be alluringly deceptive. But he knows that the self-aware use of illusion is one of the keys to the process of healthy social self-imagining. He sees the full extent of the paradox involved in using theatrical illusion as part of a critique of illusory temporal existence, but he also sees that this is the richest and most satisfying way to formulate that critique. As a dramatist, he accepts the responsibility of seeking the delicate balance between illusion and reality, without forsaking either.

Basilio, King of Poland, father of Segismundo, is a scientist in the literal sense. He seeks and would be content with empirical knowledge. He wants to verify his astrological predictions and so arranges test circumstances for his son. If his costume seems medieval, his science is coincident with Renaissance concepts of scientific method. He might be Galileo, convinced of the reduction of nature to geometry and mathematics. He works from observation to theory to practice. His predictions do not fail. On the contrary, he ensures their success. But he does not see that his scientific method deceives him. Basilio has observed and theorized and predicted, but he has failed to produce an adequate critique. He errs by failing to scrutinize the observer as part of the observed, by unwittingly writing himself *out* of his experiment. He works on the assumption that he has been objective – and he has – but his failing lies in his ignorance of the subjective. His science is an "illusion of technique," as William Barrett said in a recent book of that title. He is content with the illusion of domination by objective understanding where *self-understanding* is the crucial factor.

Renaissance thinkers waged a steady and often vigorous war against the lingering astrological *Weltanschauung* of late Antiquity and the Middle Ages. Giordano Bruno created the characteristic symbol for the trend in his *Lo spaccio della bestia trionfante*. The constellations of the zodiac appear to men to be the ultimate arbiters of fate because man is vulnerable to illusions. He must learn instead to orient his life according to the "inner light" of moral conscience and self-consciousness. We must, as Bruno writes, "put in order the heaven that intellectually lies within us." (In order to accomplish this, man must learn, as Segismundo does, to "purify the drive within.")[5] As in Pico della Mirandola's critique of astrology (*In astrologiam*), Calderón sees that the astrologer tends to hypostatize the purely geometrical apparatus of thought. He tends to misconstrue as real what is ideal, granting ontological status to what should be but a mental tool for thought. Because man is subject to illusions, he accepts the presence of abstract forces; he believes, for instance, that physical effects derive from simple location. Unlike Basilio, Pico conquers astrology by asserting the superiority of the will over location or matter, by allowing man to assert his will in the chain of intelligible forces that pervade the universe. This is the germ of Segismundo's claim in his opening monologue, an affirmation of the power of the will over mind and matter:

> ¿y yo, con más albedrío,
> tengo menos libertad?　　　　　　　　　　　　(I, 502b)

(And I, who have a freer will, why should I have less liberty?)

Basilio tries to submit an entire society to science. He wants to plan, to think, and to control. He understands the State as a kind of substance; he takes the social order as matter which can be dominated. Insofar as his experiment with Segismundo is undertaken with political intent, he confuses the natural and social orders. He fails to see that the lasting structures of power are consequent on self-dominance, that authority is strongest where it renounces force, that clemency is the greatest virtue of the potentate. Basilio likens the State to a theatrical work of art. Where the will is uncontrolled, the State disintegrates; Fate plays tragedies under the canopy of justice:

> El dosel de la jura, reducido
> a segunda intención, a horror segundo
> teatro funesto es, donde importuna
> representa tragedias la fortuna. (I, 525a)

(The canopy of justice, reduced to a second purpose and second horror, is a funereal theatre where vexations Fortune puts on tragedies.)

The social order cannot be submitted to scientific controls. Revolution and the tragedies of war are wholly unpredictable. There are spheres of human action and motivation which, for ill or for good, lie outside the domain of science. Calderón's unequivocal example of enduring rule at the close of *La vida es sueño* is possible only as Segismundo uses the faculty of the will where human understanding fails. The final act of the play is, in fact, premised on doubt: "Cielos, si es verdad que sueño . . ." ("Heavens, if indeed I dream . . .") (I, 530a).

What Calderón seems to be consistently saying is that no understanding, no vision is justified or complete unless the frame of the viewer is incorporated into the field of his vision. The play is like a lesson in optics; the characters are case studies in points of view. Basilio, Clarín, and Segismundo are at different distances from reality; they organize different foci. But the crucial matter is the degree to which their vision is self-critical. The lesson is thoroughly humanistic. Each character approximates or surpasses a purely rational response to temporal illusion – that of skeptical doubt – but only Segismundo learns the subtleties of perspective: that the methodical separation of subject and object is insufficient. Segismundo transcends rational doubt or certainty because he knows that he, as much as what he sees, may be illusory.

Clarín is exceedingly close to the world about him. He can make no sense of the teeming surface of reality that surrounds him. He has no capacity for perspective, no understanding; he lacks a point of view. He barely sees the world at all. Clarín is a coward, afraid to approach the world. He has no control over himself or his circumstances and therefore suffers the accidents which are dealt him. His most memorable act is his flight from the revolution. He dies an accidental death, a death at the hands of chance, a death which does not dignify him.

Basilio errs in a way opposite to Clarín's. He is too far from events. His point of view is too cool, too distanced. He is too calm and composed, too much in control. His insight is great, but he relies too heavily on domination by intellectual mastery. In fact, he has overlooked the limits of his own understanding. He uses understanding to control those about him, but not to master himself. Basilio pairs his own vision with a cosmic perspective: he tries to read in the stars the signs of fate. In so doing, he ignores the human will. He raises his son in isolation; he enforces a division between man and nature; and Segismundo emerges a brute.

Segismundo is the only character who learns the paradoxical nature of vision. He learns to see himself in order to see others, he learns self-understanding in order to understand the world, self-domination and control in order to lead the state. When he finally achieves power and control, he is clement, magnanimous. Segismundo alone seems to know that understanding, when premised on self-understanding, is never domination, that self-reflection adds a crucial assurance and clarity to human vision.

Since Lionel Abel discussed *La vida es sueño* as an example of "metatheatre," there has been a tendency to suppose that Basilio is the sole "dramatist" of the play and that he alone orders the relationships of the characters about him. He is taken to be part Prospero of Shakespeare's *Tempest*, if less benevolent, part Hamlet, albeit not vengeful or mad. But, more important, Basilio is a failed dramatist. His state cannot sustain itself against the intrusions of political chaos. He cannot maintain order in the world he has fashioned. His "characters" rebel against him and his production fails. Where he wanted to script a comedy, affairs take grimly tragic turns. Segismundo in the palace is the image of all he hoped he would not see in his son.

As the restrained prince of the final scenes, Segismundo is the only character whose understanding and whose actions involve a self-critique. He is the ideal "dramatist," the exemplary author of a role: he orders relationships according to a deeply humanist ethic, taking man, the human person, as the basis of the social fabric. His point of view, his judgment, and his actions are appropriate first to himself and then to the other characters in the play because he is self-critical.

In Segismundo, Calderón outlines the human capacity for dramatization as mediation, as self-imagining and reflection. This, in turn, is the highest claim he can make for his own art: Calderón uses illusion in a self-consciously justified way. If theatrical metaphors – indeed the whole theatrical "idea" – pervade his work, this is because he as dramatist implicitly writes himself *into* the picture he represents. Whereas Plato could exile the poets and image-dealers from his ideal state, Calderón had no choice but to confront the ambiguities of the artistic illusion: as a dramatist, he had to find a way to "save the appearances" if only to press them into the service of a practical philosophy, viz. art. He sees the aesthetic experience as one way to transcend philosophical doubt, as a springboard to a self-critical moral and social philosophy. Rosaura, emblematic of beauty's image, leads Segismundo not just to realize his attachment to some higher goal, nor just to remember the markings of beauty written on his soul, but to place his abilities in the service of society as clement head of State.

The self-conscious use of illusion is a deep vein in Calderón's work. He continually recognizes that the viewer and the viewed are both caught up in illusion, and that the theatre itself is the locus of these ambivalent polarities. It is a crucial moment in the play when Segismundo faces up to temporal illusion; but his awareness of illusion enables him to savor the world, just as we, as spectators, can profit from Calderón's work only if we recognize that it is ephemeral:

> . . . llegué a saber
> que toda la dicha humana,
> en fin, pasa como sueño,
> y quiero hoy aprovecharla
> el tiempo que me durare.   (I, 533b)

(I came to see that all human happiness, in the end, passes like a dream, and so I want to enjoy it for the time I have left.)

In a world that is itself an illusion, a dream, part of a history that may be foreordained or accidental, neither the renunciation of illusion nor its uncritical acceptance is an adequate response. The matter is infinitely more subtle. Illusion fosters deceit, but self-conscious illusion allows for its enjoyment. Illusion must regulate itself, find its proper equilibrium as against the world of transcendent reality.

Calderón's *comedias* are shot through with messages and exempla of willful restraint and self-consciousness. Yet what most uniquely characterizes his disposition is his use of illusion in the resolution of the

You keep saying this but you don't explain how it is achieved.

problem itself. He restores the balance between illusion and reality by illusory means, incorporating the theatre into the process of its own critique. The form of the representation thus becomes a vehicle of self-criticism. His thinking is itself theatrical, embracing the critique of illusion in an illusory space.

In its three-act structure and tripartite shape, *La vida es sueño* gives the impression of a dialectic. The impression is only partly founded. Calderón has nothing to do with Hegel; his sense of the possibilities for fulfillment inherent in each being is Aristotelian. But as in dialectical thought, he uses ideas as levers to overthrow themselves, or as pulleys, to hoist themselves up from within. In *La vida es sueño*, there are inversions of premise and conclusion; the title is in fact a misstatement of the theme of the play. In a manner more akin to Kierkegaard than to Hegel, Calderón's dialectic terminates in Segismundo's voluntary abrogation, the culmination of his self-critique, the overcoming of his skepticism. Calderón refuses simply to invoke the clichés of Christian faith in response to temporal illusion; the play is no litany of formulaic response. Unlike Descartes, who found a single principle of doubt unilaterally applicable to the whole of sensory experience, Calderón sees the problem of deceit and illusion in its social, political, and personal terms, as a problem of ethics. Moreover, he adjusts the question of belief and its solution according to the possibilities offered by representational space. He takes the experience of the sensory world, the aesthetic experience itself, as the foundation of a moral philosophy. This is where the play is unique: it uses the theatrical wrappings in which philosophical problems are posed – indeed, toward which they are directed – in order to resolve the problems themselves.

How?

Segismundo marks the three nodes of the play in his monologues. He starts with a complaint to Heaven. He has been repressed physically, deprived of political freedom, and of self-knowledge; he has been reared apart from his father. He seeks to overcome his repression. He wants freedom and understanding: "Apurar, Cielos, pretendo . . ." ("Heavens, I demand to know . . .") (I, 502a). His father Basilio, the astrologer king, also wanted knowledge; he wanted to know the future of his son, and to do so he tried to read the book of nature. The effort is not itself suspect, but Basilio is too wise, too confident in his wisdom. He is falsely confident in his knowledge, deceived by the allure of certainty. The action he takes – keeping his son prisoner – is ill-advised.

Segismundo retracts his complaint in Act II. He learns self-control. ②
"reprimamos/esta fiera condición" ("Let us repress this beastly
nature") (I, 522a–b). His self-repression is conjoined to his skepticism: life is, or may be, a dream. We shall never know. But better not
to take this world as ultimate than to presume with Basilio that we can ✓✓
circumscribe it completely. Far better to doubt than to accept the
world at face value. And there is a certain security in skeptical doubt,
a complacency in the use of doubt to separate subject and object.
Indeed, the man who lives by doubt may in fact be less courageous
than Descartes would have him seem: his doubt serves as an
unchanging response to all circumstances. As Segismundo is returned
to the tower, he enjoys the limited but undeniable pleasure of
skepticism. He has found a personal contentment, a restfulness, that
he did not know at the opening of the play.

But the security of the skeptic is just as false as the arrogant 2a →
confidence of the man who has not learned to doubt at all. And the
world will not allow this false confidence to last for long. The arch
skeptic, the true Pyrrhonian, is incapable of action. Skeptics die of
weakened nerves and moral cowardice. They do not make good
heroes. Segismundo learns to surpass the limited contentment of the
skeptic. He is called into action by the revolution. He learns that he
must live in a social community. He has responsibilities to the State:
he cannot stay at rest in the tower. There are circumstances –
revolution foremost among them – that cannot be met by the method
of skeptical doubt. The circumstances of war and social upheaval
demand a translation of philosophy into praxis, and the skeptic has no
practical philosophy. He has no ethic and sees no need for one.
Segismundo's final speech is directed to the "illustrious court of
Poland" for a good reason: it shows his awareness of the social and
political exigencies of embodied existence. The skeptic may be right:
"Cielos, si es verdad que sueño . . ." ("Heavens, if indeed I
dream . . .") (I, 530a–b); but his defensive stance, his guard against
deceit, is itself illusory. He needs prudence, the capacity to initiate
action and to judge; but he lacks the self-awareness which precedes
clemency.

For Calderón, as for Descartes, the business of doubting, the
proposition that "life is a dream" or the work of an evil genius,
implies accepting a large onus. It is not enough to sleep, perhaps to
dream, or to be drugged like Segismundo in the tower. The freedom
thus gained is transient, delusory. Descartes wrote that

just as a captive who in sleep enjoys an imaginary liberty, when he begins to suspect that his liberty is but a dream, fears to awaken, and conspires with these agreeable illusions that the deception may be prolonged, so insensibly of my own accord I fall back into my former opinions, and I dread awakening from this slumber, lest the laborious wakefulness which would follow the tranquility of this repose should have to be spent not in daylight, but in the excessive darkness of the difficulties which have just been discussed.[6]

Segismundo cannot grant himself the luxury of the sleep of illusion. He must awaken to the darkness of the problems at hand, to the revolution which awaits him.

Like Segismundo, Descartes accepted the possibility that the sensible world may be an illusion: "Let us assume," he wrote, "that we are asleep and that all these particulars, e.g. that we open our eyes, shake our head, extend our hands, and so on, are but false delusions; and let us reflect that possibly neither our hands nor our whole body are such as they appear to us to be" ("Meditation I," p. 146). This is the first step in the Cartesian search for the first principles of philosophy, and it is the cornerstone of *La vida es sueño*. Segismundo accepts the doubt of the skeptic in order to turn those energies to more productive concerns. Because the skeptic's doubt is undermining in intent, it is naturally more powerful than the assertion of certainty, of the claims of reason, on the part of the anti-skeptic. The skeptic cannot be met head-on; he cannot be refuted directly. But his energy, the rigors of his doubt, can be harnessed: let us assume *unfailingly* that all we see and know through the senses is the work of some evil demon, a *malin génie* who intentionally falsifies things; let us believe only what we can ascertain in the face of this unyielding, hyperbolic doubt:

I shall then suppose, not that God who is supremely good and the fountain of truth, but some evil genius not less powerful than deceitful, has employed his whole energies in deceiving me; I shall consider that the heavens, the earth, colours, figures, sound, and all other external things are nought but the illusions and dreams of which this genius has availed himself in order to lay traps for my credulity; I shall consider myself as having no hands, no eyes, no flesh, no blood, nor any senses, yet falsely believing myself to possess all these things; I shall remain obstinately attached to this idea, and if by this means it is not in my power to arrive at the knowledge of any truth, I may at least do what is in my power.   (*ibid.*, p, 148)

It was Kierkegaard who questioned the skeptical process of self-doubt and said that it must finally abrogate itself: "It can be vanquished only by a breach of continuity, a qualitative leap."[7] This is the leap that Segismundo makes as he is clement toward his father and merciful toward his subjects.

Any actual influence of Descartes on Calderón is improbable; affinities of this type are difficult to demonstrate, far more so to ascertain. Calderón is not known to have read any of Descartes' writings; yet, just as in Racine and Corneille, the presence of a tacit Cartesian spectator seems implicit in the theatre of Calderón. Calderón uses the theatre as a place to exercise the cool scrutiny of the mind, as a locus for the detached contemplation of the passions and emotions. But he finds that the theatre is never adequate for these tasks; never is a purely mental space able to contain the bodily passions. Hence the images of physical containment which burden the characters in plays like *El mayor monstruo* and *Los tres mayores prodigios*; hence, in *La vida es sueño*, Segismundo's need to overcome the confinement of the cave of ignorance through the exercise of the will, not simply of the intellect; hence this insistence on transcending the world of matter not by the mind but by the spirit:

> ¿y teniendo yo más alma,
> tengo menos libertad? (I, 502b)

(And I, who have a greater soul, should I have less freedom?)

When Descartes divided mind from body in dualistic fashion, he sought a rationalistic solution to the human condition. For him, the theatre is the primarily mental space in which the mind can contemplate the body and thus dominate the passions. The theatre offers the opportunity for what one critic called the "dispassionate contemplation of passion."[8] But at the same time it necessarily arouses and excites those passions. The theatre becomes, for the audience, a place to enjoy a deliciously ambiguous pleasure: on the one hand, the joy of emotions, the fruition of the passions released therein, and, on the other, the moral satisfaction gained from their containment and domination. For Descartes – as in the passage below – that containment works by virtue of primarily mental forces; for Calderón, the intellectual motive, the capacity of the understanding, is transcended by a spiritual vault:

When we read of strange adventures in a book, or see them represented in a theatre, which sometimes excite sadness in us, sometimes joy, or love, or hatred, and generally speaking all the passions, according to the diversity of the objects which are offered to our imagination; but along with that we have pleasure in feeling them excited in us, and *this pleasure is an intellectual joy* which may as easily take its origin from sadness as from any of the other passions.[9]

Unlike Cartesian rationalism, Calderón's transcendent drive is able to resist the simply "intellectual love of God" toward which Spinoza later pushed. It is true that in temper Calderón resembles Spinoza more than Descartes: like Leibniz, and like Calderón, Spinoza inherited from Scholasticism an astounding capacity for organization, a supreme will to order; indeed there is hardly a more organized philosophical work than the *Ethics,* a cross-weave of subdivision, a lattice of cross-reference, a whorl of atomization wrought of created life. But Spinoza could not bear to consider, as Descartes and Calderón both did, that the sensible world might be an illusion, the fabrication of a devious evil spirit. He was convinced that God must be reasonable, and he sought therefore to resolve the vast and contradictory qualities of nature. As in the metaphors of Segismundo's first monologue, or of Rosaura's opening speech – in the comparisons of horse to bird and fish, of man to the beasts of nature, of streams to silver serpents – Spinoza saw each entity in nature as gifted with large doses of the will to subsist, each ordered toward self-preservation, each struggling against the flattening effects of the philosophical reconciliation toward which his own thought in fact tended: "Each group of particles in nature, from the simplest to the most complex, strives, before all else, to maintain itself, and to preserve its identity: man, animals, trees, stones, even the remote emptiness of the heavens can be known in their identity because the energies which compose them are devoted above all else to this effort of self-preservation."[10] Spinoza sensed the energies which yoke together contraries and subsume differences under the auspices of an Absolute Being. But because he tried to reconcile all of nature – if only in order to *identify* it – by the powers of the mind, he discovered the more subtle and poignant fact that substance does not always fit form, that there may be a mismatch of convention and nature, that the order of the mind may be a source of great unease. In Segismundo's first monologue, there is a related sense of fracture running between man and nature: Segismundo is isolated as different from the beasts; this is part of his coming to self-knowledge. But unlike Spinoza, Segismundo identifies himself according to the qualities of his soul and his will, the faculties which allow him to transcend himself in the final Act of the play. If at the start Segismundo suffers a gnawing suspicion that his self-love may go unsatisfied, if, as Narciso in Calderón's mythological play, he feels orphaned, he is consoled by the fact that he has more than merely mental powers at his disposal.

Segismundo's heroism is not consequent on any rational certainty gained in response to the dreamlike illusion of life. The ambiguity remains, despite the powers of the mind. Instead, Segismundo's success is dependent on various intangible, if not illusory, factors. He pits his will against conditions which may be occultly written in the stars; he is saved by the silhouette of Beauty–Rosaura; he grants the possibility that the very world in which he lives may be an illusion. To extract from *La vida es sueño* an ascetic indictment of the temporal world, to reduce the play to the maxim of its title, is to ignore the richest aspect of its theme and its most salient formal feature. Calderón does not reject illusion; rather, he indicates that illusion is absolutely necessary to existence on earth. The play is no attack on "ideology" in the Marxist sense; as in the *auto El gran teatro del mundo*, Calderón looks past social ideology – the costumes and the masks which all men wear – and trains his eye on those spheres in which the human will and soul hold sway; his play is an ambivalent celebration and critique of illusion. His theatre is transcendent in thrust because it works on the principle that the key to man's salvation lies in a wide embrace of illusion. If the root metaphor of his *auto sacramental* were in force, if his "idea" of the theatre were that the world is a stage, we should say that his theatrical "idea" is an idea about life itself. Read in conjunction with the metaphor of his *auto*, which intones the topic of the *theatrum mundi*, the maxim spelled out by *La vida es sueño* is not just that life is a dream, but that the theatre is a dream, and that it is therefore a locus of value as well.

Calderón in relation to Descartes. }
& Spinoza. {

2

La dama duende

"¿Era dama o torbellino?"
("Was that a lady or a whirlwind?")

Cosme, in *La dama duende*

In *La vida es sueño* and in plays which resemble it either formally or thematically (e.g. *El gran teatro del mundo* or the *comedia En la vida todo es verdad y todo mentira*) Calderón develops the paradox of illusion through a dramatic action that is global in its scope, archetypal in its suggestions, and sometimes straightforwardly allegorical as well. Elsewhere, I have called this the "encyclopedic" design of Calderón's theatre.[1] Indeed, if we take Francis Fergusson's judgment that Dante's *Divina Commedia*, rather than any work of theatre, represents the single most accomplished version of the theatrical "idea" in Western culture, it is not difficult to see how a work like *La vida es sueño* can be said to embody this theatrical idea in compact form.[2] In addition to the absorption of skepticism, which Calderón achieves through his use of the *theatrum mundi* trope, the play represents the grand arc of a complete action which writers ever since Aristotle have seen as the mark of accomplished drama. In this sense, *La vida es sueño* is Calderón's most Aristotelian play, the shape of its action being the exact reverse of that which Aristotle saw as appropriate for tragedy, but retaining the wholeness and order which characterize the well-made plot.

La dama duende, which I shall discuss here, as well as *El galán fantasma* and *El secreto a voces*, which I shall discuss in the following sections, show a vastly different conception of dramatic form from *La vida es sueño*. As I shall explain, some of these differences can be accounted for in terms of Calderón's early Tirsian affinities, but if Calderón did learn from Tirso, the lessons remained with him throughout his career. Even in his later years, we find Calderón composing fast-paced *comedias* of equivocation, minor intrigue, and deceit which

24

resemble some of Tirso's work. My concern here is to show how, for *La dama duende* at least, Calderón was able to transpose the thematics of illusion into a form which differs so vastly from what we have seen so far. Calderón's phantom lady flits across the stage like a bundle of veiled motion, a volatile packet of erotic energy, chameleon-like in her *duende*-like nature. She is indeed like no other female character he was to imagine, and her femininity is central to the themes and theatrical techniques of illusion in this play. Unlike Rosaura of *La vida es sueño*, the wives of the bloody honor plays, or the "terrible mothers" (Everett Hesse's phrase) like Liríope of *Eco y Narciso*,[3] Angela is supple and vivacious, potent with desire, ready to partake of illusion, yet mature enough to experience the wondrous process of personal growth through interaction with others.

Critics have been rather at a loss to define the play generically or stylistically. It can be seen as an honor play, as one variation on tragedy, or as a cloak-and-dagger play; Angela could be Calderón's version of Proteus. Conclusions have yet to be drawn, but there is no doubt that *La dama duende* is vastly different from the dramatic conception embodied in *La vida es sueño* and the allegorical *autos*. Still, the play can be related to the rest of Calderón's work. The interplay of illusion and reality is his constant theme; the value of personal integrity is unchanging in his canon; the devices of role-playing and self-dramatization are set in motion in countless plays, and we will find all of this in *La dama duende*. What distinguishes the play is the fixing of identity through process and change, the definition of "self" in terms of "other." Like Proteus, Angela is unstable, volatile, multiform; she unfolds before our eyes, gaining integrity and gradually fixing her identity through a near-daemonic capacity for "otherness." Her sobriquet is no accident; she is indeed phantom-like. And it is through her growth in the embrace of illusion, her shadings of role against self and society, that the dramatist is able effectively to engage his audience in theatrical credulity and deceit.

Cosme, the *gracioso* of the play, asks the crucial question concerning identity cited above. The very possibility of questioning identity, the very fact that self and self-image are divided for Angela, are clues to her feminine composition. The play concerns not so much her affirmation of identity over image as her discovery of self through the demands of interaction with others. Calderón gives the illusion of the process of human growth, of the emergence and gradual maturation of Angela's identity, through tricks of theatrical chiaroscuro, the counterpoint of illusion and reality, of skepticism and good faith, of disclosure and deceit. The question of identity is itself a remarkable one considering the nature of the Spanish *comedia*. Readers of Shakespeare, Racine, and Corneille know identity crises in a variety of different guises. Who is Hamlet if not someone who questions who he is? Who is Lear? Even Corneille's Cid finds his self-definition tried in the conflicting demands that weigh on him. But the keynote of the *comedia*, which is more Marlovian than Shakespearean in temper, is struck in a phrase of self-affirmation and assertion, a slogan of epic derivation that acts as a talisman of personal value for those who are able to affirm it: "soy quien soy." I am who I am, and simply because I am, because I was so born. I am who I am, that is, not by acquired wealth, and not by social station, and not by public office, but because my blood is pure. This is the irreducible matrix of the hierarchical and static values of caste, and especially of the dominant social caste, which built the *comedia* as a form of national self-imagining. But there is something Angela can say which few others on the Spanish stage can and which marks her as unique: "*Who* am I?" The phrase is of necessity spoken in hushed undertones against the litany of social self-assertion. For her it is no sign of weakness. Angela finds satisfaction by defining herself in a negative way. In Angela, Calderón has created a character with the ability to say, like Shakespeare's Iago, "I am not I."

Angela's very lack of fixed definition is her single greatest resource. She is endowed with psychic mobility. Because she can be other than who she is, she is able to respond to the changing personal and social circumstances in which she finds herself. She can adapt herself, turn circumstance to her advantage, fashion freedom from limitation, resource from constraint, wholeness and integrity from social convention and stricture. Unlike Calderón's rigid and self-asserting males, Angela is responsive. Where others would be crushed by adherence to established social codes, or vanquished morally by easy acquiescence, Angela flourishes and matures. Calderón has fashioned from her negativity a remarkable pattern of growth.

Ostensibly, Angela is society's waste, a widow owing her husband's large debts. Born of a bureaucracy which, by 1629 (the date of the play),[4] was becoming not only unwieldy but useless and corrupt, she can only fit into conventional moulds of social definition against the background of male control and domination. The servant Rodrigo explains:

Ya sé que su esposo era
Administrador en puerto
de mar de unas reales rentas
y quedó debiendo al Rey
grande cantidad de hacienda,
y ella a la Corte se vino
de secreto, donde intenta,
escondida y retirada,
componer mejor sus deudas.   (II, 241b–2a)

(Yes, I know that her husband was collector of the Royal Ports and left a large debt owed to the Crown, and so she came secretly to the Court where, withdrawn and in seclusion, she hopes to settle her accounts.)

Her problem in the play is to find a way to reconcile herself to a society which would seem to have no place for her, to realize the potential she has within her, to purchase personal liberation where her credit is low. How does this happen?

Calderón places Angela within a doubly valent space. The personalized space of the house in which the play is set is the exact obverse of the outward space of self-assertion of the male-dominated society. Angela knows how to mould the inwardness of the house to her designs. Set against Manuel, who likewise has come to don Juan's house to stay, juxtaposed to his steadfast skepticism and unfailing good sense, Angela unveils a multivalent, protean personality. Her femininity is founded on the forms of change more than whimsy or caprice.

The play thus becomes a dialectic of positive and negative, inside and out, male and female, of reversible roles and values. Calderón teases these contrasts out of a deceptively "inward" theatrical space. He uses the stage, and the house which he imagines set within the stage, as a place to summon up and to resolve these passionately driven ambivalences. His understanding of identity and sexuality is dependent on the physically circumscribed, contained space in which the human passions play. If the world is a stage, the theatre is a body. The assuagement of the passions and their reconciliation to the body, the reunion of spirit and sensibility, follow on the recognition of the phantom-like, daemonic quality of the body itself, of the physical matter to which the spirit is tethered. The integration of body and spirit is made possible by the polyvalent capacity of theatrical space.

Philosophically, Calderón inherited these and the related concerns of metaphysical dualism from conflicts of the Platonic and Aristotelian elements embedded in Thomistic thought. For the Platonist, psyche and soma were originally separate and fundamentally different entities; the unity of the two, any conflation of body and spirit, sense and intellect, is necessarily illusory. For Aristotle, the soul is simply the "entelechy" of the body, the "form" which it achieves. Like Aquinas, Calderón recognizes the need for spatial illusions and physical "phantasms," if only in order to lend support to pure spirit or pure thought. He makes physical, theatrical space supple enough to integrate and house what we would call soul, spirit, or psyche.

Gaston Bachelard thought that houses were the intrinsically privileged places of personal psychology.[5] Calderón sees the house as offering Angela the chance to fulfill both her spiritual and her passionate needs. Only in the house, in contrast to the external world, only in this interior space which is divided from the outside space by a permeable membrane, can such satisfaction be found. Angela comes to her brother's house and is shut within it, a prisoner. The house is meant to shield her from any of the possible transgressions of the external world. She is kept there so that her honor will remain intact. The house is, in Bachelard's fine phrase, "cast into the hurricane" of the world about it: "Faced with the bestial hostility of the storm and the hurricane, the house's virtues of protection and resistance are transposed into human virtues. The house acquires the physical and moral energy of a human body" (p. 46). It is the house, and within it her room, that Angela's brothers have built as a shield to protect her physically and morally.

But for a woman of her energy, the house is a prison which threatens to rob her of her freedom. She begins to wilt and wither within:

> . . . Que yo
> entre dos paredes muera,
> donde apenas el sol sabe
> quién soy . . .
> . . .
> Donde en efecto encerrada
> sin libertad he vivido,
> porque enviudé de un marido,
> con dos hermanos casada.   (II, 242a–b)

(For I am dying, shut in by two walls, where the sun hardly knows who I am . . . Where, in effect, I live enclosed and with no freedom, widowed of a husband, and married to two brothers.)

Like any shield, though, the house and its walls are vulnerable to penetration:

que no ha puesto por defensa
de su honor más que unos vidrios,
que al primer golpe se quiebran.   (II, 242a)

(The only thing guarding my sister's honor are a few panes of glass that a
single blow could shatter.)

The particular irony here is that the flaw is built into the construction.
The house of males is itself a threat to Angela's honor, but it is Angela
who penetrates the partition between her room and Manuel's.
Calderón takes the situation as incongruously comic, but the humor
derives also from the illusory dangers raised by the impropriety of a
woman in a man's room. Angela sees the opportunity to satisfy her
impetuously budding curiosity. For Manuel, the closet dividing the
two rooms, which is, as he says, "compuesta de vidrios" ("made of
glass") (II, 262b), is thoroughly confusing. The glass is in fact
ambivalent; it conceals and reveals at the same time, and Manuel is
reluctant to give credence to the phantom he suspects.

Angela may be temporarily deprived of her freedom, but she
herself is, like the environment in which she is set, doubly valent. She
sees that the chambers of the house are intimate space, and that
phantom-like concealment, not self-revelation, is the key to her
success. Instinctively, she understands that what appears to confine
may in fact liberate. She knows the rules of an honor-conscious
society. As she writes to Manuel, she insists on the social need for
secrecy: ". . . que el secreto importa, porque el día que lo sepa alguno
de los amigos, perderé yo el honor y la vida" ("secrecy is essential,
because the day any one of my friends finds out, I will lose my honor
and my life") (II, 249a). She can speak in vague periphrases,
guarding her words, hiding herself just as she conceals her male
visitor:

Ang.   Señor, mi padre es aquéste.
Man.   ¿Qué he de hacer?
Ang.   Fuerza es que vais
        a esconderos a un retrete.
        Isabel, llévale tú,
        hasta que oculto le dejes
        en aquel cuarto que sabes,
        apartado; ya me entiendes.
        . . .
Ang. [a Beatriz]
        Ya hasta que se sosiegue
        más la casa, y Don Manuel

vuelva de su cuarto a verme,
para ser menos sentidas,
entremos a este retrete.   (II, 265a–b)

(*Ang.*   Sir, that's my father. *Man.*   What should I do? *Ang.*   You must go
and hide in a closet. Isabel, take him away and hide him in that separate
room you know about; you know what I mean . . . *Ang.* [*to Beatriz*] And
until things settle down more in the house and Don Manuel comes out from
his room to see me, let's go into this closet so that we won't be heard.)

While the private rooms of the house offer her a chance to reveal an
authentic self, the public, social demands of honor vie with these
inward, personal values. Intimacy may become secrecy, sincerity
sham, candor concealment. If Angela can succeed in an environment
like this, it is only because she is a master of role-playing and illusory
ways. If the social paradoxes of an honor-conscious society would
force her to forsake her true inward *ser* for a public persona, she learns
that she must fabricate a role of her own imagining. She takes
advantage of the ambiguous space of the house in order to preserve
her honor and still satisfy her desires.

Not only the setting of the play, the house itself, but also the objects
scattered throughout its interior are essential to the theatrical illusion
of the play and thus to Angela's success. Rarely was Calderón so
concerned with the selection and placement of stage properties. Two
rooms, a mysteriously moveable cabinet and door separating them, a
travelling bag and a basket of clothes: all are powerful images of
inwardness. They are dense with the intimate lives of the characters
around them, laden with desire. In passing through the *alacena* and in
searching through Manuel's bags, Angela penetrates the forbidden
space of personal intimacy. Initially, she is fueled by erotic desire.
When she first enters Manuel's room with Isabel, the two rummage
through his clothes. But as a phantom force, she operates at a physical
distance, leaving for Manuel lures to charm and trap him. These seem
all the more pleasurable to Manuel, given the *gracioso*'s fear of the
phantom. Angela is seductive, but her love is, here, immature. It is
external; it seeks and offers the gratification of the senses. She is intent
on attracting Manuel by charming him. Thus she deploys a cast of
images of feminine intimacy as lures.

In Act III, for instance, Angela acts as a priestess of love, director of
a courtly rite, chief dramatist of a staged ritual. The scene bespeaks a
thirst for intimate communication where social convention reigns. It
is set initially with napkins, conserves, and water, and with female

attendants "haciendo reverencia todas" ("all bowing in reverence"); the ladies bring glasses, boxes of sweets, napkins – feminine objects, captivating lures. Edwin Honig saw this as a "mythological ritual allied to the initiation and fertility rites out of which the oldest comedy sprang."[6] That description may be excessive, but the thought is essentially right. This is a psychic world of Angela's making, a private world, richly symbolic of her needs, even if it is an illusion. Manuel enters her space, and she ensnares him: he is convinced that she is a *grande dame*. Angela relies on these accoutrements because she cannot approach Manuel openly. Society would not allow her such an assertive role. Moreover, her love has yet to grow; she has yet to surrender these props and face up to the fact that she, a widow, feels love.

Angela does not grow in isolation. [She uses Manuel as a springboard to achieve the unity of self, the final fusion of dramatized role and inward self.] She is a maker of illusion within an illusory world, and she uses Manuel's steadfast good sense and skepticism as constant forces to lead her to self-realization. Throughout the play, Manuel is remarkably stable. His *entereza* would be epic-like were his actions themselves not so slight. He refuses to distinguish interior and exterior or to accept illusions. He binds interior self to external appearances. As he relates near the beginning of the play, he acted nobly and magnanimously toward don Juan; the claim is not a boast. He lives up to the role of noble and exemplary courtier and is justified in seeking formal recognition. Unlike his friend don Luis, for whom honor means nothing more than the hollow external forms and symbols in which it is couched, Manuel enacts a number of virtues. The social forms of courtesy have real meaning for him; they are part of his moral equipment for living. They mean more to him than to some members of the Court:

> . . . Si tuviera
> necesidad mi valor
> de satisfacciones, crea
> vuestra arrogancia de mí,
> que no me fuera sin ella.
> Preguntar en qué os ofende
> [en qué os agravia o molesta],
> merece más cortesía;
> y pues la Corte la enseña,
> no la pongáis el mal nombre
> de que un forastero venga

a enseñarla a los que tienen
obligación de saberla.   (II, 240a)

(If my valor were in need of excuses, then let your arrogance think that it was
not I but she. To ask how I offend you [how I injure or affront you] demands
greater courtesy; and since courtesy is taught at Court, don't let it be alleged
that a stranger came and demonstrated courtesy to those who ought to know
what it is.)

It is against Manuel's honor that Angela is able to fashion herself as
a complete person. But in the final analysis he is weaker than she. If he
is not vulnerable personally or emotionally, this apparent strength
may hide a deeper failing. Manuel is too unshaken, too unperturbed,
too much a bastion of good sense, always in control of himself. But
because he has none of the capacity for illusion that Angela has, he is
not fulfilled with the richness that she is. In some ways he is naive.
Never risking being ruffled, no matter what Angela may say or do, he
must forgo most of the sheer fun of illusion and role-playing which
gives her satisfaction.

Manuel is the straight man in a comedy. It is his business to let the
others have fun while he denies himself the pleasure. We laugh at his
expense. When he writes to Angela and signs his letter "El Caballero
de la Dama Duende," in overt parody of Don Quixote's letter to
Dulcinea, it is we who reap the enjoyment. He balks at Cosme's
suggestion that the house is inhabited by a *duende*. And when, in Act II,
he seizes Angela and cries out:

Angel, demonio o mujer,
a fe que no has de librarte
de mis manos esta vez   (II, 261a)

(Angel, devil or woman, I swear that you won't escape from my hands this
time)

he is unable to comprehend the puns. For him, interior and exterior
are never really divided. His constant aplomb denies him the personal
liberation that is possible for Angela. He is incapable of the joy of
illusion. An extremist, he is either too skeptical or too naively
credulous toward the world about him. He lives a univocal existence
in a flat, lacklustre world of *entereza*. Only for that reason do we resist
hailing his heroism as he helps bring unity to Angela's divided self.

Angela reveals herself in slow, gradual steps, each time taking a
new role in response to the moment, each time resolving more clearly
the image of her authentic self. Social demands humanize her, and

this humanization is the source of her resounding success as a character. She learns to use convention to see her plans fulfilled. Convention and authenticity work hand in hand for her:

> Yo te escribí aquesta tarde
> en el último papel
> que nos veríamos presto,
> y anteviendo aquesto fué.
> Y pues cumplí mi palabra,
> supuesto que ya me ves
> en la más humana forma
> que he podido elegir . . .   (II, 261a)

(I wrote to you that evening in my last letter that we would soon meet, and anticipating that, I came here. And thus I kept my word, for you now see me in the most human form I could take . . .)

She has an uncommon negative capacity, an ability to efface her self and substitute for it the *duende*. While the other characters are continuously *affirming* who they are, while they are striving for assertive self-definition, Angela takes a more oblique path. The negative valence of her personal capacity could hardly be stressed enough. In Act III, when Manuel meets a now elegantly dressed Angela, she describes herself in a string of negative terms:

negative personality.

> No soy alba, pues la risa
> me falta en contento tanto;
> ni aurora, pues que mi llanto
> de mi dolor no os avisa;
> no soy sol, pues no divisa
> mi luz la verdad que adoro,
> y así lo que soy ignoro;
> que sólo sé que no soy
> alba, aurora o sol . . .   (II, 264a)

(I am not the morning light, since in all my joy I have not laughter; nor am I the dawn, since my weeping does not tell you of my sorrow; I am not the sun, since my light [mind] does not descry the truth that I adore, and thus I know not what I am and only know that I am neither morning light, dawn, nor sun.)

The turning point in Angela's development comes when she discovers her reliance on someone other than herself. She comes to realize that she exists in a social world and that her actions affect others. She knows that she has a greater responsibility than simply to efface herself. She owes Manuel the declaration of a more stable self; she grows at his expense, and she must shed her roles for his sake. The play transcends the usual ambit of comedy of intrigue because of Calderón's remarkable sensitivity to the reciprocal needs and demands that his characters place on one another.]

> *Ang.* Y así os ruego que digáis
> señor Don Manuel, de mí
> que una mujer soy y fuí
> a quien vos sólo obligáis
> al extremo que miráis.
>
> *Man.* Muy poco debe de ser;
> pues aunque me llego a ver
> aquí, os pudiera argüir
> que tengo más que sentir,
> señora, que agradecer.
> Y así me doy por sentido.
>
> *Ang.* ¿Vos de mí sentido?
> *Man.*   Sí,
> pues que no fiáis de mí
> quien sois.
>
> *Ang.*   Solamente os pido
> que eso no mandéis; que ha sido
> imposible de contar.   (II, 264a)

(*Ang.* Thus I beg you Don Manuel, to say about me only that I am a woman indebted only to you to the extent that you can see. *Man.* That must be very little, since although I see myself here, I could object that I have more to regret than to be thankful for. And so I feel offended. *Ang.* You, offended by me? *Man.* Yes, since you won't confide your identity in me. *Ang.* That is the only thing I beg you not to ask, since it is impossible to say.)

When in the final scene of the play Angela is forced to reveal who she is, she sees the painful effects of her actions on Manuel. She realizes that in her attempts to work surreptitiously within the constraints imposed by her honor-conscious brothers she has placed the honor of another in serious danger. It is here, finally, that she recognizes that Manuel needs her for his salvation. Calderón is merciful toward his straight man and will not let him suffer at the hands of a cruel honor-code. Calderón's play is rich in that liquor which Lady Macbeth saw in her husband, the "milk of human kindness." Angela's verses ring of repentance and the play thus achieves a healing effect. There is reconciliation in the confession:

> ¿Quién creerá que el callarme haya hecho daño
> siendo mujer? Y es cierto,
> siendo mujer, que por callar me he muerto.
> En fin, él esperando,
> a esta puerta estaba, ¡ay Cielo!, cuando

yo a sus umbrales llego,
hecha volcán de nieve, alpe de fuego.
. . .

Por haberte querido,
fingida sombra de mi casa he sido;
por haberte estimado,
sepulcro vivo fuí de mi cuidado;
porque no te quisiera,
quién el respeto a tu valor perdiera;
porque no te estimara,
quién su pasión dijera cara a cara.
Mi intento fué el quererte,
mi fin amarte, mi temor perderte   ✓   (II, 271a–b)

(Who would think that, for a woman, keeping silent would have done any harm? And it is certain that, as a woman, I suffered death to keep silent. And so, he was waiting at this door (oh Heaven!) when I came like a volcano of snow, like an Alp of fire, to its threshold . . . Because I loved you, I was a phantom in my house. Because I cherished you, I was the living tomb of my cares, for the one who might lose the respect of your valor would not love you, and the one who would speak her passion face to face with you would not cherish you. I wanted to cherish you, my purpose was to love you, my fear was of losing you.)

At the end of the play, the public and personal demands of honor are reconciled. The customary tension of personal concealment and public affirmation is resolved. Angela's self-relevation is the key to this reconciliation. She must deny herself the roles to which she has long been clinging and accept herself as who she really is. She must abandon illusion: she is a woman caught in the intricate web of circumstances ruled by love and honor. Throughout the play, Angela has resisted the crucial formula of affirmative self-definition; she pronounces it only at the end: "Que ya resisto, ya defiendo en vano/decir quien soy" ("In vain I now resist and refuse to say who I am") (II, 271a). But this is no standard honor play. The apparent threats to Manuel's and Angela's honor have been illusory throughout. Nor is there any strong autocratic figure dominating the action. Instead, Calderón looks at the familial relationship between siblings. Edwin Honig saw in this a "flicker of incest." But it is only a flicker, a teasing illusion, not a real threat. The flame of human passion is relatively cool here; it will burn hotly enough in the bona fide honor plays. This is not Racine, where incest is indeed a danger. Calderón chose familial relationships for other reasons. He shows us peers, in whose homogeneous relationships he sees the possibility of an equilibrium which eludes authoritarian, honor-conscious fathers and their vulnerable daughters.

The techniques of illusion, when adapted to the serious honor play, are not nearly so successful for the characters. On the contrary, illusion is at the root of the disasters of at least two of Calderón's honor plays, *El médico de su honra* and *El pintor de su deshonra*; the latter title alone should have been a tip to critics. *La dama duende* has a comic tone and rhythm. The theatrical illusion allows the characters to grow in love. It is only when this growth is complete that the illusions can be destroyed. The play ends with reconciliation on all levels: the comic incongruities are resolved, the false threats to honor are neutralized, familial relationships are set at ease, Angela is reconciled with her authentic self, honor is reconciled with love. The play summons up and destroys illusions, and as this happens theatrically the characters grow in compassion. It is not a virtue for which Calderón is famous. But in this play at least, Calderón instills sympathy for his characters, for Angela and for Manuel, and really only for the two of them together. Out of conflictive demands – desire and honor, pleasure and restraint, reality and illusion – he shapes a balanced whole. √√

3

Calderón and Tirso: *El galán fantasma*

> "¿Quién eres, hombre?"
> "¿Quién soy? Un hombre sin nombre."
>
> ("Who are you, sir?"
> "Who am I? A man with no name.")
>
> *El burlador de Sevilla*

On the grounds of the reading just given, *La dama duende* is one of Calderón's most successful plays. In it, he discovered and mobilized the near-magical powers of self-transformation that could be wrought through the deft use of theatrical space. The form of the theatre and its stage, which hint of interiority and even of sexual intimacy, are part of an illusion which can be embraced and finally dispelled in the interests of moral order. But that order is not, as in some of the allegorical *autos*, a transcendent world of the spirit; it is the male-dominated social structure within which Angela moves and to which she is subject. Calderón refuses to bend this order in response to Angela's needs, in part because he is genuinely interested in the human trials which such difficult accommodations entail, but also because he seems to sense something in the male psyche which was, at root, rigid and unswerving; in contrast he sees the female psyche as relatively supple in its composition. This was not, as it might seem, a generic response of *comedia* writers to the social circumstances of seventeenth-century Spain, although for evidence of this we shall have to look outside Calderón's work. Indeed, Tirso's Don Juan, who offers the negative self-definition of himself as a "nameless man," provides the most convincing support for the claim that *comedia* as a genre may admit a male hero as supple as Calderón's Angela. As I shall say, however, Don Juan is exactly the inverse of the characteristic *comedia* hero; in comparison to Calderón's Astolfo, the hero of *El galán fantasma* who may be compared to his phantom lady, he is still an exceptional creation.

37

Since Don Juan was first conceived in 1614 or 1615 by Tirso he has lent his name and legend to versions by Molière, Mozart/da Ponte, Zorrilla, Grabbe, Pushkin, Anouilh, and on some counts at least a hundred others. He is like no typical male hero of the Spanish *comedia* because he is able to subvert the social structures of power and identity and say, rather like Philip Sidney's Astrophil or, more closely, Shakespeare's Iago, " I am not I." Where Calderón's males are characteristically steely and rigid, Don Juan is temperamentally, psychically, and above all sexually, supple. The exuberance with which he flouts morality, and which in Tirso's version damns him to hell, has provided for his survival as a myth. In the end his negative self-definition has given him a more enduring claim to fame than any of the other memorable characters of the Spanish Golden Age theatre. Among the others – Gutierre of *El médico*, Juan Roca of *El pintor de su deshonra*, Segismundo, Lope's Peribáñez – only Guillén de Castro's Rodrigo, the Cid, has transcended the genre, and he not solely on the strength of Guillén de Castro's play.

Pedro Salinas saw Don Juan as the Baroque inversion of Renaissance Venus; for Ortega he is the vitalistic obverse of Socratic irony and reason.[1] What to my reading is most impressive about Tirso's Don Juan is the fact that his sexual conquests are so dextrously cunning and his power games so nearly self-effacing. He is a master of illusion, the self-dramatist par excellence, and he is able to pursue his own desires by a shrewd capacity for empathy with others. He achieves dominance and mastery by insinuating himself into whatever context may surround him. Don Juan stalks and takes his sexual prey as a benevolent *caballero*, reaping huge profits from individual and collective trust: "Tan largo me lo fiáis," as if to say "Trust me a while longer." The phrase is spoken by a man who invariably seems innocent, nearly naive, which is of course the posture of every confidence man.

Since Don Juan defines himself in negative terms and seeks only the satisfaction of his ego, he risks no injury to his personality and no perdition of a deeper moral self; his appetites are large and he consumes his quarry with gargantuan lust. But this also means that Don Juan's desires can never find fulfillment. One would have to look, in the theatre, to Marlowe's Tamburlaine, tearing up huge chunks of the map, to find an appetite of comparable energy and size. But since there are no models within the *comedia* to explain these aspects of Don Juan's character, one must look instead to the broader cultural conditions which might have made it possible to imagine him; these were the very same conditions which made possible the existence of the *comedia* as a genre, that is to say the structures of social power in force in Golden Age Spain. Don Juan is the anti-*caballero*. He finds his way to the core of established power structures – family, honor among gentlemen, orders of chivalry, King and Court – in order to subvert them. Thus he is one of the few authentically dangerous figures ever imagined on the Spanish stage of this period, and his threatening power is at least equal in force to the strength of the social bonds he rends. Where other *comedia* villains are overtly evil and threaten only certain social strata or institutions, Don Juan is unilaterally subversive. His treachery is rooted in his capacity for self-dramatization and illusion, for playing roles and imagining himself *other* than what he is. Appropriate cultural terms of comparison would be some of Cortés' strategies in the taking of Mexico; in both instances a reigning power structure is threatened by subversion. Cortés' capacity for situational improvisation, for military and political conquest in the manner of Don Juan's sexual conquest, through the flexible adaptation of self to circumstance, through role-playing and the strategic use of illusion, set him apart as a military man from the more bloodthirsty conquerors like Pizarro and Nuño de Guzmán. Able to insinuate himself into the circumstances at hand, Cortés proved to be an effective leader; he was for instance able to take shrewd decisions privately and give the appearance that they had come voluntarily from those under him.[2]

In a recent study of the "improvisation of power" in Shakespeare's *Othello*, Stephen Greenblatt cites a related incident from Peter Martyr's *De orbe novo* (1525).[3] Martyr tells how the Spaniards of Hispaniola were able to subvert the entire population of a neighboring island in the Bahamas (then the Lucayas). Tactically, the account is reminiscent of Cortés among the Aztecs, who believed that he was Quetzalcoatl. Greenblatt adopts the term "empathy" in its sociological sense to describe this strategic capacity to see oneself in the other's position, for the purposes of military, cultural, or interpersonal subversion. As regards Don Juan, the capacity for empathic projection, i.e. for identifying oneself with another, is at the heart of what I have called his negative self-definition. It shows up most clearly in the play in the specific strategies of his self-dramatizations. As a *burlador*, Don Juan is an impostor, a mountebank, and he plays roles from the very start of the play. The work in fact begins on a note of equivocation, with Don Juan as the Duque Octavio. He impersonates the Duke and then excuses his actions to his uncle: "Mozo soy y mozo fuiste," as if to say "you were once like this too." Calling on his store of "empathy," he lets his uncle think he imagines himself in his place, and thus retains control. Later he supplants the bridegroom at the wedding feast. He steps into the role of his friend, the Marqués de la Mota, seizing opportunity from the equivocations of others. Tisbea, the fisherwoman, is his only real challenge, but he defies her scorn and fans her fiery passion.

After each performance, Don Juan runs. "Ensilla, Catalinón" ("Saddle up, Catalinón"): this *estribillo* of motion is the emblem of his energy, the spur of desire which pricks his ego. He runs after each conquest because his appetite is insatiable; it is his only way to self-definition because his ego is itself so highly mobile. He is male energy in perpetual motion, a whirlwind of libidinous drive, and if he should stop moving he would cease to exist. In this he again represents the inversion of the reigning social order. Unlike most Western societies, which have been characterized by their remarkable mobility, both for the society as a whole geographically and for the individual or class within society, Spanish culture throughout the Golden Age demonstrated the marks of "traditional society."[4] In as much as the hierarchies of caste were relatively static, they inhibited overt development of the more mobile sensibility characteristic of other societies in the West. Yet underneath, or in the shadows alongside the hierarchies of caste, we find the possibility of challenging not simply individual social institutions but the reigning caste order itself. Apart from a few of the *conquistadores* in the New World, Tirso's Don Juan is unique in giving expression to this treacherous possibility.

Seen in these terms, there are major differences between Tirso's imagination in *El burlador* and Calderón's in *La dama duende*, only some of which could be accounted for in terms of the sexual differences between the main characters. Still, Calderón's early plays owe large debts to Tirso, and *La dama duende* is to be counted among those that show this indebtedness. On the whole this group of plays is uneven in tone and shape; it includes Calderón's *Lances de amor y fortuna, Los cabellos de Absalón, El mayor monstruo del mundo, A secreto agravio, secreta venganza, El encanto sin encanto, El secreto a voces* and, of special interest here, *El galán fantasma*. Some of their most significant affinities with Tirso's work are to be found at the level of plot, but as I want now to discuss it was in terms of overall dramatic conception that Tirso was of importance to Calderón in his early years. When Calderón began writing in the late 1620s, the Lopean stage had reached maturity. Tirso was already making fundamental changes in the constitutive principles of the genre. He built worlds of intrigue, kinetic shapes, fast-paced worlds of phantoms, shades, darkness, and deceit. He mastered the art of intricate plotting. His characters were imagined as not so much intelligent as ingenious and resourceful, gifted with the ability to improvise ways of response. Like Don Juan, they have a singular capacity for losing themselves, to play the roles demanded of them by their circumstances, to mine theatrical illusion, in order to find fulfillment, even if this means nothing more than the satisfaction of their base drives.

Tirso attempted to mobilize some of the same psycho-sexual energy we find in *El burlador* for the female characters of two plays which bear directly on Calderón's *El galán fantasma*: *La celosa de sí misma* and *Amar por señas*. His intuitive understanding of the female psyche was considerable, but neither play matches *El burlador*. Like *La dama duende*, these plays lack the subversive threat which enlivens *El burlador*. Tirso tried to explore the limiting consequences of role-playing, social improvisation, and theatrical illusion, but his characters are weakened because they are morally admirable: they relinquish their self-dramatizing drives, they forsake illusion, and they are saved. Hence they are worthy of none of the tragic admiration which we feel for Don Juan at the end of *El burlador*.

In *La celosa de sí misma*, Don Melchor falls madly in love with Magdalena, a lady whose identity is unknown to him, and whom he recognizes primarily by a snow-white hand which he once had the pleasure to glimpse unveiled. If he is impetuous, Magdalena maintains a tough outer varnish of pretense. The "scornful disdain" with which she greets Melchor is courtly and practiced. The dual ironies are entirely predictable: it had already been arranged for Melchor to marry Magdalena, the very lady whose heart he cannot seem to win; Magdalena is enamored of Melchor. Although she has no suspicion of his love for her, she makes plain her feelings to her confidante. She remains an unattainable beauty in his mind, and he a gallant stranger to her.

Magdalena creates an image of Melchor that is purely of her own fashioning. In the face of reality, the image seems to pale: "que si le amé forastero, / doméstico y dueño ya, / dudo, al paso que le quiero" ("for if I loved him as a stranger, now, lord and master at home, I

doubt that I'll love him right away") (II, 1459b).[5] In order to sustain
the illusion, she must engage Melchor in situations that will lead him
to believe that she is indeed the intriguing lady of the snow-white
hand. The role of mysterious stranger she wishes Melchor to take is
fruit of the role that she has created for herself: that of the lady loved
by such a man. Magdalena is duple. She is both herself and a
fabricated image of herself, and she takes advantage of Melchor's
willingness to sustain the illusion. Throughout, Tirso underlines the
irony that the two are meant for each other by prearranged design.

Magdalena finds that Melchor is more interested in the mysterious
lady she pretends to be than in the Magdalena whose hand he has
been promised. Her role is not something from which she can detach
herself. She perceives herself in terms of her role, and her role vies with
her deeper self. As she reveals to Quiñones, she is divided within:

> . . . yo, Quiñones,
> soy amada aborrecida
> desdeñada y pretendida.
> ¡Mira mis contradicciones!
> Cubierta, doy ocasiones
> a su pasión amorosa;
> vista, soy fea y odiosa;
> enamoro y desobligo;
> y compitiendo conmigo,
> de mí misma estoy celosa.   (II, 1470b)

(Quiñones, I am despised and beloved, courted and scorned. Just look at my
contradictions! Veiled, I fuel his loving passion; seen, I am ugly and odious. I
inspire love and I offend. Competing with myself, I am jealous of myself.)

She has created an image for herself, and in the space between self and
self-image, the monster of jealousy rears its ugly head. Perhaps her
willingness to fashion a false image of herself stems from a deep
discontent. There seems to be no way out of the vicious circle of role-
playing and illusion; here, she is jealous of the created image. When
she finds that Melchor's cousin is in love with her, she must
perpetuate her role as someone she is not.

The only character in the play comparable to Magdalena is
Quiñones, her confidante. Jealous from the start, she would rather
have Melchor marry another lady, Angela, than see Magdalena wed.
Quiñones plays on Angela's most vulnerable sentiments, love and
jealousy. For a brief time, Magdalena competes with Angela, a
usurper of her role, an image of Magdalena's created self-image. But

Angela is not strong enough to play the part for long. She quickly abandons her role. Magdalena must do the same if she is to win Melchor. But, for her, to abandon a role is to grow through self-sacrifice, in the context of social restrictions. Magdalena sheds her role: she comes to terms with herself, and she accepts the imposed demands of the society in which she lives. Thus it is not her role that saves her, but the fact that she succumbs. The role is not the personally creative force that it was for Calderón's *dama duende*, nor the brilliantly tragic force that it was for Don Juan Tenorio. None of the characters of this play have the psychic energy of Don Juan or the *dama duende*. They are either calculating social strategists, or comic figures, who may or may not know themselves. But they are not sufficiently strong supporters of truth and self-identity, nor do they cling to illusions enough to merit heroic exaltation or destruction.

Amar por señas is a further Tirsian play that relates to *La dama duende*. The understanding of concealed desires, the intellectual and psychological manipulation among characters, the use of role-playing and illusion in social intercourse, are remarkable here, but still there is an obstinate margin between this play and greatness. Don Gabriel is cast as an overzealous *galán*, with a certain *quijotismo* about him. (His lackey Montoya is quick to inform us of the fact.) Gabriel is smitten by Beatriz, and she in turn generates and controls the circumstances of his love. As a covert force, she is a powerful character. But she lacks the sheer presence which might make her memorable. She operates at a distance. Early on, Ricardo is sent to detain Gabriel and Montoya, to take their belongings, and to state that he has been ordered to do so by a nameless lady who loves Gabriel. Asked if it might be any of three specific ladies, including Beatriz, Ricardo responds with a coyly enigmatic statement: "porque es una de las tres, / y de las tres no es ninguna" ("because she is one of the three and of the three she is none") (I, 1722a). Gabriel and his servant are held doubly captive: they are detained within a house in the forest, and they are unable to decipher the enigma.

Tirso wants to stress the mental and psychic aspect of Beatriz' control. Gabriel is advised in an unsigned note to "conjeturar por señas cuál de las tres primeras damas es la que en Palacio os apetece por amante" ("guess by signs which of the first three ladies is the one who in the Palace wants you as lover") (I, 1777a). But these are theatrical ploys, and not altogether successful ones. The riddles are neither sufficiently profound nor entirely humorous. Were the play in all respects a piece of Saturday entertainment, the cavil would matter little. But Tirso is driving at some deeper insight into the life of the psyche and the passions that he tapped in making Don Juan.

The play works best where it most resembles *La dama duende*. Trapped within the room of a house, Gabriel is Beatriz' object of worship. Edwin Honig spoke of "rites of love" in connection with *La dama duende*: they are in full force here. Beatriz supplies her prisoners with ample food; she lowers the viands on a winch, as a ritual of feeding. Ironically enough Montoya sees her seemingly magical powers in religious terms, whereas her driving motive is erotic.

> . . . ¡Oh soror,
> la más callada obradora
> de cuantas amor registra!
> Hágate el Cielo ministra,
> abadesa, correctora,
> guardiana, archibispesa,
> pontificia, preste Juana.   (I, 1778b)

(Oh sister, the most silent worker of all those whom love counts among its numbers! May Heaven make you minister, abbess, corrector, guardian, archbishopess, priestess, pontifical Juana.)

The role-playing in a play like this is teasing, but Tirso has serious motives. Beatriz is forced to shed her role and to become reconciled with her deeper self, just like Angela of *La dama duende* and Magdalena of *La celosa de sí misma*. Tirso saw all the advantages of shrewd character control and of Celestinesque dialogue in making this play, but he also saw that the stage, the theatrical space itself, could be a powerful setting for the dramatization of the fluctuations of human psychic and erotic desires. The spatial awareness in "blind" works like Lope's *La Dorotea*, Rojas' *Celestina*, and in the novels of Richardson or Dostoyevsky, is a function of a purely verbal reality. Tirso has the added advantage of representational space in which to probe the changing makeup of his characters. The sense of ritual, despite the comic sheen, is achieved largely by serious representational effects. And the illusion of growth follows on the shadings of dark and light, the divisions within the self, that are reflected in the spatial rapprochements and separations set forth on the stage.

Calderón's phantom man is less the counterpart to his phantom lady than one might at first expect. More equivocal in tone than *La dama duende*, *El galán fantasma* brings intimations of the fantastic to the world of conventional comedy of intrigue. The supernatural turns out to be completely mundane and explicable, more a conventional illusion of the theatre than the product of a deep intuition of some otherworldly realm. To be sure, a play like this is impressive as a representation of interior, human space, an inhabited world, a personal life; but it is excessively conventional. The important matter is to determine whether there is anything which justifies this conventionality, or whether Calderón is guilty of abuse. Is his understanding of the male personality on a par with his penetration of the female psyche in *La dama duende*, or with Tirso's unleashing of volatile male sexuality in *El burlador*?

Astolfo, the hero of the play, is not as convincing a phantom as Angela was. From the very start, Julia saps energy from his role. It is through her initiative, her masquerades and clandestine maneuvering, that she and Astolfo are able to meet. For a brief while, she is fearful of threats to Astolfo's life (indeed, for a time she thinks he has been killed). But on the whole she is strong-willed and persuasive. Her will prevails over Astolfo's. She dominates him by a diction and rhetoric which are singularly effective:

> Y, pues, que yo vengo así
> a persuadirte, a rogarte,
>
> . . .
>
> yo ruego lo más difícil,
> concede tú lo más fácil.   (II, 638b–9a)

(And, since I come thus to persuade you, to beg you, . . . I beg what is most difficult, you should concede what is most easy.)

There is a tunnel that runs underground between the house of a friend, Carlos, and Julia's house. The lovers use this passageway for their secret meetings. Carlos, who is in love with Laura, facilitates the lovers' comings and goings. But, whereas in a play like *La dama duende* the characters seem to move with and within their setting, melding their plans and designs with the spatial resources they find at hand, this communicative space, unlike the partition in *La dama duende*, is not personalized enough to provide a convincing illusion of the characters' inner growth. Calderón was looking to create a sense of enclosure, of environmental containment; the Duke for instance notes the cool, enveloping darkness: "En esta noche fría / émula hermosa de la luz del día" ("In the shade of this cool night, beautiful copy of the day's light") (II, 644a); but his verbal scenery is backed by worn Renaissance convention. We should expect more of the Duke. He is a proud man, self-assured, yet convinced that Julia loves Astolfo and not him. He is jealous like Tirso's Magdalena, and he perpetuates and confirms his own passion. But he does not show any capacity to mould himself to changing circumstances and so to see his real wants fulfilled. He is a static, presumptuous prop.

Calderón puts his hero Astolfo through rigorous training in the art of situational invention. In the garden scene, he reacts impetuously to Carlos. He moves to the balcony, drops down from there to the garden itself, and confronts the Duke; one can easily imagine the scene played on the loft and elevated platform of a contemporary open-air stage. In the ensuing skirmish, Astolfo falls wounded. As he will later confess to Julia, "celoso una noche entré / y salí muerto" ("One night I went in jealous and came out dead") (II, 656a): his jealousy killed him. Actually, he is not killed, but only wounded, yet his situational death is crucial because it gives him a needed entrée into vital circumstances for the remaining action of the play.

What is surprising about Calderón's arrangement of the roles in this play is that the hero is one of the weaker and more vulnerable characters. Carlos is self-confident and bold. Enrique, Astolfo's father, is diffident but worried; he bends to the demands of social convention, yet he is instrumental in saving his son's life and in caring for him as he recovers from his wounds. He knows, as is shown in his words to Laura below, that social conventions naturally limit speech and actions, and he knows how to accommodate his actions to the surrounding social context. Conscious of the dangers of gossip, he is able to protect the privacy of what he has to say. Ingeniously, he suggests that a door be left ajar:

> No la cierres, que podrán
> escucharnos detrás della;
> que el que quiere decir, Laura,
> cosas, y más como éstas,
> adonde importa el secreto
> tanto, hace mal si la cierra,
> pues no sabe quién le escucha   (II, 647a)

(Don't close the door, since they will be able to hear us behind it. For, if we want to say things, Laura, above all things like these where secrecy is so important, it is worse to close the door, since one never knows who listens in.)

If he is an emotional man, as he reveals in private conversation with his daughter, he is also astutely aware of the public settings which restrict frank self-relevation.

Enrique, more than his son, is Calderón's success in this play. He

continuously alternates between social feint and cover-up on the one
hand and authentic self-expression on the other. The two modes of
behavior set each other off. His monologue at the beginning of Act III,
for instance, is one of Calderón's many remarkable uses of seemingly
silent self-reasoning. But such rational controls are as much illusions
of the dramatist's making as they are tacit governors of a character's
true self. Logic orders the emotions and gives the appearance that
they spring from inner necessity. Enrique verbalizes his rational
process:

> Mas no hay de qué recelarme.
> Si quejoso me imagina
> de su rigor, ¿no será
> más cierto pensar que ya
> hacerme honras determina
> que disculpen su rigor?
> Sí, pues que no puede ser
> otra cosa . . .   (II, 658b)

(But there is nothing to fear. If I think I am offended by his cruelty, would it
not be better to think that he is now seeking to do me honor, which will
excuse his cruelty? Yes, for it can be nothing else . . .)

One can see here a bud of the verbalized suspicions that are so
prominent in *El médico de su honra*. Calderón was deeply interested in
the uses, the limits, even the perversions of logic, and when the Duke
bellows that logic and reasoned speech are beneath his attention, we
wonder if the boast makes any sense at all: "Yo puedo formar
discursos; / pero no temer peligros" ("I know how to make speeches,
but not how to fear danger") (II, 660b). In a world so tightly
controlled by convention, frank statements seem boorish.

Once Astolfo is presumed dead, Calderón studies the reactions of
Carlos, Juan, and the Duke to the possibility that he has reappeared
as a phantom man. Carlos has arranged a secret meeting with Laura,
and as he is about to leave, his servant Candil tells him of a mysterious
man who has come to call. Julia has sincere emotions guiding her
perceptions, and she is ready to believe that she sees Astolfo's ghost.
But this sincerity is a source of illusion. When Astolfo appears, Julia is
frightened. Terrified at the apparition, she faints. When she recovers,
her verses to the Duke underscore her belief in the ghost. A long block
of *silvas*, they betray confusion, surprise, belief, and the doubts of
reason. The phrasing is halting. She is breathless:

> En este (¡ay Dios!) no sé (no tengo aliento)
> cómo diga, jardín o monumento;
> en este (¡ay Dios!), no sé (¡desdicha dura!)
> cómo diga, sepulcro de hermosura . . .
> Mas ¿qué dudo, luchando yo conmigo?
> Monumento, señor, y jardín digo.
> . . .
> No puedo hablar . . . Yo vi, yo vi bañado
> en sangre y polvo a Astolfo, que abortado
> de su sangre nacía.   (II, 653b–4b)

(In this (oh God!) I don't know (I'm out of breath) what to say, garden or
cemetery; in this (oh God!), I don't know (cruel misfortune!) what to say, a
tomb of beauty . . . But what do I doubt, fighting with myself? A cemetery,
sir, and a garden I say. I cannot speak . . . I saw, I saw Astolfo bathed in
blood and dust, brought to life aborted from his blood.)

The most effective moments of the play come in verses such as these,
which try to be serious. Yet the overall tone remains equivocal, and
the gross exaggeration defuses the power of the play. One can hear a
giggle ripple through the audience; they know full well that there has
been no death. The illusions in the play are both comic and serious,
which is technically intriguing, but the ambiguity of tone is a major
flaw.

Like Julia, the Duke is ready to believe that the apparition is really
Astolfo's ghost. His passions have preconvinced him. Because he is
jealous of Astolfo, he is never convinced that his love for Julia would
be reciprocated. Even after Astolfo is "dead" he feels his love for Julia
threatened. Octavio challenges his sentiments:

> Si tú mismo confiesas de esos modos
> que murió, y es verdad que anoche todos
> su entierro vimos, ¿cómo en esta parte
> un muerto puede darte
> celos?   (II, 649b)

(If you yourself admit that he died that way, and if it is true that last night we
all saw his burial, how then can a dead man make you jealous?)

Yet Astolfo's ghost remains a nearly tangible projection of his own
"mayor monstruo," his jealousy. Passion creates illusion, as Carlos
well observes: "sería ilusión de tu ciega fantasía" ("it must have been
an illusion of your blind imagination") (II, 655b). Jealousy is a
passion whose business is deceit.

Astolfo himself is only brought back to life, figuratively, as he
confesses his jealousy. The action begins to unwind, and he reveals

himself to Julia at the end of Act II, confirming the thematic
connection between his "death," his phantom existence, and his own
jealousy:

> puesto que celos y muerte
> dicen muchos que es lo propio.   (II, 656a)

(since many people say that death and jealousy are the same thing.)

As the confession of jealousy leads to the destruction of illusion, the
speech brings us into a world of exceedingly formalized and
conventional diction. In this world, Astolfo is not a convincing
character. Dramatically, he is his own undoing. Once he conquers
passion, he has little real use for the situational intelligence and
improvisation that he has learned. His capacity to dramatize himself
and deal in illusion, to be a phantom, is in the end useless. Calderón
sees the tension between illusion and moral virtue, but the conflict
works against the illusion which Calderón himself needed to make a
successful play.

It is not Astolfo, but Laura and Carlos, who are sustained by their
naturally deceptive behavior. Taken by surprise at Enrique's unexpected return, the lovers must improvise a plan. We know that
Enrique would not hesitate to let the full force of his sentiments be
known if he were to find the two alone in his house. But their spon-
taneous response is disguised by its disappointing conventionality:
Laura hides Carlos in a closet. Utterly perturbed, she speaks to the
audience in *apartes*. But she cannot lower the mask entirely and put her
fears aside. She misreads Enrique's concern over the fact that he is
concealing his son. She sees only her own preoccupation that Enrique
might discover Carlos, superimposing her cares upon his:

> *Enriq.*   Pues, ¿no basta
>   saber, Laura, que escondido . . . ?
>   Déjame, que hablar no puedo.
> *Laura*   [*Aparte*]
>   A declararse conmigo
>   iba, y al decir que sabe
>   que Carlos está escondido,
>   le volvió a atajar el llanto.   (II, 661b)

(*Enriq.* Well, wasn't it enough, Laura, to know that hidden . . . ? Leave
me alone, I can't say it. *Laura* (*Aside*) He was going to speak his mind to me,
but when he said that Carlos is hidden, his tears cut him off again.)

When she learns of Enrique's true concerns, she uses a bit of female
psychology to convince him to allow her to visit Julia:

> *Laura*   Las mujeres nos decimos
> más fácilmente a nosotras
> todo aquello que sentimos.
> Yo iré a visitar a Julia,
> y a darle de todo aviso.   (II, 662a)

(*Laura*   We women can tell each other what we feel more easily. I'll go visit Julia and inform her of everything.)

She is one of the more successful engineers of illusion in the play. Yet her designs are for the short term. They are limited to those moments when she feels endangered. She can react to pressing immediate exigencies, but she does not execute plans to achieve more far-reaching goals.

This underscores a broader weakness of the play. Astolfo is the only character with constant designs, and he would prefer to achieve those in straightforward ways, were that possible. If at the start he suffers from limitation by adverse circumstances, in the end he learns to find the measure of accommodation needed to save himself. He is steadfast in his love for Julia. He is reluctant to leave her alone, vulnerable to the Duke; he suggests that he and Julia hide in the tunnel as the Duke approaches. But he is less active than reactive, more ruled by the situations that others determine than by the ones he himself creates.

Perhaps it was not possible to imagine a successful counterpart to the phantom lady. What Tirso did with Don Juan was to allow his character to gain complete and total control over others – recognizing no controls for himself – by a subversive capacity for role-playing, illusion, and dramatization. But Tirso had the relative advantage of Don Juan's moral corruption. He had no need to school him in plain-dealing and steadfastness. On the whole, Calderón's males are more impressive in the honor plays, where they are block-like and rigid rather than in comedies like this, where the hero is accommodating.

In resolving the action, Calderón falls back shamelessly on convention and stock tricks of plot design. The plot is tied into a seemingly irresoluble knot until just before the end. In the *Arte nuevo*, Lope advised leaving the denouement until the last possible moment; he would have applauded the technique here. Astolfo is found by Laura, unexpectedly, in Carlos' house, and Laura is in turn discovered by Astolfo. The Duke mistakes Laura for Julia and discovers that Julia is in Carlos' house. Enrique and Astolfo finally have no choice but to reveal Astolfo's presence and the true nature of the *galán fantasma*. What remains of the illusion is destroyed. The antagonist is brought to his knees, figuratively speaking, his *soberbia* castigated; the hero is justified and praised. But there is no climax of personal growth, no psychological development, no sense of reconciliation.

In short, the play is self-defeating. The theatrical illusion and the moral theme are no help to each other. Calderón has a right to believe in poetic justice, but he owes his audience something more than conventional advice. At his best, he is able to give us poetic justice laced with moral concern, and still tempt us to delight in the theatrical illusions, themselves antithetical to the ideals of moral disclosure. At his *very* best, Calderón works out a subtle critique of illusions through theatrical representation. But it is important that the paradoxes cross in perfect order; partial magic will not work. Throughout his career, Calderón was sensitive to the ambiguities of illusion and the self-conscious possibilities of the theatre. He was at work, from the first to the last, mining the dualities of the theatrical image. But he did not continue for long in this vein. His late *comedias de salón* are cut from a different cloth, and fulfill a different critical function.

4

El secreto a voces: language and social illusion

"The stage is a concrete physical space which asks to be filled, and to be given its own concrete language to speak."

Antonin Artaud

Lope de Vega once remarked that if at the opening of *La Celestina* Melibea had not asked Calisto the simple question, "¿En qué Calisto?," Fernando de Rojas' closet drama would not have existed at all. Lope was acute in his judgment, having spent decades writing and revising his *Dorotea*, a dialogue novel in the vein of Rojas' work. Melibea's comment is not coy. She is young and innocent, and this is a first love. She speaks the line with complete candor. But the consequences which Rojas spins out in the remaining dialogue of the *Celestina* – the personal silences, the collective lies – are as deadly, as poisonous, as anything imagined by a Chekhov or a Kraus. Rojas is sensitive as no other writer is to the personalized tempers, the distinct ranges of hearing, possible in and through language. The *Celestina* takes in the gamut of styles and registers. In the Golden Age canon, only the *Quixote* can match its range. But Cervantes had nothing of Rojas' ear for the spoken word. Rojas is scathingly subtle at the numbed nerve-ends of language, in cliché, precisely where it is most difficult to keep the touch of feeling alive. He lets his characters eat away at the verbal varnish of social self-presentation; they then find that their lives run to disastrous ends. In its language (there is nothing more) the work is a devastating critique of the Spain of Rojas' day.

The *Celestina* is not a play. Rojas gives the illusion of intimate, lived space, simply in the implied perspectives of his characters' voices. Their words are laden with forces directed from one self to another; they originate in a spatially determined if "blind" awareness, and they end in another. They are spoken before no public. No audience *overhears* what is said on the stage because there is no stage; the overhearings are consigned to the space in which only the characters'

52

voices resonate. The work resembles drama, but it is not theatrical. Stephen Gilman saw it as a proto-novel rather than as a work of theatre.[1] The insight is all the more true if we speak with specific reference to the Spanish stage. While in the *Dorotea* Lope achieves a sense of dialogue akin to that of the *Celestina*, the characters of his *comedias* are given to speaking in long monologues; Leo Spitzer called the characters of the *Dorotea* "*Konversationsgeister*";[2] they provide an interpersonal audience for each other and are each other's personal space of (over)hearing.

A *comedia* like *El caballero de Olmedo* owes a large and obvious debt to the *Celestina* in characterization, but Lope's theatrical idiom and social perspective are nearly antithetical to those of Rojas. On the whole, the *comedia* uses language in a public guise. The characters speak in a national idiom, and understandably so: Lope fashioned the *comedia*, following the example of the Valencian dramatists, out of the native ballad tradition. But the scenic factor was crucial in determining the path that the *comedia* took. The verbal space of the *comedia* is complemented by an actual, public space. This technical difference between a dialogue novel or a closet drama and a theatrical representation alters the language in inestimable ways. The *comedia* grew up in open-air theatres, in *corrales*, where communication could be visual as well as aural, but where elaborate stage effects were for a long time unavailable. The efforts of nineteenth-century editors with a penchant for scenic division and description mislead when they indicate that a work like *Peribáñez* is set in the "living room of Peribáñez' house" at the beginning.[3] Like most of Lope's plays, *Peribáñez* exists in verses directed toward a massed audience, not in an environment which envelops its characters. It was not until after 1635 that the *comedia* became an indoor affair. The genre then underwent a mutation in construction. It changed from what a contemporary critic, Suárez de Figueroa, would have called *comedias de ingenio* to *comedias de cuerpo*. The former were purely verbal; he recalls that some could be mimed, if not acted, by a single voice. The latter needed stage machinery and visual effects.[4] In Calderón's late pageant-plays, in his mythological plays and *comedias caballerescas*, the spectacle and scenery are essential to the theatrical intent. Calderón writes as a showman, intent more on bedazzling his audience visually than on revealing to them the shared intimacies characteristic of novelistic dialogue.

Even in *La dama duende* and *El galán fantasma*, the theatrical and

personal illusions, the role-playing and dramatization, are dependent
on imaginary spatial divisions, objects, or tokens, which maintain an
illusion of personal space: walls, cloaks, closets, tunnels. Calderón
never manifests his sensitivity to spoken language or conversation in
the ways that Rojas does. On the contrary, he uses the studied tones of
pretense and social reflex, courtly and artificial conversation, in
purely theatrical ways. He fits language to the fact of the stage,
making language a show and conversation a spectacle for display. He
works out his social imagining and linguistic critiques in representational ways.

El secreto a voces is seldom read or discussed, which is unfortunate; we
need a summary to facilitate any meaningful treatment here. The
setting is quintessentially courtly: Parma, Italy. Enrique, the Duke of
Mantua, has come incognito to visit the Duchess Flérida, his avowed
love. But Flérida loves Federico, a lesser member of the court. She
must conceal her love because of his inferior social station. Laura,
Federico's peer and admirer, has been promised to Lisardo. Flérida is
jealous; she grows suspicious of Federico's actions. Ironically enough,
she enlists the assistance of Laura and of the *gracioso* Fabio in order to
pursue Federico. Laura and Federico, in turn, are forced to find ways
to express their secret love within the social limitations imposed by
Flérida. Federico must invent ways to meet Laura, and he must
persuade Laura's father Arnesto to allow him to marry his daughter –
without publicly declaring this to Arnesto. The plot is a marvel of
entanglement. Flérida presides over the others and restricts their
actions, and they in turn must seek to fulfill themselves within the
context of her vigilance. As with all such knotted plots, any attempt to
loosen the tangles only entangles things more. The sole solution is to
be found through conversion, by cutting the knot. Flérida's jealous
ambition becomes self-limiting: she recognizes Enrique as the Duke of
Mantua, renounces her interest in Federico, and offers her hand to
the Duke. Once this path is cleared, Federico and Laura are able to
marry as well. There is no deepening of character as the plot moves
along. Flérida's change is sudden; it is a reversal of her ways, a
recantation, not a real enrichment.

Although there is no semblance of personal, inward space, or of
novelistic dialogue, the language of the play remains fascinating in
theatrical terms. From the start, Calderón is aware that he is working
in representational space: to take advantage of this fact, he creates a
dialogue of display. The opening is taken up with music and song and

with verbal equivocation. How can we use language if, every time we speak, the words get in the way? What good are secret words of love if language betrays? What good to be sincere if sincerity cannot be affirmed?

> Razón tienes corazón:
> lágrimas el pecho exhale.
> Mas ¡ay, que inútiles son!
> Que a quien la razón amando no vale,
> ¿qué vale tener amando razón?   (II, 1206a)

(Heart, you are right: let my breast be tearful. But oh, they are of such little use! For if language is useless in love, what does it matter if I am right [have the words/reason] in loving?)

The sigh is as practiced as anything in *Astrophil and Stella*. But whereas Sidney's persona strikes only verbal poses, these are graphically theatrical. The puns themselves get in the way of the lament. The wordplay on *razón* is untranslatable, but no matter; it leads us to an interesting point: Calderón is looking to the theatre as a way to dramatize and enjoy, if not to mend, the breach between speech and reason that concerned almost every Renaissance thinker who had read Cicero.[5] The verbal etyma themselves – *ratio, logos* – are richly ambiguous and suggestive. But Calderón has an advantage unavailable to Lorenzo Valla, Luis Vives, Petrarch, Poggio, Bruni, or Salutati: a theatre. He deploys language in representational space, sending verbal signs shooting through space. As words become things, thought and speech are indissolubly wed. The character relationships of the play are thus moved by the clash of substantive words.

The lovers carry each other's miniature portraits, signs and symbols of affection. They use pictorial images as forms of tacit communication. But Flérida suspects their love. She confronts Federico with the fact. During a moment of deftly placed distraction, Laura sees the danger and switches the portrait she holds for the one Federico has been carrying. Laura saves Federico from chastisement, but does nothing to diminish Flérida's suspicions. The scene ends in a draw for all involved: Flérida gains no further information and Laura and Federico make no significant advances in their attempts to express their love. In view of the manifest danger presented by Flérida's jealous motives, there seems to be little hope for genuine communication in any form in this play.

Yet Enrique tries to communicate with Flérida. To do so he writes letters and sends a proxy, Federico. One critic said that letters like this

in Tirso represented "inadequate means of communication."[6] Use of
the written word suggests a blockage of the verbal channels. In *El
secreto a voces*, where the characters are all striving for authentic
communication, the written word marks a social constriction, a
societal limitation placed on frank and open speech. But Calderón
derives technical benefit from this limiting fact, for "representational" language is a viable ploy on the stage. There is of course a
tension between what is good for Calderón's characters socially and
what is useful to the dramatist theatrically, but he does not sacrifice
his characters' morals to his theatrical ends: he allows them to recant
their ways of concealment and deceit.

   In many ways, the written word is more interesting than studied
courtly speech. We would rather read a letter than listen to false talk.
In Act I, Flérida, Enrique, Laura, and several others convene – ladies
on one side, men on the other, to discuss a topical question: "What
is love's greatest sorrow?" ("¿Cuál es mayor pena amando?")
(II, 1210a). The exercise is a show of social dexterity. The staging itself
suggests a courtly ballet. Calderón shows us language reduced to
quotidian diversion, to mere social coding. Heidegger would call such
language "prattle" (*Gerede*), Roland Barthes *babil*, that mere "foam
of language which forms by the effect of a simple need."[7] This is talk
thick with varnish, courtly and effete, such as may come from reading
too much Castiglione.

   The verbal games are fun, but the personal effect is paralyzing
because the social code is too constricting. Federico and Laura seek a
more personalized form of expression. They invent a private code: at
the flash of a handkerchief they will speak secrets aloud; they will give
voice to private desire by circumventing the public code, flaunting
their relative freedom in the face of constraint. Federico gives the
details of the plan:

>   Siempre que quieras, señora,
>   que de algo tu voz me advierta,
>   lo primero será hacerme
>   con el pañuelo una seña
>   para que esté atento yo.
>   Luego, en cualquiera materia
>   que hables, la primera voz
>   con que empieces razón nueva,
>   será para mí, y las otras
>   para todos . . .   (II, 1222a)

(Whenever you wish, my lady, to tell me something, the first thing to do is to signal me with your handkerchief so that I will pay attention. Then, whatever you say, the first word with which you begin a phrase will be for me, the rest for everyone . . .)

This is semiotic *ingenio*, not psychological dexterity. In comparison to the communicative resources used in *La dama duende*, *El secreto a voces* moves *ingenio* to the surface. Calderón intends this as an exhibition of virtuosity. Language is not just a two-track mode of communication, but a show all in itself. The trick is so difficult, though, that Calderón risks losing touch with his audience. He must confirm the message with discursive underlinings:

> Feder. "Mi bien" es muy imposible,
> "señora", de conseguir;
> "alma" es mía el padecer,
> "y vida" mía el morir.
> Laura [*Aparte*]
> "Mi bien, señora, alma y vida . . ."
> de sus voces entendí.
> Feder. "Está" mi amor tan tirano,
> "cruel" tanto mi sentir,
> "fiera" tanto mi esperanza,
> "infeliz" tanto mi fin . . .
> Laura [*Aparte*]
> Lo que dijo ahora fué:
> "Esta cruel fiera infeliz" . . .
> Feder. "Hoy", que a costa de la vida
> "me" tiene fuera de mí,
> "embaraza" mi temor
> "el hablarte" en esto a ti.
> Laura [*Aparte*]
> "Hoy me embaraza el hablarte."
> Fler. Pues ¿para qué lo decís?
> Feder. "No" me culpes, ni conmigo
> "vayas" enojada así;
> "pues" será mi muerte, haciendo
> "al jardín" sepulcro vil.
> Fler. Está bien.
> Laura [*Aparte*]
>   En todo dijo,
> si lo puedo repetir:
> "Mi bien, señora, alma y vida",
> "esta cruel fiera infeliz"
> "hoy me embaraza el hablarte":
> "no vayas, pues, al jardín."[8]   (II, 1228a–b)

In comparison to Calderón's theatrical exploitation of language, Lope de Vega's technique was less representational, more lyric in bias. One thinks of *La dama boba*, perhaps his finest *ingenio* creation. The play is a lesson in poetics, an education in love and the world through language training. Finea, the play's engaging heroine, learns to master semantics, to feign *bobería* by playing on words, and so to sway circumstances to her advantage. She makes herself into a pun, a hybrid creature, a *boba ingeniosa*. At the outset, she is unaware of the polysemous possibilities of language; she is naive. But in the final scenes she is master of the double meaning, a geminate creature (Nise calls her a *sirena* in Act III, v.659). Finea's awareness of her own *bobería* is consequent on her mastery of language, its tricks and illusions; she sees that the richness of reality itself depends on these illusions. As Lope's linguistic *ingenio* exalts itself through Finea, as Finea learns to discern verbal image and reality, we savor the real as much as the image of the real. (Bruce Wardropper astutely noted that mirror imagery is important in the play.)[9] Through a poetic finesse that simply out-graces Calderón, Lope heightens the claims of reality and illusion both. His own poetry funds their mutual benefits: he knows that language itself can be the source of their increase.

In *El secreto a voces*, wordplay becomes an obstacle to communication and gives rise to hypocrisy. It is not the gateway to a world of multivalent richness and many-sided meanings as in *La dama boba*. The *gracioso* in Calderón's play tells a proverbial story which makes the point: a priest in Macarandona was outraged with the priest of neighboring Agere when he responded, in Latin, *gratias agere*. Fabio's recommendation to Federico, based on the parable, is to further his own goals by maintaining double loyalties:

> Si tú dos feligresías
> tienes de amor, ciego dios,
> cumple con ambas a dos.   (II, 1229b)

(If love, blind god that he is, gave you two charges to look after, be sure to serve them both.)

In *El secreto a voces*, the characters become creatures of language. Dialogue itself is converted into a game in communication. Self-reasoning, soliloquizing, is left for the *gracioso*. The first beneficiaries of this are the spectators; the characters do not grow and blossom like Lope's Finea or Calderón's Angela. Federico and Laura are vehicles for Calderón's dazzling show of linguistic skill. Their fiery stichomythia at the end of Act II is linguistic pyrotechnics, intended for spectacular effect.

Calderón reveals virtuoso technical powers in this play even as he presses the social point. Under Flérida's censorial auspices, the cunning interplay of secrets and voice becomes a pointed critique of social convention. In Act III, when circumstances prevent Federico from speaking to Laura in any way, coded or not, he has recourse to purely nonverbal means of expression: he makes noises at the window to signal his presence to Laura. But "the wind deceives a thousand times" ("El viento engaña mil veces") (II, 1242a), as he tells Flérida, who pries for information. The wind, words, and physical signs alike are deceiving – so much so that when Laura is forced to confront Federico, she must openly deny him. In such severely constrained social circumstances, the truth is fragile when spoken outright. The characters look for moral reassurance and seek self-defense in verbal *apartes*. Not only language, but nonverbal communication as well falters and misses its mark: the noises that Federico made at the window forced the confrontation with Flérida in the first place.

Calderón shows us a world in which it is impossible to speak clearly and openly. Language is weakened as the common ground of society; it fails even as a medium for transmitting information. Occasionally, as in Fabio's monologue at the beginning of Act III, or in Flérida's private reflection after she has gained control over Fabio, we hear the eruption of authentic personal expression. But when characters speak in cryptic codes language is best adapted to illusion and deceit. Flérida is the societal censor. She has forced the other characters to abandon conventional language and seek nonverbal ways of expression. Where she is in power, no one can do what Federico says to Laura's father, "hablar claro." Indeed, those very words of declared authenticity are a trick of Federico's to win Laura's hand.

The *gracioso*, a pivot for the social and linguistic pressures, is himself caught in the cross-currents of manipulation and deceit staged by his master Federico and the Duchess Flérida. Flérida works with Celestina's tools: she has the capacity to make others think that she sympathizes with them, that she sees and understands their needs. She wins Fabio's complicity by a familiar lure – the glitter of gold – which at once loosens his tongue:

> *Fler.* Tomad aquesta cadena.
> *Fabio* Sí haré por cierto; y no ignoro
> que, por ser vuestra y de oro,

será por extremo buena.
Por hablar rabiando estoy.   (ii, 1213a)

(*Fler.*   Take this chain. *Fabio*   Indeed I will. And I know that since it is yours and made of gold, it must be extremely fine. I'm just dying to tell.)

Flérida's sway is powerful. She has sealed her pact with Fabio on her own terms. She has broken the crucial bond of master and servant. Now Fabio is a pawn to be used in her schemes. He supplies all the needed information: that Federico was in Parma when supposedly in Mantua, and that he carries Laura's portrait.

The play ends only as Flérida overcomes her jealousy. The pattern is familiar to readers of Calderón. Twice in the final act, she speaks the formulaic phrase of self-definition, "soy quien soy," first in an *aparte*, as if gathering inner resolve, and finally as an assertion of personal value: "que yo valgo más que yo . . . / . . . Que soy quien soy" ("Since I am worth more than I . . . For I am who I am") (ii, 1244a). She achieves self-domination and relaxes control. She represses jealousy and willingly accepts Enrique. She allows the social tension to subside. On a strictly moral plane, her actions are admirable, but theatrically the ending is weak. As Flérida relinquishes control, she removes the need for artificial social communication. She asserts herself, and she loses her cunning abilities. As she sums up her value in the *estribillo* of self-affirmation, she becomes real to herself. Morally, philosophically, sociologically, we applaud. But we leave the theatre less satisfied than when we entered. There is simply too much pleasure to be reaped from the theatrical illusion for it to be sacrificed for the morality of convention.

5

Toward tragedy

The Calderón who looks out at us from seventeenth-century engravings is not a happy man. The face is stern, the figure restrained, serious, nearly grim. No one thinks of Calderón as a great comic writer, and rightly so: *comedias* like *La dama duende*, *El galán fantasma*, and *El secreto a voces*, which stand at the comic extreme of what he wrote, are not occasions of high laughter. In comparison to Shakespeare or Lope de Vega, Molière or Alarcón, Calderón's sense of humor is restrained. He does not have the festive, saturnalian spirit which animates Shakespeare's comic world. In his hands the conventions of social occasion produce sumptuous court entertainment, but not mythological mirth. In tone, Calderón is reserved. Self-mockery, the lighthearted reversal of literary tradition which underlies Shakespeare's *As You Like It* are not within Calderón's temperamental range. He respects tradition too much and accepts its limitations.

Lope's *comedias* are informed by a different drive. The unifying capacities of passionate, but innocent, human love lend a verve to his verse and a celebratory tone to the action of his plays. Even a work like *Fuenteovejuna*, which is comic in rhythm, if not humorous in tone, depends on the joyous energies released by the drive toward harmony. The marriage of Laurencia and Frondoso is the thematic embodiment of the unifying capacities which Lope sees in human love. Not so for Calderón. Eroticism – as in *La dama duende* – is suspect. In the grim honor plays, the erotic impulse is openly destructive. For Calderón, love is bounded by social constraints; for Lope, it is the groundwork of social harmony. Even bodily, Calderón's heroes internalize their passions, which for that reason so easily run to jealousy, and thence to self-destruction.

How can he write comedy at all if his world is so seemingly "loveless," as one recent critic says?[1] Are Angela, Flérida, and the

61

galán fantasma deeply unfulfilled? To look beyond the comedies: is Segismundo, in renouncing Rosaura, and marrying Estrella, dissatisfied? Is the marriage of Gutierre, the infamous "surgeon" of his honor, a perverse form of punishment for him? Does Calderón imply that he will suffer in his marriage with Leonor? Certainly, Calderón recognizes the constraints of human love; more clearly than Lope or Shakespeare, he sees the price that love exacts. In some cases, as in the honor plays, love is bought at punitive rates. Segismundo, Angela, Flérida, and the *galán fantasma* are all reconciled to their social contexts, as is Gutierre in *El médico*, but Calderón is genuinely interested in the cost of that reconciliation.

More than either Shakespeare or Lope, Calderón knows that love is not freestanding. "Love" for Calderón means not only Eros but *agape* – Christian love, which sees in human love the love of God. Only for this reason are the human sacrifices and denials justified or bearable at all. Calderón can afford to exact the high price of love because he knows that human love is not autonomous. Moreover, he sees human love as naturally limited; like all passions, it is destined to create monstrous illusions. But Calderón sees the possibility of salvation in Christian love. In this light he esteems the greatest of love's demands: self-sacrifice.

As Flérida conquers herself (there are parallels with Segismundo), as the *galán fantasma* comes to life through self-denial, as Angela finds herself by losing her beguiling role, the personal interests are subordinated to stable, institutionalized social structures: marriage, the well-ordered polis, harmonious family life. These collective orders are the repositories of truth for the individual, guides to clear self-perception, templates for responsible action. Rather than celebrate the free reign of Eros, Calderón works toward the reduction of illusion, the sublimation of human passion through its accommodation to the constraints of social existence. Thus where Lope would use the theatre as a form of celebration, in a way closer to Shakespeare's "festive comedy" (C. L. Barber), Calderón uses the theatrical form of comedy to social and moral ends, as a way to engage his audience in the interrelated problems of love and self-sacrifice, self-understanding and action, perception and ethics. These are given shape according to his directly theatrical imagination: the nature of role and the problem of identity, the perils of illusion, the formation of perspective, the ambiguous pleasure of the spectacle itself. In Calderón's hands, comedy is for social criticism, for the resolution of identity crises, for self-discovery, for learning how to use and limit illusion. The value of his comedy depends on what we may, parenthetically, enjoy. If in Shakespeare's comedies we experience an essential deepening of the emotional "felt life" (Henry James), Calderón sees the root purpose of comedy as lying in the comic resolution, in the strengthening and toughening of reality as such.

The sacrificial investments made in reality by Calderón's characters are well made because the theatrical space in which they move is broad enough to embrace illusion while it seeks anchor in some ultimate, immutable ground. Calderón's characters work unfailingly toward felicitous plot resolutions, even where human sacrifice is necessary, because certain rewards will befall them from a wholly different realm. His comedies use irony, if at all, as a stabilizing, grounding force. The butt of irony is often the theatrical illusion itself, through whose dismantling the comic incongruities are resolved. Where tragic irony tends to dissolve truth into an ironic mist, comic irony resolves its polarities, as Wayne Booth says, "into relatively secure moral or philosophical perceptions or truths."[2] Calderón's irony is Christian in manner of function, and in doctrine as well. Death brings life, self-sacrifice yields increase, suffering gives cause for joy. Calderón's comedies reveal a serious sense of life,[3] a radical will to ground illusion.

What is the process by which comedy allows us to master reality? How is the use of illusion placed in the service of reality? In plot structure, the comedies we have seen are romance-like; in fact, *La dama duende* and *El galán fantasma* derive from an actual romance, the *Partinuples de Bles*.[4] I shall say more about romance in connection with Calderón's later plays, but for the present I want to point out that what is unavailable in prose romance is the theatrical form to which the comic resolution is bound in Calderón.

In *La dama duende*, Calderón establishes among his characters, as between audience and stage, interactive layers of proximity to and distance from the sham illusion of the *duende*: Cosme, the over-credulous *gracioso*, believes firmly in the phantom; as his credulity is undercut by Manuel, the *duende* recedes from the spiritual confidence of the audience. Manuel is himself comic in assuming such "good sense" throughout Angela's role-playing; the audience cannot accept his perspective and judgment unequivocally. Angela's roles, particularly as the *duende*, clothe the illusion in comically distancing garb. Through these estimations of the phantom, Calderón is able to entertain the illusion of the *duende* and at the same time to strengthen and uphold its complement, the stable and whole person of Angela. In *El galán fantasma*, the effects are more ambiguous and for that reason not as successful. Astolfo's role involves him in comedy of situation, but he is at the same time our stable dramatic indicator of the nature of the illusion. Although the comic distance does not allow for as strong a reinforcement of self as in *La dama duende*, Astolfo nonetheless places the illusion at a spiritual distance from the audience: his role is an obvious sham that he tries to conceal. The other characters are able to affirm themselves emotionally – the fatherly rage of Enrique, the flagrant jealousy of the Duke, the amorous interests of Laura – vis-à-vis a reality that we, like they, are trying to define and fix.

In Shakespeare's or in Lope's hands, a similar use of levels of distance from the theatrical illusion serves not so much to strengthen and stabilize reality as to deepen our awareness of the ambiguity of reality itself. Shakespeare's comedies range broadly, to be sure, from the situation comedies (such as *The Comedy of Errors*), to comedies of character (such as *As You Like It*), to comedies of transformation (such as *The Winter's Tale* or *The Tempest*). But the comic perspective, the discrepant awareness, is achieved by a subtle manipulation of the balance between reality and illusion, audience and stage: in *The Comedy of Errors*, for example, by supplying the spectators with sufficient information to understand the situation of two sets of identical twins each existing as master and servant, while the characters themselves do not realize this; in *As You Like It*, through a series of dramatic indicators which undercut the characters and distance them from us rationally; and in a play like *A Midsummer Night's Dream*, by a magical transformation, a captivating trick of illusion, that transforms the natural world.[5]

As You Like It (which derives from Thomas Lodge's *Rosalynde* and, possibly, from the anonymous *Tale of Gamelyn*,[6] and not from the Partonopeus romance to which it nonetheless bears some resemblance) is a work similar in form and genre to Calderón's "phantom" plays. Orlando rebels against his brother and flees to the forest of Arden, where he pines for Rosalind, whom he had momentarily encountered at a court wrestling match. In the forest – a kind of illusory world apart, where men "fleet the time carelessly, as they did in the golden world" (i. i. 124–5) – Ganymede (Rosalind in disguise) acts as a maturing force on Orlando's passion and allows his amorous sentiments to deepen. Consequently, Orlando is able to forgive his older brother and realize the noblest qualities of his character. At the outset (I. iii), Rosalind hesitates to admit the seriousness of her love; taking the role of Ganymede, Rosalind loves by proxy. She keeps the reality of her love at the safe distance of illusion. But, as at least one critic says, "she, like Orlando is 'schooled' in affection as she twice observes in Phebe's disdainful repudiation of Silvius (III. v; IV. iii) the cruelty of feminine pride in mocking sincere overtures of love."[7]

The comedy emerges as Shakespeare counterpoints this development of character by a number of incongruities, wrapping illusion in humorous tones. Touchstone mocks the Petrarchan conventions of Rosalind and Orlando (II. iv; compare the parody in III. iii); William's reluctance to approach Audrey offsets Orlando's role (but, of course, William loses his beloved); Phebe's disdain – as in IV. iii. – is a parody of Rosalind's self-assured pretension. Larry S. Champion said that "all such devices block the spectator's emotional involvement and thus create the distance necessary to the comic vision."[8] As in the relationship between Rosalind (Ganymede) and Orlando, each character undercuts the other; the two provide their own mutual context of incongruity. Calderón achieved something of the same effect in La dama duende. Angela, her roles, and Manuel provide each other with an interpersonal context, and place Angela at the distance from the audience that is necessary for her personal growth. She sheds her roles, forsaking illusion for the reality of her authentic ser. In El secreto a voces, Flérida succumbs to reality because of her own deceits.

At the serious end of the theatrical spectrum Calderón is manifestly different from Shakespeare in temper and technique; but there are divergences in the two dramatists' comic use of illusion as well. In Calderón's comedies, the disjunction of stage and audience creates the illusion of a space in which reality is affirmed. The obvious paradox is wondrous while it works, but it is only natural that the situation should bring about the destruction of illusion. In his best plays, Calderón sees that reality is strengthened through love. Within an illusory world of his own making, the dramatist frames the images of guile and deceit which magnetically attract our emotions; yet, through the incongruous or comic characters, we are never completely lost in that world, never fully taken in by illusion. C. L. Barber has written of As You Like It that "the reality we feel about the experience of love in the play . . . comes from presenting what was sentimental extremity as impulsive extravagance and so leaving judgment free to mock what the heart embraces."[9] In Calderón's world, the freedoms are not so wide and the moral demands are more stringent. Reasoned judgment must in fact reject what is most emotionally seductive.

The "complementarities"[10] of reality and illusion, the countervailing interests of judgment and emotion, are adapted to wholly different ends in the non-comic plays. In Shakespeare's *Titus Andronicus*, Marcus laments of Titus' distraction:

> Alas, poor man! grief has so wrought on him,
> He takes false shadows for true substances.   (iii. ii. 79–80)

The same might be said of Hamlet as he sees his father's ghost, or of Richard II, whose hoary ideas about kingship prove inadequate in the face of the "true substances" set in motion by Bolingbroke. Certainly the contrasts between fact and fiction, reason and feeling, substance and the shadows of deceit, supply most of the generative energies of plays like *El médico de su honra*, *El pintor de su deshonra*, and *A secreto agravio, secreta venganza*. Calderón is at least as powerful a builder of contrasts as Shakespeare; he marks antitheses with absolutely clear lines. More than Shakespeare's characters, though, and even more than Descartes, Calderón's characters want to sweep away any interfering "secondary qualities." Perhaps for this reason, and because Calderón himself wants to be able to draw clear lines, his characters *suffer* the separations of mind and body, reason and passion, illusion and reality.

Barber wrote of Shakespeare's early tragedies – *Romeo and Juliet*, *Titus Andronicus*, *Richard II* – that the movement away from mirth is fueled by energies analogous to those which move comedy. Theseus in *A Midsummer Night's Dream* says that

> The lunatic, the lover and the poet
> Are of imagination all compact.   (v. i. 7–8)

In tragedy, though, the imagination gives voice to an inner world of deeply felt, emotional life:

Tragedy is conceived as the contradiction between a warm inner world of feeling and impulse and a cold outer world of fact. Imagination, as the voice of this inner world, has a crucial significance, but its felt reality is limited by the way the imaginary and the real are commonly presented as separate realms. Imagination tends to be merely expressive, an evidence of passions rather than a mode of perception. (pp. 159–60)

Barber saw in Theseus' distinction a formula for discerning what is merely "apprehended" from what is fully, and rationally, "comprehended." More than Theseus, who maintains a unified rationalistic perspective, Calderón wants to understand the consequences of such distinctions and the sources of their breakdown. In his serious drama, in plays like *El médico de su honra* and *El mayor monstruo del mundo*, the irrational world of the phantom passions, the world of unmediated apprehension, will be put to rest. As I will discuss in the chapter to follow, Gutierre's bizarre actions as "surgeon of his honor," his confected role, feed on the shadow-mass of suspicion. The body of his wife could not be a more "true substance." Calderón intuits Gutierre's action, in the closing scenes, via irrationally "apprehended," emblematic images: Mencía's sacrificial body and Gutierre's bloody hand. The outcome of the surgeon's actions destroys what his imagination had fabricated, but Calderón is reluctant simply to demolish the dark products of fantasy. In *El mayor monstruo* we shall see in Herod's "monster" a variation on the theme of jealous passion. His insubstantial affections seem to confine him within tangible space, not so much blinding him to reality as forcing him physically to butt up against its limits. Herod is a man of large appetites; most of Calderón's jealous lovers are. Fed by fantasy, his cravings work their way inward; they swell within the Tetrarch, while externally he is constrained within real space. Calderón intuits the mind-body split theatrically: he underlines the distinctions between illusory space – which can be the most highly personalized and imaginative of all spaces – and substantive physical space. In those of Calderón's *comedias* that tend toward the tragic extreme of the genre – in plays like *El médico de su honra* and *El mayor monstruo del mundo* – the imagination is not consigned to the mere "expression" of reality. On the contrary: imagination is, by definition, a way of seeing via images; it is a means of perception. "Reality" and "illusion" are terms to help us appraise what we see. More than expression, Calderón seeks through the theatrical imagination to strike a balance of judgment.

6

El médico de su honra

> *Ludovico*   . . . Una imagen
> de la muerte, un bulto veo
> que sobre una cama yace:
> dos velas tiene a los lados,
> y un crucifijo delante.   (I, 344b–5a)

(I see an image of death, I see a form lying prostrate in bed: two candles beside it and a crucifix at the head.)

> *Gutierre* trato en honor, y así pongo
> mi mano en sangre bañada
> a la puerta; que el honor
> con sangre, señor, se lava.   (I, 348b)

(I deal in honor, and thus I place my blood-bathed hand on the door; for tainted honor, sir, is cleansed with blood.)

The images that Calderón conjures up at the end of *El médico de su honra* – Doña Mencía's prostrate figure awaiting death, and the bloodied hand of Gutierre her husband – are almost unforgettable theatrical encounters. The words evoke vivid presences which fix our attention. They are images, visible emblems. Just as the bloodied hand which marks Gutierre's door is a rubric of his actions ("Los que de un oficio tratan, / ponen, señor, a las puertas / *un escudo* de sus armas") ("Those who practice a profession, sir, place *a coat of arms* on their door") (I, 348b, emphasis mine), so too Mencía's corpse becomes emblematic of his crime. Calderón looks to incite the *admiratio* of his audience during these two final moments; he drives toward the naked, unmediated apprehension of these images. He elicits a primary emotional response of wonder, horror, dread, and, perhaps, pity. *El médico* is the ultimate honor play; it is by definition meant to stir the passions, to "move everyone forcefully."[1]

Yet the play has provoked no small degree of reasoned scholarly debate, despite the violent and non-rational images of the final scenes.

Calderón is not content simply to bring us the brute fact of human cruelty; he wants to show the clash and the balance of forces exerted by human judgment and reason. The central problem revolves around King Pedro's apparent pardon of Gutierre. The King seems to advise Gutierre to follow this course of action in the future: "sangrarla" ("bleed her"), he tells him, should all other recourses fail to dull his suspicions. Is Calderón condoning Gutierre's action? The clemency of King Pedro seems brutal. Menéndez y Pelayo tried to understand the whole group of honor plays with this harsh implication in mind:

> A secreto agravio, secreta venganza, El médico de su honra, and El pintor de su deshonra are radically immoral in the eyes of absolute ethics, although they may have a certain relative and historical morality, and although they may have served as good examples, for the rigor with which even the slightest suspicion is punished, and we should add that this very draconian rigor proves, to a certain point, that infractions were rare.[2]

His attempt at moral relativism betrays its own unease. Gerald Brenan, whose attitude was similarly extreme, rejected the play out of hand, assuming that "this secret and premeditated murder of an innocent wife is held up to us as a course to be followed."[3]

No one seems to know for certain if Pedro is the Cruel or the Just King in this play. Parker and Sloman find him cruel.[4] Their inference is that neither Calderón nor the audience approves of the pardon. A. Irvine Watson exonerates Pedro, and to a certain degree Gutierre as well, and sees the King as "tragic victim of a cruel social code."[5] Watson, like Parker, poses the question in terms of theatrical genres: is the play a tragedy or not? We should answer that question first – but in order to do so we need to appraise the moral constitution of the hero and the judgment of the judge. The generic possibilities seem limitless. We can redefine tragedy, with Parker, or, with Watson, make infinite distinctions between comedia and comedy, black comedy, melodrama, tragedia patética, tragedia morata, and so on. Polonius' catalogue of the players' repertoire in Hamlet, ii.ii would be a fair estimate of the possibilities.

I invoke the critical controversy surrounding this particular play because it is, as Menéndez y Pelayo saw, representative of a group, and because that group has for many become representative of Calderón's reputation world-wide. Calderón is known for his rigid and bloody honor plays, even if they account for only four or five percent of what he wrote. The way we see El médico is crucial to the way we see Calderón: is he clement or just? Is he himself as dramatist trapped by the social codes which are catastrophic for the characters of these plays?

Bruce Wardropper thought it was possible to understand the play as a kind of "dramatic poetry."[6] The action is spun out of a metaphor that Gutierre carries too far and misapplies. The title itself is an invitation to this kind of reading. But I would go further in this vein and ask of *El médico* not what its lessons are, nor what the absolute guilt or innocence of its protagonist is, nor what the capabilities and intentions of the kingly judge are. Not first. First I would ask the simply stated question: in what way is this play made, and how does it exploit its own theatricality? How does Calderón weave so deeply challenging a moral sensibility into the poetry of the play? How does he weld these formidable theatrics to the problem of human justice and reasoned judgment? With regard principally to Gutierre and Pedro, two facts seem to emerge. The action moves from intrigue and dark illusion, concealment and deceit, to a world of public spectacle and emblematically displayed images, such as those of the final scene. Gutierre and Pedro follow contrasting paths with regard to the roles they play in these diverging worlds. In the final moments of the play they meet: Gutierre's poetically fashioned role brings disaster, and Pedro assumes the responsibilities of a public role, that of king and judge.

The play opens with a Calderonian signature occurrence, the fall from a horse. The event is a seed of disorder. As the King's brother Enrique is thrown to the ground, don Arias comments on his physical state: "A un tiempo ha perdido / pulso, color y sentido" ("All at once he lost pulse, color, and feeling") (I, 317a). Pedro sees to it that his brother is sheltered, but leaves the scene quickly. For Arias, this is evidence of his "fiera condición," his "beastly nature" (I, 317b). Calderón seems already to be driving toward a moral evaluation of his characters, and the play is successful, in large measure, because he is able to awaken our sense of judgment from the start. But the difference between Pedro and Enrique is not ostensibly one of character. It is a difference of role. Pedro remains distant and aloof, intent on what we learn later to be less-than-kingly concerns: "que aunque este horror y mancilla / mi rémora pudo ser, / no me quiero detener / hasta llegar a Sevilla" ("But although this horror and blemish might be an obstacle for me, I don't intend to stop until I reach Seville") (I, 317b). Calderón intends that role-playing should be the basis for our moral evaluation of the characters. Here, Pedro is little more than a name, a virtually vaporous figure in contrast to Enrique who has suffered a jarring physical mishap. We know of Enrique's past passion for Mencía, Gutierre's wife. Pedro has no past and at the start plays no recognizable role. Enrique is notably human, corporeal, embodied; we note his "pulse, color, and feeling" after his fall. In the verses he speaks to Mencía, he signals his own vulnerable humanity: he looks at her and thinks of death ("¡Ay, don Arias, la caída / no fue acaso, sino agüero / de mi muerte!") ("Ay, don Arias, this fall was no accident, but an augury of my death!") (1, 320a).

Calderón begins to take interest in Pedro's emerging role in the following scenes. The fact itself is worth noting. It is not usual for a king to be as involved in the intricacies of clandestine plotting and palace intrigue as is Pedro in El médico. His dubious involvement in the details of the sublunary world should tip us off. Calderón's King Pedro plays a dual role. He is not only judge and figural head of state but a mortal human being. In the course of three acts, Calderón explores his contrasting roles, first as man and finally as king. His Pedro grows into a figure who is finally able to meet his social role, a role sanctioned in the comedia tradition. This assumption of role is all the more notable in contrast to Gutierre, who assumes a purely personal, illusory role. Whereas Pedro as judge transcends his humanity, Gutierre is destroyed by illusion; he is in the end less human than the King.

The ambivalences and poignant complexities of Pedro's role first come to the fore in Act 1 as he interviews Leonor, Gutierre's former betrothed. Pedro is, momentarily, the aloof administrator, wasting few words – "Pocas palabras gasta" (1, 323b) – as one of the pretendientes comments. But he becomes personally involved when Leonor appears. Since honor is the question she brings to him, he must deal with her in private. His interest in a "caso de la honra" demands secretive action. He must move in the covert world of social intrigue. But, in so doing, he relinquishes his royal stance. He cannot, as detective, pronounce on and administer human affairs. He delves into the mundane world, and helps sustain the illusions which one would hope that he, as King, would resolve.

The scene with Coquín, the gracioso who interrupts Leonor's plea, confirms the duality of Pedro's role and the intentional moral ambiguity. Leonor had addressed Pedro as "Justiciero" (1, 323b), but Pedro threatens the jester with bodily harm if he should not make the

King laugh. Inconclusive as that may be, the King offers a grand reward for success. We do not know if Pedro is Cruel or Just. At the very least, Calderón seems to have sensed the advantage to be gained by juxtaposing King and jester. In Act II, Coquín mocks the King as bereft of the quintessential human capacity, that for laughter. But Coquín himself is drawn into the intrigue – not by Pedro but by Gutierre. In certain ways, the *gracioso* is a hinge for the role-playing of the two main characters.

In the scene with Leonor, Pedro vacillates between royal and merely private human roles. He meets her in public but he hears her plea in private. As Gutierre approaches, Pedro is the one to suggest that Leonor should hide behind a curtain. Ostensibly, Pedro does this in the interests of impartiality and justice – "Podrá, so conmigo os ve, / conocer que me informasteis / primero. Aqueste cancel / os encubra . . ." ("If he sees you with me he will know that you informed me first. Hide behind this curtain") (I, 324b) – but this is also a likely historical allusion to Philip IV, who had small windows cut into the council chambers in the Alcázar of Madrid so that he could follow political discussions undetected.[7] In the final act of the play the King will again act as a force sustaining intrigue, and in much the same way. Gutierre comes to him, addressing him in all the kingly terms ("castellano Atlante," "español Apolo" – this latter epithet recalls Philip IV's association with the sun, which was considered the fourth planet[8]); Gutierre presents him with the dagger, but Enrique enters and so Pedro must hide Gutierre, much as he hid Leonor in Act I.

The scene is crucial. As the King returns the dagger to Enrique, royal blood is spilled. Pedro's thoughts run to death; he envisions his own demise at the hands of Enrique. Not only is the King a key actor in the palace intrigue, but he allows his suspicions to rule him. Indeed, he seems much like Gutierre. The image of his death anticipates Gutierre's final verses ("*Bañado* me vi *en mi sangre*, / muerto estuve . . .") ("I saw myself dead, *bathed in my own blood*") (I, 341b, my emphasis); insofar as the image of his own blood marks him as human, he resembles his brother Enrique. Pedro takes the role of mortal man in these palace intrigues; as such, he inhabits a natural body, rather than the "corporate body" of which he, as King, should be head.

Calderón's dramatization of Pedro's dual role is strongly reminiscent of the medieval notion of the king's "two bodies," a juridical appropriation of a mystical fiction. The concept was widely known, and remained popular, at least among political theorists, in the Spanish Golden Age. In *El concejo y consejeros del príncipe* (1559), for example, Fadrique Furió Ceriol explained that "every prince is fashioned as if of two persons: the one is the product of nature's hands, insofar as he partakes of the same existence as other men; the other is by grace of fortune and divine favor, made for the government and protection of the common weal, for which reason we call him a public person."[9] Shakespeare was deeply aware of the notion, and drew large consequences from it in *Richard II*. Ernst Kantorowicz in fact called that play the "tragedy of the king's two bodies."[10] The contrast with *El médico* is illuminating. In the opening scene of *Richard II* Shakespeare gives us an image of kingly confidence and authority, of masterful arbitration, of judgment beyond man-made law: "We were not born to sue, but to command" (i. i. 196). The kingly word lifts the sovereign above the limitations of human time:

> How long a time lies in one little word!
> Four lagging winters and four wanton springs
> End in a word: such is the breath of kings.   (i. iii. 213–15)

The sacramental component of kingship, the king's atemporal body, does not guarantee the king's decisions. In fact, Richard is inept in his kingly role. He neglects troubles at home and is preoccupied with civil wars in Ireland. He stands ready to seize the dying Gaunt's property, and, with reckless abandon, to make a battlefield of England's sheltered isle. In light of these failings, his "other body" and human role become all the more vulnerable to the effects of time and change: "Let's talk of graves, of worms and epitaphs," are his words in Act III (ii. 145).

In the great deposition speech we see the calamitous results of his inability to meet the demands of a kingly role – a role that Calderón's King Pedro is, by contrast, finally able to accept. Richard relinquishes all the symbolic accoutrements of kingship in trade for the effects of the poor common man:

> The king shall do it: must he be depos'd?
> The king shall be contented: must he lose
> The name of king? 'o' God's name, let it go:
> I'll give my jewels for a set of beads,
> My gorgeous palace for a hermitage,
> My gay apparel for an almsman's gown,
> My figured goblets for a dish of wood,
> My sceptre for a palmer's walking staff,

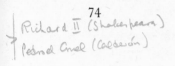

My subjects for a pair of carved saints,
And my kingdom for a little grave,
A little little grave, an obscure grave   (III. iii. 144–55)

If *Richard II* is the tragedy of one who is "in one person many people" (v. v. 31), then Calderón avoids that tragedy for his Pedro, who in the final scene resolves the complexities of his role. Structurally and formally, *Richard II*, like *Lear*, is built on the conflict between public and private worlds. They clash in the kingly figure. Richard's imprudence in public affairs of great consequence reveals that beneath lies a private person of little substance, one who is quickly reduced to the "shadow of his sorrow." The images of the poor man's world are soon tucked into a "little little grave." Shakespeare's play has a two-movement, linear shape, marking the fall of Richard and the rise of Bolingbroke. Richard himself sees the pattern:

> Now is the golden crown like a deep well
> That owes two buckets, filling one another,
> The emptier ever dancing in the air,
> The other down, unseen and full of water:
> That bucket down and full of tears am I,
> Drinking my griefs, whilst you mount up on high.
>
> (IV. i. 184–9)

As Richard falls, history opens to a new dynasty. Bolingbroke's guilty hands must be washed, but this is a cleansing for renewal and change.

Calderón closes his play with emblems, visual images that suggest the timelessness of ritual: Mencía's corpse with crucifix and candles and Gutierre's *escudo*. Calderón returns us from the mundane world of intrigue to a world of imaginative apprehension and ritual order. The eventual historical succession, though prophesied, is left neatly out of the action of Calderón's play.[11] This is not a history play in the Shakespearean mould. There is no intuition of historical change and succession, no sweeping movement across time. It is "religious" theatre, in the sense in which Kitto argued the case for *Hamlet*.[12] Calderón has a sacramental understanding of nature and of kingship that drives toward the resolution of Pedro's role and moral reconciliation for Gutierre.

Pedro's two acts of palace intrigue mentioned above are punctuated by a telling incident, marking his role as that of mortal man during this part of the action; it is a prelude to the moment when his actual, natural body is injured by Enrique's dagger, occurring just after Gutierre has noticed the dagger in his house. The King arrives at the Alcázar of Seville late in the evening. He has been reconnoitering in the city of Seville, observing incognito the comings and goings of his subjects; the incident recalls Pedro's intentions to visit Seville, as stated in the very first scene of the play. The motif of the ruler who wanders his kingdom's streets by night is topical, especially in the Golden Age theatre, and there is probably an historical allusion to Philip IV's escapades with Olivares here as well (Philip was a noted hunter, and held court at the Alcázar of Madrid). As in Lope's *El infanzón de Illescas*, Calderón's King Pedro vacillates between aloof administrator and common subject:

> Toda la noche rondé
> de aquesta ciudad las calles,
> que quiero saber así
> sujetos y novedades
> de Sevilla, que es lugar
> donde cada noche salen
> cuentos nuevos; y deseo
> de esta manera informarme
> de todo . . .   (I, 332a–b)

(All night long I haunted the streets of this city to find out about my subjects and to learn news of Seville, a place where new things happen every night; and I want to keep informed of everything this way . . .)

Pedro is not the "Júpiter español" of whom Leonor sought justice, nor the "español Apolo" to whom Gutierre will bring his concerns, but Argos, who keeps vigil over his subjects. This is the image don Diego chooses for him. Insecure and fearful, Pedro has no privileged, royal perspective. How ironic, then, that Coquín suggests the King might have been amused by taking a role in a *comedia*:

> Fuera hacer tú aquesta tarde
> el papel de una comedia
> que se llamaba "El Rey Angel".   (I, 332b)

(You were to play a role this afternoon in a play called *The Angel King*.)

Late in Act III Diego and Pedro are once more in the streets seeking stealthily to gain information to judge Gutierre's case. Ludovico is in the distance, but they cannot see him well. The scene is dimly lit. Under the uncertain light cast by the moon, Pedro is confused:

> . . . A darme
> confusión; que si le veo
> a la poca luz que esparce

> la luna, no tiene forma
> su rostro: confusa imagen
> el bulto, mal acabado,
> parece de un blanco jaspe.   (I, 345b)

(. . . This confuses me; for although I see him in the scant light that the moon scatters, his face has no shape; the form is a confused image, poorly defined, and seems of white jasper.)

In order to pursue his investigation, he conjoins clandestine searchings and the type of covert intriguing he used in the palace. He does this in order to arrive at sound judgment, but nothing could in fact be less kingly; he is misguided in his role. With Diego, he stalks Gutierre's house:

> . . . Y pues el día
> aún no se muestra, lleguemos,
> Don Diego. Así, pues, daremos
> color a una industria mía,
> de entrar en casa mejor,
> diciendo que me ha cogido
> cerca el día y he querido
> disimular el color
> del vestido; y una vez
> allá, el estado veremos
> del suceso; y así haremos
> como Rey, supremo juez.   (I, 347a)

(Since morning has not yet come, let us go, Don Diego. Thus we will carry out a plan of mine to enter the house in a better way, saying that daylight caught me nearby and that I wanted to change my clothes to a different color, and once there, we will observe the state of the matter; and thus we will act, like a King, as supreme judge.)

The clash between his covert actions and his declared role as "supremo juez" could not be more marked. Diego confirms his interest in the plan: "No hubiera industria mejor" ("There couldn't be a better plan") (I, 347a).

In face of the stark fact of Mencía's death, Pedro adopts a perspective of greater detachment for the final moments of the play. He summons prudence – Aquinas defined the virtue as "clear-sightedness"[13] – in order to adjudicate. He is "spectator" to the crime, as Margit Frenk rightly observed,[14] to which must be added that he looks at these images morally, not just visually. The purely emotive, felt response to the "prodigio que espanta" ("frightening wonder"), to the "espectáculo que admira" ("amazing spectacle")

(I, 348a), is facile, but Calderón wants more. Prudence is in order ("la prudencia es de importancia," *ibid*.). Pedro assumes his kingly role, and so assumes the social responsibilities, the moral vision, which weigh on him. Calderón is nearly always concerned with a critique of false confidence in illusions and irresponsible role-playing, but he is not always as sensitive to the onus of role.

Gutierre, for his part, misconceives his role. He takes a role fashioned from the vapor of words and assumes it in relation to his wife. His poetic understanding of social responsibility in effect perverts his role as spouse. He understands love as a sickness with possible cures and honor as cleanliness of blood, as well as if not better than any other character in the *comedia* tradition. But he is unable to see that these conventions also demand an awareness of his responsibilities to others. Gutierre is blind; he lacks prudence. He takes his earthly role with unfailing rigor as ultimate. For this reason, Pedro pities him.

Gutierre confuses public and private languages and roles. He adopts convention and makes it real. His wife Mencía, by contrast, is all too aware of the necessary contradistinctions. When Enrique approaches her house in Act I, she guards her words closely; where honor is in peril, silence is in force. When alone, she speaks with abandon, but in public she is courteous. Yet she is victimized; she must suffer for Gutierre's obtuseness and for society's rigid demands.

In Gutierre we see the intensity of human reason reach catastrophic proportions. He considers his profession as a science (*ciencia*). He argues like a logician, and uses his own life as a case for the *aplicatio*:

> Escúchame un argumento:
> Una llama en noche oscura
> arde hermosa, luce pura,
>
> . . .
>
> Aplico ahora: yo amaba
> una luz . . .   (I, 322b)

(Listen to an argument I have. A flame burns beautifully, shines purely, in a dark night . . . Now I apply it: I loved a burning light . . .)

He forms a drama for himself based on poetic invention, and acts in accordance with an illusory role. He grows suspicious, and reasons with himself. His doubts well up and his judgment is muddled. He forgets that language and convention are social, and thus he preempts the second person. Gutierre's discourse in Act II is one of Calderón's masterpieces of monologue art, moving from the illusion of rational self-control, to solitary complaint, to the direct address of personified honor:

> Pero cese el sentimiento,
> . . .
> Pero vengamos al caso,
> quizá hallaremos respuesta.
> ¡Oh, ruego a Dios que le haya!
> ¡Oh, plegue a Dios que la tenga!
> . . .
> A peligro estáis, honor,
> no hay hora en vos que no sea
> crítica, en vuestro sepulcro
> vivís, puesto que os alienta
> la mujer, en ella estáis
> pisando siempre la huesa.
> Yo os he de curar, honor
> . . .
> [Sea] la primera medicina
> cerrar al daño las puertas,
> atajar al mal los pasos.
> Y así os receta y ordena
> el médico de su honra
> primeramente la dieta
> del silencio . . .   (I, 334a–5a)

(But let this feeling cease . . . But let us get to the point, and perhaps we will find an answer. Oh, would God there were one! Oh, would God I had one! . . . Honor, you are in danger. There is no time at which you are not in critical condition. You live in your tomb, and since woman gives you life, in her you are always stepping on the grave. Honor, I must find a cure for you . . . Let the first medicine be to close the doors to harm, to cut off the steps of evil. And thus the surgeon of his honor first prescribes and orders you a diet of silence.)

The medical metaphors are the same in Act III, when Gutierre addresses King Pedro. But the surgeon's prescription of silence is poisoned by its own chemistry. Self-concealment and intrigue, purely personal concerns, are no longer at issue. Gutierre has murdered his wife, and he is numbed with shock. He exposes to the King the role he has invented, confessing his crime, if unwittingly, as he flaunts the deed:

> Un médico, que lo es
> el de mayor nombre y fama,
> y el que en el mundo merece

inmortales alabanzas,
la recetó una sangría,
porque con ella esperaba
restituir la salud
a un mal de tanta importancia.
Sangróse, en fin . . .   (I, 347b)

(A doctor, who is of the greatest renown and fame, who in this world merits
immortal praise, prescribed her a bloodletting, because with this he expected
to cure a very grave illness. In short, she was bled . . .)

In his uncanny pride at the fact, Gutierre seems like Hamlet, mad just
a touch, "north-north-west."

Moved to a modicum of self-awareness by his actions as creator and
actor in a poetic psychodrama, and recognizing, finally, that his
rhetoric was real, he achieves a kind of sublimation in the final
spectacle. As the images are displayed before us, verbally and
visually, they shimmer as pure presences, more phenomenological
than representational. At the end of the play, the stage itself seems a
timeless world, a place of numinal essences. It is no longer a place of
concealment and intrigue, or of temporal illusion; it is an arena of
almost religious ritual. More than *Hamlet*, where religion turns out to
be a worn conundrum of medieval beliefs, *El médico* has overtones of
ritualistic sacrifice. Instead of the muted cadence of drums, we are
given over to a barely rational spectacle. The final challenge, which
Pedro faces, is to advise a reasoned course of action given the spectacle
of cold-blooded murder, and to judge the price of forgiveness for
Gutierre, who cannot judge for himself.

Let us look now at the exchange between Gutierre and Pedro, the
crucial moment of pardon. Pedro has accepted his kingly responsibilities; he has tempered the demands of his role with human
mercy and compassion. He is, in the root sense of the word, a *prudent*
judge:

Gut.	¿Posible es que a esto le haya?	[i.e. *una remedia*]
Rey	Sí, Gutierre.	
Gut.	¿Cuál, señor?	
Rey	Uno vuestro.	
Gut.	¿Qué es?	
Rey	Sangrarla.	
Gut.	¿Qué decís?	
Rey	Qué hagáis borrar	
	las puertas de vuestra casa,	
	que hay mano sangrienta en ellas.	(I, 348b)

(*Gut.* Is it possible that there is one [i.e. a solution for this]? *King* Yes, Gutierre. *Gut.* What, sir? *King* One of yours. *Gut.* Which, sir? *King* Bleed her. *Gut.* What do you say? *King* That you cleanse the doors of your house, since there is a bloody hand on them.)

This is more than a simple pardon or excuse. Pedro knows that Gutierre will act in the same way in the future. He is conscious of human weakness. Pedro does not condone or condemn the brutal act per se. Calderón took care to avoid exclusive options: human justice is more complicated. The forgiveness is bound up with cleansing, and takes on a sacramental aura.

Pedro's words call to mind those of Bolingbroke at the end of Shakespeare's *Richard II*, the final verses of that play:

> They love not poison that do poison need,
> Nor do I thee: though I did wish him dead,
> I hate the murderer, love him murdered.
> The guilt of conscience take thou for thy labour,
> But neither my good word nor princely favour;
> With Cain go wander through the shades of night,
> And never show thy head by day nor light.
> Lords, I protest, my soul is full of woe,
> That blood should sprinkle me to make me grow:
> Come, mourn with me for that I do lament,
> And put on sullen black incontinent.
> I'll make a voyage to the Holy Land,
> To wash this blood off from my guilty hand.
> March sadly after; grace my mournings here,
> In weeping after this untimely bier. (v. vi. 37–52)

The simple difference, though, is that Shakespeare was probing the modern theme of revolution, while Calderón was looking at guilt and innocence in relation to collective social needs. This is why the complexities of role are so important to Calderón. With respect to their roles, Gutierre and Pedro cross; the final scene is the moment of recognition, the social and theatrical anagnorisis. Pedro confronts his socially imposed role, accepts it, and tempers his judgment with prudence; Gutierre stands starkly in face of his invented role as "surgeon of his honor," in need of Pedro's clement judgment.

Rather than teach a moral lesson – Calderón can be homiletic when he wants – *El médico de su honra* depends on theatrical representation to uncover the social demands implicit in individual existence. He uses the devices of theatrical representation – role-playing, intrigue, illusion – to understand the facts of human violence and sacrifice and the demands of prudent judgment and forgiveness.

Regardless of whether these demands are met (as in Pedro's case), or are ignored and lead to catastrophe (as for Gutierre), Calderón reinforces the social conditions which bear on human life. He seems to sense that platitudes about role can blind us to the realities of lived experience, that unenlightened role-playing will only bring disaster. He presents no unequivocal triumph; he admits human vulnerability. He sees the propensity of character and of the flesh to commit offenses, and he meets human frailty with sacramental cleansing. Pedro's absolution is the source of moral renewal (just as Bolingbroke's ascendancy is the source of political change), and it allows for new transgressions.

Shakespeare similarly saw social revolution as a cyclical process. But, because his focus is on the secular world, the cycles he sees lose any sacramental aura. It was in the second tetralogy that Shakespeare achieved the transition from a sacramental to a secular understanding of nature and of kingship. Ricardo Quinones said that "we witness the drama of transition from a sacramental and ceremonial view of nature and of kingship, represented by *Richard II*, to a more secular, realistic view . . ."[15] Otis Green thought exactly the opposite of the Spanish Baroque: i.e. that "the transition from a sacramental to a secular view of nature was *not* accomplished during our period."[16] Yet there is in *El médico* an order of cyclical social understanding, a sacramental view of the fabric of society and of the mechanisms of collective healing, of "nature" in this sacramental sense, that set it apart from *Richard II*. The play suggests a cycle in its structure, and Calderón's critique of illusion puts secular and religious, temporal and ultimate worlds into interdependent play. The work is a consideration of human possibility and limitation, of personal calamity and collective transcendence, finally, of the ineluctable demands and responsibilities of rational existence. As Calderón knew, these could be shown nowhere better than in the theatre.

7

Herod and Hercules: theatrical space and the body

El médico de su honra is certainly one of Calderón's more suggestive plays. In it, as in all his best work, he invests the stage with an enormous range of functions. The theatrical metaphor of role, the poetic formulae of honor, the intimations of ritual and sacrifice are not merely figurative forms, poetic contrivances. Calderón sees that the stage has the power to make these notions concrete, real, that representation implies a bodying forth of the autistic gestures latent in language and thought. In *El médico* Calderón envelops the stark brutality of human sacrifice in a religious aura; in so doing, he tempers its raw power. Through Pedro, he solicits responses of reasoned judgment, compassion, and pity. He uses the stage as an arena for embracing these competing reactions. What distinguishes his theatrical "idea" in *El médico* from the merely "dramatic" ideas prominent in Aristotle's *Poetics* and its Renaissance avatars is the spatial factor. Only because Calderón understands the capacities and limitations of representational space is he able to bring together the redoubtable set of tensions we find in *El médico*.

As much as if not more than in *El médico*, Calderón explores the implications of theatrical representation in his Herod play, *El mayor monstruo del mundo*. By means of spatial dimensions, Calderón probes the insatiable and seemingly limitless desires of the Tetrarch of Jerusalem. In him Calderón sees the personal consequences of human acquisitiveness, the inward destruction wrought by the will to power and possession. Calderón translates into spatial terms the almost suffocating, inward constrictions which Herod suffers from belief in an illusion. In the play, that illusion is invisible; it is Herod's monster, "visible" only to him. Yet the illusion is received by the audience in terms of the personal confinements which pervade the most ample theatrical space.

The play is exotic in setting and flavor. Seventeenth-century taste developed a fondness for a variety of ancient cultures, and Calderón himself wrote a number of Biblical plays. The Herod theme was of continuing interest to him (we have two versions of the work).[1] But Calderón is attracted to the exotic for rather different reasons from those of the French or English dramatists. He seeks to reap an exuberance, a breadth and expansiveness, from the setting and thus to reinforce the contrast to the moral dimensions of his characters. Where Racine binds technique and theme in Aristotelian measure, in narrowness of focus and economy of means, Calderón is attracted by the amplitude of theatrical possibilities at his disposal. His Herod play is driven by the violent contrast between the outward show, the apparent limitlessness of theatrical means, and the inner constriction, the personal reduction in moral stature generated by the Tetrarch's all-consuming jealous passion.

The contrast with Racine is worth pursuing. Both playwrights specialize in long monologues. But Calderón's language is never a mirror of the inner life as Racine's almost always is. Racine binds that life, through language, to the representational space itself. At the opening of a play like *Bérénice*, there are inner, mental perspectives implicit in the words. The setting mirrors the thought and, as a mental action, is itself transformed into poetry. Racine is untranslatable, in the literal sense: his verses cannot be *moved* from the place in which they are spoken. They hold their scenery inside them. His characters are fixed in given places by virtue of what they say. As Francis Fergusson observed, this "place" is primarily a mental locus.[2] Language in Racine reflects the angle of vision of the mind from which it springs. It is determined by the immediate situation in which thought takes place. It reveals the most interior of all actions – the process of the human mind at work:

> Arrêtons un moment. La pompe de ces lieux,
> Je le vois bien, Arsace, est nouvelle à tes yeux.
> Souvent ce cabinet superbe et solitaire
> Des secrets de Titus est le dépositaire.
> C'est ici quelquefois qu'il se cache à sa cour,
> Lorsqu'il vient à la Reine expliquer son amour.
> De son appartement cette porte est prochaine,
> Et cette autre conduit dans celui de la Reine.
> Va chez elle. Dis-lui qu'importun à regret,
> J'ose lui demander un entretien secret.[3] (v. 1–10)

(Let us wait a moment. The majestic decor of this residence is new to your eyes, I can tell, Arsace. Often this splendid and solitary chamber is the confidant of Titus' secrets. It is here that he sometimes hides himself from his court, when he comes to the Queen to pour out his love. This door is just next to his apartment, and this other one leads into that of the Queen. Go to her. Say that, reluctant to intrude, I venture to request a secret meeting with her.)

Antiochus' words are laden with the perspective of an interlocutor. Yet another, hidden angle impinges on the verses: it is as if Titus looks on. The points of view unfold like petals. There is nothing more precise, more absolutely dependent on the conjunction of physical, mental, and verbal spaces.

Racine sustains the illusion of action with a minimum of aids. His characters move about on stage stripped nearly bare: nothing more or less than language gives evidence of the life of the mind. Thus when language dries up action is knotted. When a character suffers paroxysms of the tongue he is unable to act. The whole of *Bérenice* is Titus' struggle to say a single word: "adieu."

> . . . Hé bien, Titus, que viens-tu faire?
> Bérénice t'attend. Où viens-tu téméraire?
> Tes adieux sont-ils prêts? T'es-tu bien consulté?
> Ton coeur te promet-il assez de cruauté?
> Car enfin au combat qui pour toi se prépare
> C'est peu d'être constant, il faut être barbare.
> Soutiendrai-je ces yeux dont la douce langueur
> Sait si bien découvrir les chemins de mon coeur?
> Quand je verrai ces yeux armés de tous leurs charmes,
> Attachés sur les miens, m'accabler de leurs larmes,
> Me souviendrai-je alors de mon triste devoir?
> Pourrai-je dire enfin: "Je ne veux plus vous voir?"   (v. 987–98)

(What then, Titus, have you come here to do? Bérénice awaits you. What are you doing, foolhardy that you are? Are your farewells ready? Have you deliberated well enough? Does your heart promise to be sufficiently cruel? For ultimately in the battle being prepared for you it means little to be unyielding, you must be inhuman. Will I hold up under those eyes whose sweet languishing knows so well how to uncover the paths of my heart? When I see those eyes armed with all their charms, fixed on mine, overpowering me with their tears, then will I remember my sad duty? Will I be able to say at last: "I do not wish to see you any more?")

As Roland Barthes observed, Titus suffers a kind of epilepsy; he stammers.[4] Thus Bérénice herself must say goodbye. Racine reduces language to the bare will to speak. He gives the illusion of outward action through the interior monologue. He takes Aristotelian constraints and, by fusing mental and verbal action in these monologues, conveys a sense of expansive grandeur.

For Racine, language is the irreducible and transparent image of the life of the rational mind, suffused with a setting. Not so for Calderón. His long monologues are rhetorical rather than rational. He is aware that words seem to have the power to sway interlocutors; he knows that language is power but that, like all power, it may be illusory. Calderón endows certain of his characters with a rhetorical prowess that is also the capacity for self-deception. In *El mayor monstruo* the authentically rhetorical capacity of language, its ability to persuade, gives evidence of a refusal to submit to the purely mental, rational space to which Racine so elegantly consigns his characters. Calderón's characters seek a more ample and outward personal presence through their rhetoric; as a direct consequence of this drive, some of them suffer inward woe.

Herod, the Tetrarch of Jerusalem, would persuade Mariene to be happy, to accept his love, and to love him in return. He is an orator who uses the logic of discourse – its comparisons, examples, premises, and conclusions – in order to sway her will. But because he is jealous, his efforts to win her are tortuous. He tries to dominate her, but he has no control over himself. Hence his own language turns against him; unaware, he admits he is jealous:

> . . . pues con discursos graves
> a celos me ocasionan tus desvelos.
> No sé qué más decir: ya dije celos. (I, 459a)

(But with such ponderous speeches your unease makes me jealous. I don't know what else to say now that I've said "jealous.")

Mariene tells the Tetrarch of a prophecy of their future misfortune: that she will be the undeserving victim of "un monstruo, el más cruel, horrible y fuerte / del mundo . . ." ("The most cruel, horrible and powerful monster in the world") (I, 459b) and that Herod's own dagger will be the instrument of destruction of what he loves most.

For the characters, the prophecy is an inscription which delimits all their actions. There is nothing they can do to escape the purview of fate. The dagger itself is a persistent reminder of the limit of man's control. It brings Herod to realize that life is continuously submitted to change: "Ninguna vida hay segura / un instante . . ." ("No life is sure for an instant . . .") (I, 460a–b). Tolomeo is the first to learn that each moment of life is a unit of unknown measure. Life is marked off by contingencies; there are factors which bear directly on us but which have their origin outside the human drama. Although he does not act upon his knowledge, Herod learns that life hangs by a thread, that the thread can be cut at any instant, and that we cannot know how or when:

> La Parca, que nuestras vidas
> tiene pendientes de un hilo,
> para que el tuyo no corte
> pone en tu mano el cuchillo.
> En tu mano está tu suerte. (1, 467a)

(Fate, which has our lives hanging by a thread, places your hand on the knife so that your [thread] does not break. Your fortune is in your own hands.)

Unlike Segismundo, Herod fails to realize that the best response to fate is fashioned in relation to a transcendent world, that the question of free will ceases to be a dilemma when life is lived in the fullness which derives therefrom.

In this play, the doctrinal question of free will versus predestination is secondary. Calderón uses fate as an engine to move the plot and to bring into focus a group of moral and social questions. He wants to explore the possible responses to situations in which man is not in control of his circumstances, or of himself. He wants to find out whether there is not some independence or self-sufficiency which, as a kind of greater stoicism, might serve as a wall of defense against those situations we cannot dominate. He finds a subtle answer: inner fortitude is commendable, but not sufficient; solitary resistance, precisely because it is taken alone, is isolating; in fact, it can destroy the social solidarity which is a far stronger response to the limitations of life. Calderón also explores the workings of inner, personal space, where passions such as jealousy generate illusions, through theatrical space and time. What Calderón finds is that people can indeed be stoical here as well. They can steel up and brace themselves in order to repress the human passions (compare Segismundo's "Repriamos esta fiera condición"). But, if they do that and nothing more, they will at best be tragic figures. Longevity will not be their recompense. They will experience independence, but they will not profit from it.

In temper, Herod is reminiscent of Shakespeare's tyrant, Richard III. There is something of the exuberance of *Richard III* in this play as well. Calderón is deeply interested in the dialectics of power and self-control, reason and passion, space and human limitations. Thematically, Marlowe's *Tamburlaine* is proximate as well. As the play begins, Calderón's Herod could well be the Scythian shepherd thirsting for conquest. Tamburlaine feeds his cravings through incessant motion, as if in defiance of geography; he is guided by a repetitive, machine-like energy, which in turn dissolves the unity of his projects. Dramatically, he renders the classical unities meaningless and empty. Stephen Greenblatt said that "just as Marlowe uses the vacancy of theatrical space to suggest his characters' homelessness, so he uses the curve of theatrical time to suggest their struggle against extinction, in effect against the nothingness into which all characters fall at the end of a play."[5] Space, time, action, the character himself, are left wholly void.

Yet the intention behind the defiant energies of Tamburlaine and Herod will differentiate Calderón from Marlowe. Tamburlaine's self-assertion against theatrical limitation is part of a deep-rooted Marlovian will to question every foundation of conventional value. In his own day, Robert Greene charged him with atheism.[6] Calderón knows that, like his characters, the dramatist must in the end submit to limitations. He may be gifted with a space so ample, with illusory resources so great, that the very idea of theatrical bounds, of the restrictions of time, place, or action, may seem irrelevant, but he knows that we must all live and work within a bounded, circum-scribed world. Thus, with appropriate irony, Calderón repays his hero's limitless craving for space with personal reduction.

Indeed, from the start of the play, Herod is submitted to the constraints of space and time. These are particularly great because his appetites and desires are so large. The sheer expansiveness of his domains points up his eventual confinement. Herod would like nothing more than to enter, triumphant, into Rome, with Mariene as his wife. He would give Mariene an empire. But his power is threatened by Octavian and Mark Antony:

> . . . los dos intentan, aunque en vano,
> repartir el imperio
> que dilata y extiende su hemisferio
> desde el Tíber al Nilo   (I, 459a)

(. . . the two try in vain to divide the empire which stretches and extends its hemisphere from the Tiber to the Nile).

Octavian occupies Jerusalem, severely reducing Herod's dominion; he defeats Mark Antony and brings the Tetrarch to submission. His power increases steadily; the scope of his rule grows large:

> yo soy Octaviano, yo
> soy el que en Egipto llega
> a triunfar de Marco Antonio.   (I, 471a)

(I am Octavian, I am the one who comes to Egypt to triumph over Mark Antony.)

> Felice es la suerte mía,
> pues de Egipto victorioso,
> dilato la monarquía
> de Roma . . .   (I, 463a)

(My fortune is good, for victorious in Egypt, I extend the monarchy of Rome . . .)

As if the two were seeking equilibrium, Octavian rises in power and influence as the Tetrarch's rule is decreased:

> . . . yo soy invicto César
> de Roma; el Tíber y el Nilo
> humildes mis plantas besan.
> Yo soy tu rey y tu dueño.
> Por mí, Tetrarca, gobiernas,
> estrella eres de mi Sol,
> aunque aborrecida estrella.   (I, 471a)

(. . . I am the unconquerable Caesar of Rome; the Tiber and the Nile humbly kiss my feet. I am your king and your master. You, Tetrarch, govern for me, you are the star to my Sun, although a hated star.)

He who at the opening of the play thought to crown Mariene Empress of Rome finds himself drastically, personally reduced in power and control. He suffers defeat in terms of spatial enclosure and constricted movement:

> Yo, que ayer de Palestina
> gobernador y Tetrarca,
> no cupe ambicioso en cuanto
> el sol dora y el mar baña,
> hoy pobre, rendido y triste
> entre dos fuertes murallas
> aprisionándome el vuelo,
> tengo abatidas las alas.   (I, 473b)

(Yesterday, I was the governor of Palestine, and Tetrarch; my ambition would not fit in the space brightened by the sun or bathed by the sea. Today I am poor, tired, and sad. I am imprisoned by two strong walls, unable to flee. My wings are clipped.)

 Just as Herod suffers this diminution of power, his acquisitive appetites swell. The more he is restricted, the more his cravings turn inward. His own jealousy consumes him. Calderón understands jealousy as a passionate desire for possession on a par with political, territorial, and material acquisitiveness. Yet while all those are outwardly directed drives, jealousy works its way inward as well. It is humanly corrosive, because it is shuttered up inside the person. It finds no way to vent itself, and ends up destroying its human container:

> No, pues, mi ambición, Filipo;
> no mi atrevida arrogancia,
> no el ser parcial con Antonio,
> no mi poder, no mis armas
> me han puesto en este cuidado,
> me han puesto en esta mudanza.
> ¡El ser, sí, de Mariene
> esposo! (I, 474a)

(Not my ambition, Filipo; not my daring arrogance, nor my having favored Antony, nor my power, nor my arms have put me in these straits, have brought this change upon me. But yes, the fact that I am Mariene's husband!)

Not arrogance, not ambition, not political or military foibles so much as his jealous passion for a woman is the source of Herod's undoing.

Calderón understands the acquisitive drive in a myriad of shapes and guises; he sees wants as welded to the human constitution. Jealousy is sexual possessiveness; sexual desire is seen in economic terms. His characters want to acquire, to save, to store up, and to hoard each other as if all were involved in human trade and commerce. Mariene is a prize ("trofeo," as the prophecy spells out); when Herod is forced to submit to Octavian's rule, he is "poor" by comparison to his rival's power: "El poderoso, yo pobre" (I, 475b). For Herod, love is the desire to possess, and the word that best expresses this desire – "quiero" – is for him a sign of material, physical want. He talks of buying and selling, of high prices and low, as if he were a merchant of desire. His greed blinds him to his temporal limitations; he sees money as a way to extend his control beyond the grave. He regards Octavian as the thief of his property; Mariene is reduced to the category of "stolen goods":

> ¿Quién en el mundo ladrón
> del mismo tesoro suyo
> quiso dentro de su casa
> gozar sus bienes por hurto? (I, 488a)

(Who in the world would steal his own treasure and would enjoy his own goods in concealment within his own house?)

Mariene is quick to recognize the Tetrarch's greed. She knows she is
the object of his desire, and that his greed is larger than his will to
control it, indeed larger than his life:

> . . . avaro de los gozos,
> aun muriendo no los dejas;
> bien como el que codicioso
> amante de sus riquezas,
> porque no las goce otro,
> manda que después de muerto
> le entierren con su tesoro.   (1, 484a)

(Greedy for pleasures, you won't even leave them when you are dying; just
like the greedy man who so loves his riches that he orders that when he is
dead he should be buried with his treasure, so that no one else might enjoy
it.)

Mariene can find no adequate escape from Herod's jealous passion.
She would exile herself, were social censure not so large an obstacle.
Instead she submits to spatial confinement. In order to escape
Herod's jealous reach, she takes inner retreat. Seeking freedom from
him, she cloisters herself.

These themes are reflected in an apparent reduction of theatrical
space. The vast and open setting of Act I is marked as a public space,
suprapersonal in character, and it remains so until Herod hurls the
dagger into the sea. Man is not free to move about without restraints.
Nameless, vacant space, which he might conquer and shape to his
designs, is circumscribed by factors which he can neither see nor fully
understand. As Herod's jealousy grows, the action of the play is
contained in ever smaller spaces. Mariene addresses him as he is in
jail:

> ¿Tú, en una oscura prisión,
> funesto y mísero albergue,
> para abrazar mis desdichas
> estás tratando mi muerte?   (1, 479a)

(Are you, in a dark prison, a miserable and funereal retreat, seeking my
death in order to embrace my misfortunes?)

The final moments of the play take place in and around Mariene's
quarters. She is confined by the rival passions of Herod and Octavian.
For Herod, this only occasions a great upsurge of jealous rage. For
Mariene this is the cause of her death. She falls, in the dark, on the
dagger.

By contrast, Herod meets death as he hurls himself into the sea. He finds his grave in boundless space; his passions are dissolved in it. Figurally, this sea is reminiscent of the seas of medieval imagination and of the symbolic waters into which Icarus fell at Fortune's hand. We find it in the *Celestina* in this way, and Calderón used it in *La vida es sueño* to a similar symbolic end. In *El mayor monstruo*, the sea is an anonymous locus, suggestive of the borders of human life. The sea of fate is the abstract, generic space into which human existence must fit. Calderón senses that the adjustment is a difficult one because of the depersonalization of this space. In comparison to the sea that determines the course of life and death, human orders of value, qualitative up and down themselves, mean little. Personal and individual points of view, the structures of perception which organize reality, give it texture, and humanize it, are rendered useless where size and direction cannot be measured. The sea is then simply a place to die.

Renaissance philosophy had already reduced space to a set of coordinates, the quadrants of a map. Like Calderón's Octavian, who is in the ascendant throughout the play, Marlowe's Tamburlaine consumes abstract space as if it were food for his passions:

> Give me a Map. Then let me see how much
> Is left for me to conquer all the world,
> That these, my boys, may finish all my wants.
>
> (2 *Tam.*, v. iii. 122–4)

In Marlowe, space is relatively more abstract than in Calderón, but that is because Calderón holds hope that man can give order to space through transcendent values. For Doctor Faustus, who has bargained away eternity and salvation, hell is everywhere and nowhere and he, as a person, is devalued.

> Hell hath no limits, nor is circumscrib'd
> In one self place, but where we are is hell;
> And where hell is there must we ever be.
>
> (*Doctor Faustus*, II, i. 118–20)

Calderón's Herod resists accepting the idea that his self-consuming desires have made his own inner being into a limitless hell. His jealousy keeps him so blind to the fact that his suffering begins to take on heroic qualities. Time and again in Calderón's *comedias* we hear the conventional metaphors of the "little world of man." For Herod, Calderón's metaphor of human apocopation becomes strikingly real. His inward suffering and misery are sensed personally as the foreshortening and condensation of all human misfortune.

soy epílogo breve
de las miserias humanas.   (1, 473b)

(I am a brief epilogue of human misery.)

Herod stands in a long line of suffering rulers whose heroism is
defined in terms of their pathetic reduction. Marlowe's Edward II
suffers and dies in a sewage-filled dungeon; this is only one of his
connections to the "little little grave," to the talk of "graves, of worms
and epitaphs," of Shakespeare's Richard II. The suffering Herod is
one of Calderón's most interesting characters. Until the very end he
refuses to learn that the egotistical advance, the acquisitive politick-
ing and military conquest of his youth, now practiced by Octavian,
are not limitless. He may be defeated, but he is fearless in the face of
his opponent. He feels his limitations, but he is heedless of them. His
actions follow a course preordained not only by fate but by his own
inner constitution. When he challenges Octavian, in the final scene,
". . . Yo no me oculto. / Búscame" ("I do not hide. Look for me")
(1, 489a), he is valorous, foolish as he might also be. But there is
something essentially foolish about heroism itself. In the last moments
of the play, he defies his single greatest limitation, space. His death in
the sea – not in some tiny grave – is in fact ennobling. This is one of
Calderón's finest plays; appropriate terms of comparison are the best
Herod plays in world literature – those by Tirso, Hebbel, and
Voltaire. In Calderón's *oeuvre*, it is easy to find excellence where the
heroes are Segismundo-like and dominate themselves; it is rare to find
greatness where the hero draws strength from an inner flaw, from the
monstrous, self-destructive, illusory passion of jealousy.

There is perhaps only one case comparable to Herod's, that of
Hercules, which Calderón dramatized in *Los tres mayores prodigios*.
What is immediately remarkable about that play is the amplitude of
the theatrical conception. Three myths – Jason and the Golden
Fleece, Theseus and the Minotaur, Hercules and Deianira – were
represented on three stages by three separate theatrical companies, in
the manner of a triptych. The Hercules story occupies the final act of
the play, and was played on the central stage. The play was
performed in 1636, and it was one of the first occasions on which
Calderón had such a wealth of resources at his disposal. Ironically,
though, he seems to discover the limitations of space for his characters
at the very moment when he is discovering the breadth of represen-

tational space for himself. The play covers Asia, Europe, and finally Africa, as Jason, Theseus, and Hercules look for the Centaur. The flagrant violation of the Aristotelian unities is here marshaled to serve the creation of a physically inward, passionately derived illusion: jealousy.

Hercules, the strongest man in the world, suffers the same burning passion that limits Herod. He has traversed all Africa in search of Deianira. But the fathomless space, a space which diminishes Africa, lies within himself. How long can his body contain its wretched heart?

> Solo sé que el corazón
> a pedazos se me arranca
> del pecho, y que pavorosa
> no me cabe dentro del alma. (1, 1588b)

(I know only that my heart is torn out of my breast in pieces, and that shuddering so, it does not fit inside my soul.)

The spatial confinement of passion is an insistent motif in the play. His prodigiously strong body is constricted by the Nessus shirt, which, Hercules is unaware, is dipped in poison. He is deceived by the poison shirt just as Herod is deceived by his jealous rage. Calderón translates suffering in terms of physical constraint: "Los vestidos me parece / que me aprietan" ("it seems that my clothes press in on me") (1, 1588b).

Hercules' self-immolation is reminiscent of Tamburlaine's wounding of himself for the edification of his sons, vaguely parodic of the Christ-like pelican feeding its young with the blood of its self-inflicted wounds:

> View me, thy father, that hath conquered kings,
> And, with his host march round about the earth,
> Quite void of scars, and clear from any wound,
> That by the wars lost not a dram of blood,
> And see him lance his flesh to teach you all. *He cuts his arm.*
> . . .
> Come, boys, and with your fingers search my wound,
> And in my blood wash all your hands at once,
> While I sit smiling to behold the sight.
> Now, my boys, what think ye of a wound?
> (2 *Tam.* III. ii. 110–14, 126–9)

Ever since the Christian commentaries on Ovid, Hercules' self-sacrifice had been taken as symbolic of man's ability to purge the poisonous emotions. Hercules is the soul struggling with the bodily

passions, Nessus the devil who burns man with vice. The myth was
popular among Renaissance philosophers; Ficino relates it, as does
Bruno. But in Ficino's version Hercules' suffering represents self-
transcendence, a shedding of the body which leads the soul to a
rapturous contact with the divine. Ficino sees Hercules as a model for
positive suffering – as one who uses suffering to find a mental,
philosophical transcendence of corporeal limitation:

> Since it is impossible to approach the celestial seats with a corporeal bulk, the
> soul, taking thought as its guide, by the gift of philosophy, transcends
> through contemplation the nature of all things. . . . to speak comprehen-
> sively, since philosophy is a celestial gift, it drives earthly vices far away,
> bravely subdues fortune, admirably softens fate, safely uses mortal gifts,
> abundantly offers immortal gifts . . . O sure guide to human life, who first
> defeats the monsters of vice entirely with the club of *Hercules*, then with the
> shield of Pallas *avoids and overcomes the dangers of fortune, and finally takes human
> souls upon the shoulders of Atlas, frees them from this earthly exile, and returns them
> truly and happily to the celestial fatherland.*[7]

Hercules catches the arrow of passion and consumes it as the beast
draws near. He swallows fate by his virtuous and patient suffering. In
transcending the passions of the body, Hercules is freed from spatial
limitations. Ficino looked for his freedom in the mental dominance of
the physical passions, in the transcendence of fate through rational
reflection:

> Our body is attracted in a powerful attack by the body of the world through
> the forces of fate . . . and the power of fate does not penetrate our mind if our
> mind has not previously immersed itself in the body subject to fate. So no one
> should trust his own intelligence and strength enough to hope he can wholly
> avoid the sicknesses of the body . . . Every soul should retire from the
> pestilence of the body and withdraw into the mind, for then fortune will
> spend its force on the body and not pass into the soul. A wise man will not
> fight in vain against fate, but rather resist by fleeing. Misfortune cannot be
> hunted down, but can only be fled.[8]

Unlike Ficino's, Calderón's version of the Hercules myth is
determined by the theatrical space in which it is set. Calderón's
understanding of the body, of the need to transcend the passions, of
human fate and freedom, is inseparable from the limitations of space.
He knows that to flee fortune is to submit to its accident (witness
Clarín in *La vida es sueño*), that reason is not powerful enough to bend
the course of destiny (as for example with Herod), that attempts to
the contrary may bring social calamity, as in Basilio's Poland.
Calderón's Hercules absorbs the blows of fate with his body; he soaks

up the poisonous passion and takes the arrow of fate. The mind cannot dominate the body. Hercules is mad with love and enraged with jealousy; he suffers these drives physically. Calderón fuses the two attributes – *furens, patiens* – most commonly ascribed to Hercules in the Renaissance tradition. He interprets the myth with unflagging loyalty to his *métier* as man of the stage.

At the same time, we see Calderón's own opposing stylistic propensity toward "scholarism" (the word is Marlowe's) in the armature of his monologues, in the planned and patterned *versos correlativos*, in the metaphor and imagery of intellectual display. But his implicit trust in the powers of the mind is threatened by Herod and Hercules. Calderón gives the impression of an abstract understanding of things, of a will toward the dispassionate contemplation of all that is not rational. He seems naturally to seek order; his talent for ordered complementarities is large. But Herod and Hercules as we see them in these plays give us cause to question any wholesale trust in the powers of the mind; this is an attitude which we will see again in connection with *La estatua de Prometeo*. Calderón himself was too involved with the theatre for too long to forget the constraints which space places on any abstract "idea"; for him, the space of representation is welded to the theatrical idea like a body to a mind. Furthermore, Calderón lived too close to the actual centers of power of his society for too long to believe that the human passions, the acquisitive drives, could be reduced by the simple application of the mind. His interpretation of the Hercules myth, like his version of the Herod story, shows him ready to accept the fact that the material world, the human body, indeed the theatre itself, cannot be easily eluded. On the contrary: these material and spatial actualities will and must place their shadow-mass in the path of the mind, which may give rise to figments and self-deceptions. As a form of tangible space, the theatre can soak up the poison of its own illusions.

8

El mágico prodigioso and the theatre of alchemy

"All true alchemists know that the alchemical symbol is a mirage as the theatre is a mirage."

Antonin Artaud, "The Alchemical Theatre"

The notion of a theatre implies, at the absolute minimum, a specially marked space, a bounded if not enclosed arena, which holds within it a second (stage) space for the "play" or representation. The double meaning of "play" highlights some of the key concepts involved here. The "play" set on a stage has a certain closure, as with games, where the physical or simply "ideal" limits (e.g. the bounds, the rules) determine the space of play. Within the theatre, the "playing" space differs from that which is outside the theatre by two equal rotations, and by virtue of this double difference the stage partakes of an ambiguous equivalence with the first term of comparison, "reality." Ortega y Gasset was on target and characteristically lucid in his description of theatre along these lines in the more or less phenomenological idiom of his "Idea del teatro": the theatre is a visible metaphor, a locus of transformation, a place where, because of these double differences, the seeing and the seen become interchangeable. Working beyond phenomenology, Antonin Artaud, and Jacques Derrida writing on Artaud, would account for the paradoxical status of the elements of theatre in terms of the successive displacements and deferrals by which the marked space is at once equivalent to and yet different from "reality": "Closure is the circular limit within which the repetition of difference infinitely repeats itself. That is to say, closure is its *playing* space."[1]

Calderón's theatre generally works toward the equilibration of the entities – audience / stage, players / spectators – housed within the theatrical space. Especially in his pageant plays and court spectacles, he welds a bond between those who see and those who are seen. To do this, he eschews the kind of "novelistic" dialogue of more conventional mimesis. He favors long monologues, speeches which read like captioned summaries of sporadic gestures. His characters are experts at frontal acting. They direct themselves to the audience rather than to one another. They are masters not of soliloquies but of long *discursos*, of patterned, conventional monologues, spectacular in themselves. Much of what Artaud saw as the appropriate setting for the "theatre of cruelty" would have been surprisingly well accommodated by the Spanish *corrales*; his characterization matches the *comedia* in many ways:

> We abolish the stage and the auditorium and replace them by a single site, without partition or barrier of any kind, which will become the theatre of the action. A direct communication will be re-established between the spectator and the spectacle, between the actor and the spectator, from the fact that the spectator, placed in the middle of the action, is engulfed and physically affected by it.[2]

Affinities of this type may, however, veil deep metaphysical differences. Calderón expands purely theatrical space along theological lines. He completes the spectacular space with another, transcendent space, such that the two partake of the mutual obliquities of a paradox, each one undermining and reinforcing the other. It is this spatial and metaphysical paradox which distinguishes his theatrical "idea" from that of a thinker like Artaud and even from the theatrical practice of a dramatist like Christopher Marlowe, whose "theology" – if it can be so called – is diametrically opposed to Calderón's.

Artaud saw the possibility of a theatre, non-Western in outline, in which "the spectator is in the center and the spectacle surrounds him."[3] Unlike Brecht, whose "epic theatre" is rooted in Aristotelian thinking about drama if only by virtue of its insistent revolt against Aristotelian ideas, Artaud does not conserve the conventional meanings of "spectacle" and "spectator" because his concept of *vision* is different; his metaphysics runs counter to that prominent among the phenomenologists, as in Ortega's "El espectador." Artaud imagined a theatre in which "the distance [between spectator and spectacle] is no longer pure, cannot be abstracted from the totality of the sensory milieu; the infused spectator can no longer constitute his spectacle and provide himself with its object. There is no longer spectator or spectacle, but *festival*" (Derrida, p. 244). He conceived of a theatre with no content, because the form–content distinction should no longer apply to it; he looked for a theatre in which text and interpretation would be part of one self-nourishing biomass, in which the seeing subject and its object, the seen, would be grafted together: the theatre and its double should be life itself, not just a "book" nor just a "work" (the conventional labels are telling in their limitations), but vital energy, living force, more kinetic than metaphysical.

The difference between Brecht's "epic theatre" and Artaud's "theatre of cruelty," though, is the difference between the possible and the impossible. Each has its advantages and limitations. Artaud's ideas are, in practice, impossible to achieve. But Brechtian "alien-ation," the cornerstone of "epic theatre," "only consecrates, with didactic insistence and systematic heaviness, the nonparticipation of the spectators . . . in the creative act, in the irruptive force fissuring the space of the stage. The *Verfremdungseffekt* remains the prisoner of a classical paradox of 'the European ideal of art'" (Derrida, p. 244). The idea of a theatre without representation, by contrast, is not so much intended to help guide theatrical practice as to subvert the metaphysics which informs Western theatre. As Calderón's *comedia El mágico prodigioso* will help make clear, this metaphysics is nowhere more staunchly upheld than on the Spanish stage, yet the *comedia*, with its monologues and spectacular effects, does not follow the mimetic principles characteristic of Western theatre.

When Artaud looks to non-representational theatre, he sees the stage as a place of original, rather than mimetic, action. He looks to the stage as a space where "a form, once it has served, cannot be used again and asks to be replaced by another, . . . the only place in the world where a gesture, once made, can never be made the same way twice" (Artaud, p. 75). If repetition "separates force, presence and life from themselves" (Derrida, p. 245), then the theatre provides a glimpse of an original, vital force, indeed a violence, invisible under the guise of the metaphysics of Being, which may unintentionally grant ontological status to mere forms and ideas. There is an undercurrent of violence which Calderón brings to the fore in the bloody honor plays, as in *El mayor monstruo*. Calderón intuits a deep-rooted lawlessness embedded in the human psyche. This is evident not only in plays like *El médico* or *A secreto agravio, secreta venganza*; he sees it as part of the generic human condition, as imagined in the violence of birth, as in Rosaura's opening verses of *La vida es sueño*. The mercilessness of the revenge play – which Kyd for example thought to be quintessentially Spanish – was part of the *comedia* from the days of its inception; it runs deep in the work of Lope de Vega's early rival, Juan de la Cueva, who drew on key occurrences of medieval cruelty and revenge. But in Calderón the spatial containment of violence, its displacement and sublimation under the aegis of illusion, defers radical violence. The visual brilliance of the images of death we see in *El médico* gives us over to a spectacle which hints at the "autopresentation of pure visibility and even pure sensibility" (Derrida, p. 238), and which resembles Artaud's idea of the theatre of cruelty; but the ritual overtones draw us away from any direct, non-representational contact with human violence. Calderón insists on the use of human judgment to temper the passions; he sublimates cold-blooded murder under the guise of ritual and sacrifice. Metaphysically, Calderón is aware of the doubleness of representational space – that it is purely spectacular, self-justifying in its own sheer presence, but also that it is illusory and has no claim to permanent status. The conception of a play like *El médico*, as with *La vida es sueño*, is largely dependent on the intuition of this doubleness.

El mágico prodigioso, which I now want to discuss, epitomizes the attempt to reinvest theatrical space with metaphysical status by invoking the paradoxical theological proposition that all present space is hollow and insufficient. In *El mágico*, the vault of heaven stands above the stage as the dream over waking life.[4] When man is uprooted from the earth, it is only in order to be raised to heaven. This is prototypical of Calderón's staunch theocentricity and of the paradoxical, dualistic metaphysics of presence and absence ingrained in Western thought. Yet Calderón senses the particularly subtle pathos which follows on the apportionment of reality and illusion in such a way that only transcendent space can lay claims to permanence. The paradox pervades this *comedia*, and is characteristic of the genre.

The metaphysics of the Spanish stage is summed up in a phrase resonant with theological overtones: "soy quien soy." The phrase is emblematic of a presence, a permanence, a changelessness and self-sufficiency, which is in turn rendered hollow by the theology to which it is attached. In *El mágico*, self-identity is fashioned out of an affirmation of the wholeness of the body, not in epic terms, as for the Cid, but in transcendent terms, for the resurrected corpses at the close of the play. Calderón insists on the gravity of the sins of the flesh, but at the same time he sees that the sins of the body are illusory, because earthly existence has no transcendent status. Cipriano's concerns over Justina's faithlessness are unfounded; they are the devil's work.

In stark contrast to Calderón's theological theatre stands the atheist – but still theocentric – theatre of Christopher Marlowe. In Marlowe, the defiance of transcendence energizes a will not just to expand but to explode theatrical space; it brings his characters to the brink of an abyss. Marlowe tried to dissolve the social fabric from which Calderón's characters draw strength and personal status. The theatrical selves of Calderón's heroes are fashioned against a backdrop of public collectivities and institutions representing values which outstrip their individuality. The typical hero of an honor play avenges the "patrimony of his soul" as if he were guarding a public bank of values. In *Tamburlaine*, in *The Jew of Malta*, in *Doctor Faustus*, we find a seething revolt against family, Church, and State. Marlowe takes the quiddities of the Schoolmen, their disputes about Being and identity, as part of the social fabric which is rent by these individuals. Paradoxically, they identify themselves by revolt against the metaphysics of Being. Metaphysics is reduced to forensics as Faustus considers the Hamletian question – "*ōn kai me ōn*" (I. i. 12) – in light of the Ramist axiom that the purpose of logic is "to dispute well," as he says a few verses earlier ("*Bene disserere est finis logicis*," I. i. 7). Tamburlaine turns metaphysical language into outright bombast. He practices a strikingly corporeal self-assertion, striking because he stays for so long on the brink of absolute nothingness and self-annihilation, just as he rides the upward crest of his power so long. His will to be himself is dependent on destroying the social, geographical, and even theatrical spaces which house him, and on replacing mere representation by his charismatic "presence."

Marlowe's heroes fashion an existence through a displacement of their own sameness, through self-repetition; but because their repeated acts can never be absolutely identical, they ultimately define themselves negatively, as flux, perhaps in terms of some static *object* which they desire and toward which they move, but not in terms of any fixed essence. Tamburlaine craves space, Faustus wants knowledge. These characters are radically and inwardly violent: they are always being torn away from themselves. In them, there is a constant rending of the fabric of selfhood, a continual breaking of the law of identity. Marlowe's characters insert themselves into the vital space between identity and difference, illusion and reality, the social structure and its subversions. To cite a recent critic, Stephen

Greenblatt, Marlowe's theatre stands "on the brink of an abyss, *absolute* play."[5]

An admixture of philosophical Epicureanism and atheism gives a Gorgian cast to the speeches of Marlowe's characters. If their rhetoric is litany-like, their actions repetitious and machine-like – as for example in the case of Tamburlaine – they hold sway because of a power to sustain illusion as if through incantation. They are makers and masters of illusion; they seem to know that the man who sets illusion in play is in fact closer to reality than the man who tries to deny himself its pleasures; he comes tantalizingly close to his goals. But at the same time these characters suffer a tragedy of the appetite. Because there is no real gratification for the *libido sciendi*, and because the status of metaphysics has been reduced to the matter of disputed question and answer, they lay tenacious claims on their illusions. But none of the libidinous drives finds any deep satisfaction in Marlowe's theatre. His greatest plays, *Tamburlaine* and *Doctor Faustus*, are artistically uneven partly because there is no adequate way dramatically to order the rampant desires. In *Tamburlaine*, we are always at or near a climax. In *Doctor Faustus*, we find the Baconian equation of knowledge and power demolished *avant la lettre*. The theatre itself, the actual representation, must assume the burden of offering satisfaction; yet, as Harry Levin said of *Doctor Faustus*, there must have been substantial incongruities between the seemingly unlimited possibilities invoked by the dramatic speeches "and their all too concretely vulgar realization in the stage business."[6]

Both E. M. Wilson and Harry Levin saw the connections between Marlowe's interpretation of the Faust legend and Calderón's treatment of the analogous legend of St Cyprian in *El mágico*. There is something profound in Professor Levin's affirmation that for Calderón tragedy is "intercepted by eschatology" (p. 133). *El mágico* veers sharply away from tragedy. The devil repents, the "magician" renounces his magic; Cipriano suffers martyrdom, is converted to Christianity, and is reunited with Justina in Heaven. She too has suffered martyrdom; together, they reap the rewards of salvation. In light of this transcendent space, earthly theatrical space is hollow and empty. But whereas Marlowe flouts transcendental values, Calderón looks for the completion of the theatre in heavenly space. At the end of *El mágico*, heaven stands vigil over earth, waiting to receive the martyrs into its lap. It is only natural for the tragic sense of homelessness, of uprootedness, of utter exile, to be absorbed by the transcendent space.

The action of *El mágico prodigioso*, the patterns of events and the plan to which they point, are strongly archetypal. Every bit as much as the plan of *Paradise Lost* or the *Divina Commedia*, Calderón's theatre is "encyclopedic" in outline, but Calderón materializes these archetypal patterns theatrically. In *El mágico prodigioso*, the final transcendence is a visible ascension, just as in *La devoción de la Cruz* divine mercy reaches down through the symbol of the Cross to temper human justice. Calderón sees a great cycle of creation, of life, death, and salvation, akin to that represented in the English mystery plays of the Corpus Christi cycle. But Calderón is insistent on the original drama of violent creation and its aftermath. In *El mágico*, Justina's birth, as told by Lisandro, was the violent occasion of her mother's martyrdom ("fuiste parto de un cadáver") ("you were born of a cadaver") (1, 627b), a neat foreshadowing of her own death by martyrdom and of her transcendent re-birth. Calderón's materialization of the transcendent is replete with all the paradoxes of the great Christian mystery of the Incarnation and of the simultaneous praise and deprecation of the body enunciated by the Catholic Church.

Calderón's vision of transcendence is so powerful, though, that he sees only whole and completed patterns ending in salvation. There is no lasting evil in this world: the good predominates over the evil with an unflagging rhythm; the devil repents at the end of the play. Yet in order to maintain this rhythm his stage must renounce itself as temporal and earthly illusion; it must bare its hollow heart, no matter how strikingly tangible it may render the idea of transcendence. But Calderón is more like an alchemist than a priest; and like all true alchemists he knows "that the alchemical symbol is a mirage as the theatre is a mirage." This is the only knowledge which will explain the final recantation of his devil, which otherwise seems an instance of facile homiletics. Calderón's devil knows all along that his illusions are mirages, that the temptations of knowledge and power are insubstantial. The final palinode merely confirms the fact.

> Yo fui quien por difamar
> su virtud, formas fingiendo,
> su casa escalé, y entré
> hasta su mismo aposento;
>
> . . .
> Esta es la verdad, y yo

> la digo, porque Dios mesmo
> me fuerza a que yo la diga   (1, 642a–b)

(I was the one who, in disguise, scaled her house and entered her very room in order to dishonor her, . . . This is the truth, and I say it because God Himself forces me to.)

At the start of Act III, the devil has seen his powers falter. He can tempt the human will, but he cannot force it:

> que aunque el gran poder mío
> no puede hacer vasallo un albedrío,
> puede representalle
> tan extraños deleites, que se halle
> empeñado en buscarlos,
> e inclinarlos podré, si no forzarlos.   (1, 631a–b)

(for while my enormous power cannot make a will waver, it can show it extraordinary delights which it may seek, and I can incline, if not force, the will.)

The only way the devil can find to carry through his designs is to use Cipriano's love for Justina as a wedge to sway his will. Cipriano is not aberrant; that is the flaw of Lelio, whose jealous passions, like Floro's, create illusions and lead him to believe in the devil's tricks:

> Ahora acabo de creer
> que sombras los celos hacen,
> pues no está en este aposento,
> ni tuvo por dónde echarse
> el hombre que vi.   (1, 625a)

(Now I am convinced that jealousy creates shadows, for the man I saw isn't in this room and had no way to escape.)

The devil we see in this play transforms himself, plays roles, feigns identities. His greatest temptation is to make real and actual what is designed for the hereafter. He is, like Basilio of *La vida es sueño*, a partial self-image of the dramatist. Like the devil and the alchemist, the dramatist attempts a transformation, a conversion of matter into imaginary gold. They work according to identical principles. There is a "perpetual allusion to the materials and the principle of the theatre found in almost all alchemical books" which, Artaud writes, should be seen "as the expression of an identity (of which alchemists are extremely aware) existing between the world in which the characters, objects, and in a general way all that constitutes the virtual reality of the theatre develops, and the purely fictitious and illusory world in which the symbols of alchemy are evolved."[7] Both the theatre and alchemy are "virtual arts"; neither carries its ultimate reality within it. Like the alchemist, Calderón uses the theatre to materialize some distinctly *other* plane. Like alchemy, his theatre alludes to the sublimation of matter according to principles of order and simplicity, measure and rule.

Where alchemy, through its symbols, is the spiritual Double of an operation which functions only on one level of real matter, the theatre must also be considered as the Double, not of this direct, everyday reality of which it is gradually being reduced to a mere intact replica – as empty as it is sugarcoated [e.g. "el hombre es pequeño mundo"; "la mujer es breve cielo"] – but of another archetypal and dangerous reality, a reality of which the Principles, like Dolphins, once they have shown their heads, hurry to dive back into the obscurity of the deep (p. 48).

The theatre has metaphysical roots, like alchemy, in the need to materialize rather than simply to exteriorize an essential, original drama. It is something "subtler than Creation itself" (p. 51).

Thence the primacy of bodily suffering in *El médico*, the materialization of the formulae of honor as Gutierre brings them to bear on Mencía. Thence, in *El mágico prodigioso*, the insistence on the final martyrdom and on the ascension of the bodies into heaven, both nearly alchemical sublimations of corporeal matter. Because Calderón senses the materializing possibilities of staunchly theological theatre, he is able to work from a theocentric basis opposed to that of a Marlowe and need not sacrifice the primary substance which usually stands only as a shadow behind representations, the "prime" of which the representation is a "double." Whereas Marlowe tried to forge an ontology from the metaphysics of flux, of negative identity, of subversions of the social order, and of identifications with the alien, Calderón looks to seize the permanence of Being, its presence in a realm literally above and beyond this world, in moments of emblematic stasis such as the apotheosis of the martyrs of *El mágico*. The sublimation and exaltation of Justina's violently formed body is dependent on a realm which is static *and* substantial. She experiences the "resurrection of the body," the great Christian theological myth which Calderón puts on the stage.

In *El mágico*, the Scholastic niceties are invoked with a near-convinced and believing confidence, not because Calderón wants to ironize their content, but because he knows that, left unsupported, they may be undermined. He wants sincerely to find material substance in these principles, but he fears that they may vanish in

smoke. In Marlowe, by contrast, the metaphysical rules of order of
the Schoolmen are bartered for nothing by Doctor Faustus. They are
ground to a pulp by Tamburlaine's voice.

Calderón leaves an escape clause in Cipriano's bargain with the
devil ("fue condicional") (I, 637b), which rescues the metaphysical
formulae from daemonic devaluation. Cipriano begins the play as if
he had just returned from the twelfth-century school at Chartres, not
Wittenberg. He has read Pliny. He wants to investigate "la
definición de Dios" (I, 609b). In a medieval *disputatio* with the devil,
he adds stoic spice to patristic platitude:

> . . . hay un Dios,
> suma bondad, suma gracia,
> todo vista, todo manos,
> infalible, que no engaña,
> superior, que no compite,
> Dios a quien ninguno iguala,
> principio, al fin, sin principio,
> una esencia, una sustancia,
> un poder y un querer sólo.   (I, 611b)

(. . . there is one God, all goodness, all grace, all-seeing, all-doing, infallible,
who does not deceive, above all, who does not compete, God whom none
equals, beginning, in the end, with no beginning, an essence, a substance, a
sole power and will.)

In Act III, Calderón takes up the reprise of each of these principles –
all to the devil's utter outrage. But in the end, the martyr–hero of the
play fares better with Ramist-like discourse, as he argues with the
devil, than with the incantatory, magical formulae of seemingly
prerational speech we intuit through Marlowe's heroes. As with
Cipriano's speech at the opening of Act II – "Ingrata beldad mía,
llegó el feliz, llegó el dichoso día" ("Oh my ungrateful beauty, the
happy, felicitous day has come") (I, 630a) – the rhetoric is expert but
feckless. The pathos is that the power of poetic phrasing is not enough
to make illusions real:

> Hermosos cielos puros,
> atended a mis mágicos conjuros;
> blandos aires veloces,
> parad al sabio estruendo de mis voces.   (I, 630a–b)

(Beautiful, pure heavens, heed my magical incantations; soft, swift winds,
stop at the learned clamour of my voice.)

But because the devil sought through illusory means to give Cipriano ultimate power over concrete, earthly forces, those powers are weakened; the illusion is absorbed by the transcendent space we see at the close of the play.

In *El mágico prodigioso*, theatrical representation and Christian metaphysics are part of a single paradox. The principles of transcendence are translated into spatial and material terms, regardless of the fact that space and matter may also be denied by transcendental metaphysics. Leonardo da Vinci mused that the key to power, to wealth, indeed, the key to all except death, lay in the secret power of flight: if only man could escape from the confines of this earth, if only he could loose the bonds and restrictions of space. But Leonardo considered it a delusion to think that we might achieve our freedom from the earth by means of necromancy. Like Marlowe's *Doctor Faustus*, Calderón's *Mágico* tempts with this kind of illusion. Even in setting, the play is of cosmic proportions. The coordinates are like those of *Doctor Faustus*, which are "nothing less than heaven and hell; while in the horizontal plane, at opposite ends of the stage, the conflict of conscience will be externalized by the debate between Good and Evil Angels."[8] In Calderón, these limits are invested with metaphysical significance. In the setting of Calderón's play, the insistence on qualitative levels is implicit in the ascension of the martyrs.

Complete freedom from the limitations of space is, of course, an illusion, the illusion of metaphysical power. As the devil tempts Cipriano with the view of the city in the distance, the Biblical overtones of that temptation are patent. The poignancy of *El mágico prodigioso* lies in the similarities between the devil's intent and the dramatist's. We sense it in the way the devil makes the landscape move and in the way Calderón gives material form to the principles of transcendence: it is as if we were shown that the supposedly numinous reality of heaven were only material, like the earth, and that even in heaven we will not escape the confines of space. The only other way out of the paradox, a way which in many ways satisfies less, is to declare that *both* are an illusion.

9

The illusions of history

In arguing, as I have done so far, that Calderón's theatre incorporates
illusion as a necessary part of the same illusions it criticizes, and that
in seeking to limit illusion Calderón proposes its embrace, I have been
looking at the different theatrical adaptations of the thematics of
illusion in specific *comedias* of his (e.g. role-playing in social and
theatrical terms, theatrical representation as a form of magic, space as
endowed with stage-like limitations). There are further forms of
illusion, also developed in theatrical terms, which I shall discuss in the
chapters to follow: political authority in *En la vida todo es verdad y todo
mentira*; the sensory world in *Eco y Narciso*; the intellect in *La estatua de
Prometeo*; heroic adventure in *Hado y divisa de Leonido y Marfisa*. But I
have not yet said much about the origins of Calderón's concern with
the thematics, or the theatrics, of illusion. We know, of course, that his
work shows a deep engagement with the *theatrum mundi* conceit, and
that there are connections with the Humanist concerns exemplified in
Luis Vives' *Fabula de homine*. But there are also historical conditions
bearing very directly on Calderón's involvement with the use and the
limits of illusion; these will be my subject here.

If the *comedia* as a genre can be called a form of collective self-
reflection, which is to say a way in which a society is able to fashion
images of itself, then, beginning in the 1630s, the decade of Calderón's
mature work, the genre became a form of official, national self-
imagining as well. This is in part because performances were now no
longer designed just for the open-air *corrales*, which had been built for
the *vulgo*, but were undertaken at the newly built Retiro Palace, the
royal retreat on the edge of Madrid. Royalty could of course attend
performances in the *corrales* (although they would often go incognito)
or in the Alcázar of Madrid and at Aranjuez, but the Retiro and its
Coliseo offered a very prominent setting for regal patronage of
theatrical productions. The availability of an official forum for the

performance of *comedias* and *autos* – and especially one that was as well equipped as the Coliseo of the Buen Retiro – presented new theatrical advantages to the playwrights; Calderón in fact wrote an *auto* for 1634 about the new Palace (*El nuevo palacio del Retiro*). Certainly the productions of *Eco y Narciso* and *Hado y divisa de Leonido y Marfisa* which I shall discuss could not have been imagined without the facilities available at the Retiro Palace; indeed, it was not difficult for a dramatist to be overshadowed by the work of his stage designers. But it was not only that the Retiro Palace and its theatre helped shape the *comedia* as a genre; the reverse was true as well: the *comedia* left its mark on the way affairs were conducted in the Palace, and hence in the nation. This was only possible because life at Court, and especially at the Retiro, was itself theatrical in important ways.

Built in the 1630s, the Retiro was conceived with two interlocking purposes in mind: it was to be a showcase for the arts (not only for the theatre, but for painting and poetry as well), and it was to be a showcase for King Philip IV in his role as patron of the arts.[1] This kingly role was only one of many which the Count–Duke of Olivares helped create for him; Philip was to be the mirror of *all* the kingly virtues, as skilled at hunting and riding as at *belles lettres*. "In all Spain there is not a single private person who can ride in both styles of saddle like our master, the king," Olivares wrote, "while performing all the equestrian exercises I have described with almost equal skill. And although they did not teach him much Latin, he has some; and his knowledge of geography is outstanding. He understands and speaks French, he understands Italian and Portuguese as well as he understands Castilian; and although he cannot travel to foreign parts as he would if he were a private person, he has been round all the provinces of Spain observing them with particular care."[2] To judge by the standards of any traditional manual on the proper education of princes and rulers, these would be considered only modest accomplishments, but that is why Olivares' flattery is so striking. Like an impresario, his concern was to create for the nation, in the person of Philip IV, the image of an accomplished and self-confident ruler, when in actuality the current specimen of the Habsburg line was of only mediocre capabilities.

As Jonathan Brown and J. H. Elliott have shown in their recent study of the Retiro, Philip IV was the featured actor of official life which, with its elaborate ceremonies and the intricate requirements of protocol, began to take on theatrical proportions. Philip undertook to revise the *etiquetas de palacio*, the written rules of behavior which the Emperor Charles V had introduced in 1548, in order to maintain the highest standards of comportment in daily life.[3] Court amusements were on a grand scale, and, although not as inventive as the theatrical experiments at Florence which not too many decades earlier had given birth to modern opera, were still impressively audacious. We have records of some enormous sums which were spent on these entertainments, but these pale in comparison to the total amount expended in constructing and furnishing the Palace, some 2,500,000 ducats *exclusive* of amounts spent on festivities.[4] The finances were covered, in part, by the government's inflationary policy of minting additional currency. This alone was typical of the enormous contradictions inherent in the management of Spanish affairs in the seventeenth century: lavish, even exuberant expenditure on all manner of public spectacle, while the nation grew increasingly poor.

Brown and Elliott have said that "in the midst of poverty and defeat, the Retiro and all it contained became the symbol of bad government and of the wasteful expenditure of financial resources desperately needed to defend the Monarchy" (*A Palace for a King*, p. viii). In time, it became plain that the Palace and all its splendour were only concealing the tarnish of crisis and decline; the building materials of which the Retiro was constructed proved to be so poor that physical decay soon set in. In this context, the *comedia* functioned not only as a form of official diversion, but as a source of hope and stability for the national psyche. In so doing, however, it was fulfilling the social role which had made for its very existence. Even as early as the 1580s, when Spain's social structure was threatened by trouble with the *moriscos* and when the country still felt the threat of the Turks, the *comedia* was able to instill confidence and optimism in the general populace. In the intervening years, Spain's troubles proved to be not only social but political and economic as well, but the *comedia*'s role remained largely the same.

Modern economic historians have never been able to determine the causes of Spain's economic decline. In the wake of the American discoveries, these should have been prosperous times.[5] Why though did the riches from the American gold and silver mines seem simply to evaporate in Spanish hands? Why was it that, while most nations at war are prosperous, either from piracy or because of increased economic demand (one pundit in fact proposed that exactly what was needed was "a good war, or else we lose everything"),[6] Spain went to

[handwritten top margin: Caste as reason for increasing Spanish poverty through 1500/1600s]

ruin?[7] The answers lie in the values of caste which the *comedia* was meant to reinforce. Spaniards were not so much concerned with the quantity of wealth or with possible ways to make it grow, as with its emblematic significance. The emergent capitalism practiced by the Italians, and especially by the Genoese bankers, was founded on unfamiliar and unacceptable modes of behavior. Moneylending, commerce, and trade were indications of possible affinities with those of impure (i.e. Jewish or *converso*) blood; but, perhaps more important, the values of economic growth, of increasing – not static – worth, and of the deployment of a nuclear fiscal mass, acquired by credit, were ways of being that were at variance with the static values of a caste society.

The political economists of the day, the *arbitristas*, were in certain instances capable of the most perspicacious analyses, but the fact that their proposals were not carried out with any consistency or success testifies to the persistence of the values of caste in Golden Age Spain. González de Cellorigo, for example, was able to see that Spain could not prosper unless the nation could increase its productive capacity. To quote J. H. Elliott's analysis of Cellorigo's crucial perception when he wrote that "money is not true wealth,"

his concern was to increase the national wealth by increasing the nation's productive capacity rather than its stock of precious metals. This could only be achieved by investing more money in agricultural and industrial development. At present, surplus wealth was being unproductively invested – 'dissipated on thin air – on papers, contracts, *censos*, and letters of exchange.'[8]

Others attacked the persistent trade deficits, or what they saw as a pernicious Castilian monopoly, but no one was able to take any of these suggestions and construct from them a plan of action. The *arbitristas* have gained a somewhat undeserved reputation as madcap thinkers, largely through literary satires such as we find in Cervantes' *Coloquio de los perros* and Quevedo's *Buscón* and *La hora de todos*, but in fact many of their insights, if not their proposed remedies, were quite sane. What from our point of view seems lamentable is Spain's inability to take charge of her own destiny and alter it in any significant way.

In 1625, the elderly Count of Gondomar told the Count–Duke of Olivares in no uncertain terms that "se va todo a fondo," "the ship is going down."[9] As Elliott has shown, the awareness of national decline only encouraged national self-deception. The only tangible results of this awakening lay in the contradictory reform movement of the last years of Philip III's reign, which proposed to cure the ailing nation through a program of "purification" and "purgation."[10] This rhetoric of statecraft as bodily healing, with its bloodlettings and amputations, has obvious parallels in the Inquisitorial thought and language that were so deeply ingrained in Spanish life. But this is not alone enough to account for the fact that even the best suggestions of the *arbitristas* were met by a lassitude in praxis. The financial pressures to which the *arbitristas* were responding, along with the continued persecution of the Jewish *conversos*, the reduction of the caste structure by another third with the decreed expulsions of the *moriscos* circa 1609, and Spain's involvement with European trade, threatened the very values of caste which, since the early Middle Ages, had been decisive in determining Spanish behavior. Thus the *arbitristas* could propose – as Sancho de Moncada in fact did – that Spain should imitate her European rivals by venturing into manufacturing;[11] but this form of capital-intensive investment, with the goal of economic growth, was incompatible with the embattled values of caste.

In stark contrast to such forward-looking proposals, the *comedia* pretended to give the illusion of a nation in good health within the specific framework of the static and hierarchical values of caste – personal inviolability, the supremacy of honor, cleanliness of blood – and this in turn blocked any adjustment to the ideals of "progress" which might have been possible for Spain. From the start, the *comedia* offered the Spanish populace ways to invoke threats to the caste system, and to see those threats rebutted. The keynote of the genre, "soy quien soy" (i.e. I am who I am because I am, *personally*, by right of bloodline, not by acquired value), confirms a personal integrity, a posture of wholeness, that is as epic as the *entereza* of the Cid, and in part derived therefrom. This phrase of personal evaluation was an elixir for a national spirit wounded in caste conflict.

As the seventeenth century progressed, it was not fully evident that Spain's decline would be irreversible, that Europe as a whole was preparing for and strengthening the *class* values of a rising bourgeoisie; nor is there any reason to believe that the Spaniards who attended the first performance of *La vida es sueño* would have been any more alarmed about the future than those who had seen the *estreno* of Lope's *Fuenteovejuna*. While the expiration of the truce with the Dutch in 1621 marked the beginning of renewed problems on that front, the years 1625–6 witnessed the siege and surrender of Breda, a momentary respite in troubled times. Calderón in fact wrote one of his earliest plays (*El sitio de Bredá*) in response to the event. The work is in the Lopean mould; the characters display a capacity for epic-like action in the face of favorable and adverse circumstances alike.

Flora raises a provocative question in Act II of the play: "¿Es Bredá acaso Numancia?" ("Is Breda perchance Numantia?") (I, 130a). The resistance of the inhabitants of Breda recalls the self-sacrifice of Iberian Numantia. Indeed, the contrast of Calderón's play with Cervantes' *La Numancia* is revealing. Flora herself is shaped along the lines of Cervantes' Lira. The persistent desire for fame is reminiscent of Cervantes' allegorical Fama. In both works, the versification attempts to bring the *comedia* close to a level of classically elevated decorum. Cervantes' play is foreign to the mainstream *comedia* tradition because he did not intuit the values of the dominant caste. Nor did Cervantes make the siege of Numantia seem like a contribution to history for the public of his day. It remained a distant and unfamiliar model, an episode of Roman Iberia. Both Lope and Calderón could look to far-off times and places, but they would constantly read the past in terms of present values. In *La Numancia*, it is the vanquished Numantines who are exalted in their suffering. Willard King said that the inhabitants of the besieged city are more akin to those American and European peoples who were rapidly being submitted to Spain's imperial designs; the Roman agressors are allusively like the Spanish Conquistadores.[12]

In comparison to Cervantes' history play, which was obliquely skeptical of the Spanish imperial mission, *El sitio de Bredá* is affirmative. For Calderón, the aggressors are heroic Spaniards whose valor is exalted by their adversaries. Whereas Cervantes had offered a vision of defeat and mass suicide, of suffering and consumption from within, Calderón sees the city and its populace from without. The Spaniards pose in epic-like postures. Breda itself becomes emblematic of their heroism; it is their prize, an accomplished and self-sufficient event:

> ¡Plegue a Dios que en sus historias,
> Bredá, escriban mil naciones
> con tu ruina sus blasones,
> con tu sangre sus victorias!   (I, 122a)

(Please God that a thousand nations, Breda, may inscribe in their histories with your ruin their coat of arms, and their victories with your blood!)

The victory is, as Espínola puts it, "el sitio *famoso* / que a Bredá tenemos puesto" ("the *famous* siege that we have laid to Breda") (I, 117b, emphasis mine). The entire military campaign assumes the qualities of a pose, an act of emblematic self-presentation transferred to an event of national significance.

The *comedia* as a genre institutionalized the ways of self-presentation that were evident as early as the epic of the Cid. There are similarities of attitude linking Calderón's play and the *Cantar*. From on top of the walls of Breda, Laura looks out on the surrounding lands much as the Cid viewed with wonder the orchards of Valencia, or as Urraca in *Las mocedades del Cid* surveyed the pastoral countryside from her window:

> Llégate a ver el campo numeroso,
> que es a los ojos un objeto hermoso
> que suspende y divierte . . .   (I, 115a)

(Come see the harmonious field, which is an object of beauty for the eyes, that amazes and gives pleasure . . .)

Espínola's strategy in the siege is to send troops to Grave in order to divert attention from Breda. The Cid's taking of Alcocer comes to mind. The similarity may be coincidental; Calderón only knew of the Cid through the ballads. But there is a deeper affinity, a kinship in attitude, posture, and values between them. These strategies are appraised not in their own terms, not as intellectual maneuvers, but for the significance of the prize. They share a formal axiology.

The religious imperialism of *El sitio de Bredá* is vulgar – "¿Qué piensan estos perros luteranos?" ("What do these Lutheran dogs think?") (I, 115b) – but it transcends the immediate political conflict between Catholic Spain and Protestant Flanders. For Calderón, the slur is paired with the epic war-cry, "Santiago, cierra, España." He seeks glory for Spain and for the Church; he invokes the King as an emblematized summation of national worth:

> Solo el Rey de España reina;
> que todos cuantos imperios
> tiene el mundo son pequeña
> sombra muerta a imitación
> de esta superior grandeza.   (I, 128b)

(The King of Spain rules alone, and all the empires of the world are but a feeble shadow in comparison to this superior grandeur.)

The play culminates in a grand gesture of pity for the vanquished. Velázquez portrayed it in "Las lanzas." The scene formalizes a myth of Spanish hegemony in Europe.

Such postured responses to historical events were not limited to the arts. In 1626 Philip IV sent a message to the Council of Castile describing the state of the nation and world affairs. Together, Philip and the nation struck a pose; they crystallized a national attitude of self-congratulation:

> Our prestige has been immensely improved. We have had all Europe against us, but we have not been defeated, nor have our allies lost, whilst our enemies have sued me for peace. Last year, 1625, we had nearly 300,000 infantry and cavalry in our pay, and over 500,000 men of the militia under arms, whilst the fortresses of Spain are being put into a thorough state of defence.[13]

But, a decade after Breda, Spain's troubles turned catastrophic. In 1635, Spain's traditional enemy, France, in alliance with Holland, declared war against her. This time, however, problems with France were coupled with something far more devastating to the national ego: the revolt of Catalonia. To be sure, the revolt of the Catalans was not caused by France, but the presence of French troops was a decisive military factor. The final uprising was the culmination of anti-monarchical tendencies already evident in high-level and local politics; actual revolt began among the poorer nobility aided by bandits. The consequences were markedly different from those of the Aragonese rebellion, a more limited civil conflict put down by force. When in 1641 the Spanish troops were defeated in Catalonia, Spain had to face the loss of a portion of her nation located on the Iberian Peninsula itself. The danger was no longer to her distant empire.

At the same time, a direct threat to the unity of the Spanish nation and to the strength of the central monarchy developed at the opposite end of the Peninsula. In Portugal, which had been annexed to Spain only in 1580, general discontent crystallized in an insurrection in 1637 at Evora; in 1640, with the call for soldiers to fight in Catalonia, a revolt was sparked in Lisbon that marked Portuguese secession from Spain. In a vision as mythic as that of *comedia*, Hernando de Acuña had proclaimed to Philip II the rule of "un monarca, un imperio y una espada" ("one monarch, one empire, and one sword"); the prophecy could not have been more ironic.

The events of 1640 bring into bold relief the underlying causes of the Spanish decline: the imperfect unity which constituted the Spanish nation and the lack of a central figure able to galvanize the partisan interests. Gracián's *El político don Fernando el Católico*, written in that same year, is revealing. For Gracián, the Catholic King was an archetypal model – yet not a practical one – of the kind of ruler needed to integrate the Spanish realm: "In the kingdom of Spain, . . . the provinces are numerous, the languages varied, and the climates conflicting, and so there is needed great ability to preserve it and to unify it as well."[14] As Américo Castro said, the radical causes of the uprisings of 1640 touched the very foundation of the Spanish nation: "The separation that was so intensely reaffirmed by Isabel la Católica in her testament, between Castile and León on the one hand, and Aragón, Catalonia, and Valencia on the other, made clear the centrifugal course of the Christian kingdoms of the Peninsula, which was begun with the Reconquest and which was maintained by the Catholic Kings. A consequence of this was the uprisings of 1640 . . ."[15] Yet, as in *El sitio de Bredá*, the *comedia* was shaped to portray the Spanish monarch as reigning with singular control: "Solo el Rey de España reina" ("The King of Spain reigns alone") (1, 128b).

Azorín described Spanish history as a perpetual tumult of opposing passions. V. S. Pritchett remarked of Spain that "it is only peoples . . . who lack deep unity who will put such fatal emphasis upon it and who will corrupt the idea of unity and make it uniformity; and when we turn from the Spanish idea to the Spanish reality, . . . we see the anarchy in which Spain really lived."[16] Hence the enormous effort to impose Spanish rule on the colonies of the New World, hence the attempt to homogenize the various castes of Spanish society, hence the gravely uniform façade of the Escorial, the appearance "as of an infantry regiment drawn up in stone in the mountain" (p. 62), hence the militant Catholicism of the Jesuit missionaries and the spiritual regimentation of the Loyolan *Ejercicios*. The political and historical roots of this will to uniformity go deep; but they grow over a bedrock of separatism. Cánovas de Castillo is the common touchstone for both Azorín and Pritchett:

. . . in accepting [this] unity, each district remained as it was, with unchanged customs, with its own character, its own laws, its traditions, varying or opposed. Nor was even the footing of all the states equal: there were some of more or less equal standing, more or less privileged; some free, and some almost enslaved; for the Union had been carried out with very diverse motives, some districts coming into it voluntarily, as the Vascongadas claim to have done; others through matrimony, like Castile and León, Aragón and Catalonia; some through force of arms like Valencia and

Granada, still populated by Moors; some half by way of justice, half by force, such as Navarre. And not only so, but even within the province every town had its code, every class its law. In this way Spain represented a chaos of rights and obligations, of customs, privileges, and exemptions, easier to conceive than to analyze or reduce to order.[17]

Events subsequent to 1640 confirmed the dismemberment of Spain and her European possessions while the *comedia* continued on its course: Portugal was never recovered and Barcelona was not regained until 1652; fighting continued in the Netherlands until the Treaty of Westphalia was signed in 1648, recognizing in effect France's supremacy and religious pluralism in Flanders. Spain's traditional allies in Italy, the Prince of Monaco and the Duke of Medina Sidonia, attempted – unsuccessfully – to revolt against Castile. The Castilian military machine was being threatened, and the monarchy it imposed was faltering. This made all the more apparent the lack of a monarch who, in his person, might provide charismatic unity for a nation and an empire.

Elliott comments that "Philip III, twenty years old at the time of accession, was a pallid, anonymous creature, whose only virtue appeared to reside in a total lack of vice. Philip II knew his son well enough to fear the worst: 'Alas, Don Cristobal,' he said to Don Cristobal de Moura, 'I am afraid they will govern him.'"[18] The account of the reigns of Philip III and his successors is the story of royal favorites – the Duke of Lerma, the Count–Duke of Olivares, Luis de Haro, Castrillo, Fernando de Valenzuela, Don Juan of Austria – who sapped power from the kings. It was difficult for Spaniards, used to Philip II, to accustom themselves to government by strong-men as in the days of Juan II and Alvaro de Luna. Philip IV's attempt to govern without a Privado after the fall of Olivares was short-lived; power was ultimately given to Olivares' nephew, Luis de Haro.

At the time when Spain was most in need of a strong, charismatic monarch, of the type portrayed in countless *comedias*, the throne passed on to the four-year-old Charles II. One historian described him as a "sickly, retarded child of less than average intelligence who suffered from rickets."[19] The description of the 25-year-old King by the papal nuncio shows evidence of little improvement in the intervening years:

He cannot stand upright except when walking, unless he leans against a wall, a table, or somebody else. He is as weak in body as in mind. Now and then he gives signs of intelligence, memory and a certain liveliness, but not at present; usually he shows himself slow and indifferent, torpid and indolent, and seems to be stupefied. One can do with him what one wishes because he lacks his own will.[20]

His mother, Queen Mariana, was the official Regent with the title of Queen Governor, but she was politically powerless; Johann Nithard, her confessor, Don Juan of Austria, and Fernando de Valenzuela, the Andalusian son of an army captain, struggled for control.

Elliott describes public sentiment during the transition to the reign of Charles II as the expression of Spain's hopes for a messianic leader: "The Castile bequeathed by Philip IV to his four-year-old son was a nation awaiting a saviour . . . Castile, which had lived for so long on illusions, still clung to the more potent of them with the tenacity born of despair. A Messiah would surely rise to save his people."[21] How bitterly ironic, then, that this nation awaiting a saviour should have inherited Charles II. While no Messiah seemed likely to appear, Spain continued to sustain an illusion of grandeur reminiscent of Charles V's *idea imperial*, a grandiose *mélange* of hopes, an abstract recipe for empire not fully capable of responding to domestic problems. The dangers inherent in royal succession and the transfer of political power are often acknowledged by historians writing in the seventeenth century, but the perspective, as in the following passage from Cabrera de Córdoba's *Historia de Felipe Segundo* (1619) is thoroughly rhetorical, the recommendations insubstantial:

With no fear of God, the Empire will go to ruin if a valiant and prudent prince does not fill its needs in every way. His life is brief, and the strength of the kingdom depends entirely on him . . . if he lives long and is exposed to great changes and to the accidents which befall the governance of state over the course of time, he will ruin the state . . . Do not be surprised at the oddity that there are few good princes, for the number of good men is limited, and princes are chosen from among men; it would be much for any one of them to be excellent, and an even greater miracle if he should persevere in virtue once he finds himself raised up so high.[22]

There are no practical solutions offered here. Pressing problems are moralized away, relieved of their urgency by negative examples from the ancient Roman Empire, ascribed to the will of God or the accidents of time.

While Spain had created and maintained the image of power and self-control, it was becoming evident (although not practically recognized) that this self-image had little basis in fact. Indeed, historical and political events suggest plainly enough that the Spanish Empire was vulnerable as an entity and that the nation itself lacked a center strong enough to sustain it. All the same, the country continued to maintain the illusion of such a pivot. Even in priestly sermons we find a campaign to invigorate the character of the monarchy, an attempt to assimilate its figures of flesh and blood to the realm of the transcendental.[23] José Antonio Maravall adduced passages from Paravicino, from Ximénez de Embún, and from Francisco Xarque to support the claim. According to Xarque, "God wished to give to the House of Austria the stability of the heavens; to the Catholic Monarchy, the lasting strength of the firmament; to the kings, the firmness of the two great lights, since they act as such for Heaven and the Church; and to give the latter the permanence of Paradise."[24] This kind of political imagination points up what was manifestly *absent* at the time: a central figure strong enough to ensure precisely the *stability*, the lasting *strength*, and the *permanence* of the Habsburg dynasty in Spain, its control over the Empire, and the viability of Spain herself.

The literature of the seventeenth century is replete with generalized recipes for kings and rulers, suggesting, as was characteristic, not ways of acting, but manners of being, postures congruent with poetically formalized ways of self-understanding. Fernández de Navarrete, for example, sums up his chapter in the *Conservación de monarquías* entitled "Que el rey es corazón de la República" ("That the King is the heart of the Republic"), proclaiming:

And so Emperors, Kings, and Princes act as heads of State in order to govern the other members: they are fathers of the family in their vigilance: they are Vicars of God in their earthly providence: they are nerves that link King and Kingdom: they are rule and measure that adjust the actions of their subordinates. And, finally, they are the heart of the Kingdom, since in giving it vital fluids they maintain it in peace and justice.[25]

Maravall thought that Baroque monarchies aligned themselves politically within the capital cities.[26] But Spain chose Madrid on geographical grounds; and the political strength of the monarch was sapped by those around him, none of whom was able to anchor life in the city. Hence the nervous insecurity of a Barrionuevo: "My lord: the news is horrible and frightening!" and "My lord: the way things happen in Madrid, may God help you! What today they decide, tomorrow they abolish. Nothing is firm; everyone seeks to do his own business but no one the common good of all, and so all goes wrong;

people walk around blind, and at every step they trip and fall."²⁷ A multiplicity of interests, widely diverging points of view, and the potential weakening of central authority are natural facts of life in urban settings; but the Spanish monarchs did little to act against these tendencies.

Through the sixteenth and seventeenth centuries, the changing tenor of opinion regarding the monarch was gradual. In Lope's theatre, divine sanction does not exempt the King from possible failure; like all men, he is human; he must be trained and educated in his office. Mariana's *Del rey y de la institución real* (*De rege et regis institutione*) (1598) is in large measure devoted to kingly propaedeutics. The ideology of Calderón's theatre is different: the King need not study; government is neither taught not learned. One can see, in Herrero García's words, "we have passed from Philip II to Philip IV."²⁸ Quevedo's panegyric to the latter Philip, written in 1643 when Olivares had fallen from power, speaks eloquently of the fact. The comparisons between the Spanish King and Christ are all but sacrilegious, they are so bold: ". . . although you may not be able to raise the dead, which is the greatest miracle, you will raise the living, which is a more novel one." Quevedo looks to Philip as Saviour of Spain: ". . . your word alone . . . will place the enemy at your feet."²⁹

While the sense of what could actually be accomplished by the King had undergone a marked change by mid-century, this did not put a stop to these kinds of political illusion. In fact, it made them all the more necessary. When attention was not turned directly to providing theoretical maxims, rules, and guidelines for what constitutes the "perfect prince," or his "perfect favorite," it was turned to supplying these figures in the form of past models or to the mythification of present rulers. Saavedra Fajardo's *Corona gótica, castellana y austriaca* and Gracián's *El político don Fernando el Católico* are representative. No matter which way this evidence is turned, it reveals that the deficiencies of the throne were sensed acutely, if tacitly and indirectly.

Calderón's theatre, no less than Lope's, was the product of a society's self-imagining. But increasingly Calderón's plays were written for court audiences, who expected to be flattered, congratulated, adulated, and who would be pleased with nothing less than the most impressive and bedazzling feats of showmanship. As early as the Madrid festivities of 1636–7, Calderón collaborated with

Cosimo Lotti and Velázquez in the production of the allegorical
"Colloquy of Peace and War," which included songs and instrumental music, the new resources of the pageant play. As we saw, *Los
tres mayores prodigios* called for three separate stages floating on water
and three different theatrical companies for its production. Like the
comedia, the *auto sacramental* fell increasingly under royal purview and
tended toward gaudy showmanship. In 1635 it was declared that all
the Councils of government, as a group, would be the first audience of
the *autos*; in 1648 the *autos* were produced with four carts instead of the
usual two, this bestowing a potential for still greater lavishness upon
an already spectacular genre.[30]

Calderón's spectacles represent the solutions that the troubled
Court was attempting to fashion for a nation in historical agony. At
their best, his courtly plays resisted the inevitable temptation to serve
up wholly uncritical images to the King. But faced with the fact that
so many of the nation's problems were rooted in the failures of the
King himself, these "solutions" all too often turned out to be but
theatrical illusions, ways of escape. Barrionuevo gives us a fitting
introduction to Calderón's courtly theatre and its relationship to a
monarchy blithely ignorant of the catastrophe to which a culture was
being submitted:

So that the silk worm won't die when the sky gets cloudy and makes
threatening noises, either with thunder or lightning, the only solution is
to play guitars, strike tambourines sound timbrels, and use all the happy
instruments that people use to entertain themselves. This happens with the
King, who in the most difficult straits only cares about entertainment. In the
Retiro they put on a play called *The Restoration of Spain*, a burlesque piece.[31]

Authority and illusion: *En la vida todo es verdad y todo mentira*

In its sybaritic appeal, in its festive character, in its very subject matter – so often drawn from myth or imitative of the romances of chivalry – Calderón's courtly theatre can be described in a phrase: self-conscious spectacle. Jean Duvignaud finds the style characteristic of the European Baroque: "The theatre becomes celebration, visual delight, the representation of mysterious forces that have been freed, a visual delirium from the very moment when the spectacle is enclosed in a box, shut behind a 'closed door,' with a partition that seems artificially and clandestinely left open, by chance, to the eyes of the audience."[1] Yet precisely where theatrical form is determined in a crucial way, Calderón's later theatre breaks the mould. Despite the increasing use of *trompe l'oeil* scenery, his pageant worlds do not open clandestinely to the spectators; they do not work by chance; they are avowedly self-conscious of their own illusory status and entail a critique of the same superficiality which they flaunt. If we are to make anything of Duvignaud's metaphor, it must be revised: in the theatre of Calderón's last decades, audience and actors find themselves together behind closed doors, both within an essentially empty box. The "power of the scenic image built within [this] empty box . . . which vies with the world" (*ibid.*, p. 285) stems from the concerns of self-affirmation and critique advanced by audience and players both. As never before, Calderón's later work is inscribed within a close-knit courtly context. This was a theatre which the royal coterie used in order to fashion images for itself. At its best, it was a theatre that allowed the sovereign circle of power to fashion self-critical images and sustain the hope of sorely needed reinvigoration.

For France, Duvignaud saw a direct relationship between contemporary sociopolitical structure and theatrical form. Baroque theatre is the province of an elite surrounding the King and his immediate circle of power. It is meant to reflect a world whose magnetic center of authority is the royal person. Visually and thematically, the theatre finds its focal point in the monarch himself, both in his roles on the stage and in his physical location among the spectators. The designers of French playhouses insisted on the location of the royal box at the center of the visual rays directed toward the stage, at an optical point where the multiple perspectives converge.[2] In the *corrales* which served Spanish playwrights as late as 1640, there was no such focal point, no privileged royal node. But as official theatres were built, and as the *comedia* was placed in the service of the Crown, it became a reflection of national concerns as seen through the eyes of the King and the powerful few who surrounded him. Maravall thought that the *comedia* represented an attempt to impose a fixed social stratification. But the genre was less socially doctrinal than reflective. It was a social mirror. What seems an attempt to *impose* fixed social forms was the effort to unify a national existence that had grown increasingly polyvalent and disparate rather than tightly unified.

The time had long since passed when the theatre might actually be used to unify the nation politically. Indeed, the inherent separatism of Spanish political history would suggest that the *comedia* could never have done this. Spanish history since the Reconquest had proved that dominance by one caste or race was no assurance of the political or spiritual unity of the nation. By the time Calderón's career reached its midpoint, it was only too apparent that the monarchy was unable to perform the stabilizing functions expected of it. But the theatre was conditioned to reflect a homogeneous society centering in the royal throne. All the medieval metaphors – the king as "head" of State, the indestructibility of his corporate body, his divine right, and so on – were by convention built into the genre. Thus the theatre was conditioned to reflect something that in actuality was absent. In the Spanish court plays of the late seventeenth century, we see the image of a society devoid of a mythical center, the expression of a culture which in a crisis of authority had transferred power to the King's *privados*, in which a social elite had weakened the royal grip.

These conditions inform Calderón's *En la vida todo es verdad y todo mentira*. Superficially, the play is a late variant of *La vida es sueño*, but the plot is historical. There are versions by Corneille and Mira de Amescua which offer illuminating contrasts. Calderón organizes the action around the quest of Emperor Focas: which of the two princes, Leonido or Heraclio, is his son and rightful successor to the throne? In the covert ways demanded by the Court, Calderón teases a probingly pertinent political question out of the plot: who is the King, and how long can he sustain the illusion of authority? Focas' search for his true heir is his search for his own identity; he must find out who he is in order to cement the authority of his rule. He does not know his own parents, and finding his son will help him place himself genealogically; if he cannot, he will remain bereft of identity and without justifiable claim to power.

Thus Focas practices what Stephen Greenblatt would call "self-fashioning."[3] He looks for his identity by trying to read the signs of his family history. He wants to crown the prince who bears his marks – "para coronar . . . a quien con mis señas halle," ("in order to crown the one I find with my marks") (i, 1112b). But he suffers a crisis in his effort at self-fashioning. Returned to the place of his birth in Sicily, he recognizes the rugged terrain, but fails to perceive the similarities between himself and either of the princes. Focas is a hollow man. He is a mask, an illusion to himself. He is unable to recognize the peasants Sabañón and Luquete when they are attired in courtly dress because, as one critic commented, he himself is nothing more than a peasant in king's clothing;[4] in a telling textual variant, Astolfo, the princely tutor, calls Focas a "villano en sangre y en costumbre" ("a peasant in breeding and manners") (Act I, v. 754–5, in the Cruickshank edition). Astolfo has the "señas" which Focas gave his infant son, but he is resolute in not deciphering the information they contain.

The task of self-fashioning entails identification through imaginative devices, but Focas finds that images are useless to him. The signs he had planted have no value; his talisman is ineffectual. He tries to resolve the dilemma of identification by looking for traits of his own character in the two princes, but since he does not know himself, he cannot succeed. The princes' ignorance of their identity is a reflection of Focas' lack of self-awareness:

> *Foc.* Fieras, en quien viendo estoy
> de mi primero linaje
> la bruta especie, ¿quién sois?
> *Her.* No sabemos de nosotros
> más de que solo nos dio
> este monte la primera
> cuna . . .   (i, 1120a)

(*Foc.* Beasts, in whom I see the wild nature of my first ancestors, who are you? *Her.* We do not know anything about ourselves except that these mountains were our first cradle . . .)

Focas is a personal void peering into a vacant mirror; these are voices which echo within the hollow royal seat of power. The crucial question behind these failed recognitions points to the historical and political crisis of late seventeenth-century Spain: who was to tell the monarch that he was powerless and ineffectual?

Focas and the princes move about in a world that never ceases to reveal its theatricality. At Focas' orders, the sage Lisipo conjures up a magical palace, a stage upon the stage. Focas seeks to place theatrical representation in the service of self-identification, but he fails. Theatricality is itself a source of uninterpretable illusion for him. Unlike Denmark's Claudius, Focas remains blind to the meaning of the play within the play. Like Basilio of *La vida es sueño*, Focas errs by misjudging his own son; the error is rooted in a lack of self-knowledge. The theatrical impulse in a work like this springs from deep within a culture which, for nearly a century, had instinctively looked to the stage to accomplish its self-imagining. Like *La vida es sueño, En la vida* is an example of "metatheatre," a self-duplicating form. The theatre, the preferred mode of national identification, is thrown back on itself and becomes self-reflective; in a moment of political crisis, the theatre seems to double over and reflect its own form.

Consider by contrast *Hamlet, Richard II,* or the many other plays in which Shakespeare explores a crisis of authority mirrored in a throne left vacant by death or illegitimately usurped. Part of Shakespeare's extraordinary interest in "killing the king" (Maynard Mack) is to probe the transition of power through a broken chain of authority. But Shakespeare's perception of the crisis of authority is exceedingly forward-looking where Calderón's is reactionary. The descriptions are not evaluative. Shakespeare was the first to understand that the political crisis of authority was bound up with the theme of revolution. In the oft-cited phrase the "revolution of the times," the modern, political meaning of "revolution" is fast gaining ascendancy over its older, more physical sense. Shakespeare sees that revolutions pivot and turn on the faults of power. Much as Marlowe was before him, Shakespeare is concerned with great upsurges of power from periphery to center, and with the whorl of history created at the vortex. He perceives that torque as potentially tragic.

Calderón looks toward the restoration of order after the crisis rather than to the constant turning of revolution. He keeps to a conventional plot structure for *En la vida*, that of the just ruler replacing the tyrant, of disorder resolving into harmony. He is thus able to satisfy public needs for affirmation and still mirror critically the national crisis of royal authority. The Spain of 1650 was desperately in need of a strong ruler, and in a play like *En la vida* that need is vicariously satisfied: the just, self-aware ruler is supplied in the figure of Heraclio. This is theatrical therapy more than public congratulation. The audience celebrates at the theatre, but only after it confronts the political illusions of its circumstance. If for the bulk of the action of *En la vida* the true center of authority is absent, usurped by a virtually anonymous place-holder, the just and stable center that emerges in the final moments is an image of royal strength and confidence, of public authority founded on the tenets of reality and self-mastery.

In many ways, Calderón's preoccupations in this play anticipate distinctively modern concerns. We fear that we may be deceived by authority. In Kierkegaard, in Unamuno, in Dostoyevsky's *Grand Inquisitor*, the illusion of authority is treacherous but necessary; people cannot exist without the discipline of external rule applied to them. Freedom without authority is, paradoxically, unbearable; the illusion is crucial: "Authority is founded on the illusions of miracle and mystery and they are necessary illusions," as Richard Sennett said.[5] Perhaps man only wants to *imagine* that he is free. Calderón takes the illusion of authority – not, as in Shakespeare, the subversion of power – as the crux of his play. He fears most that the crucial link in the chain, the figure of authority, may be an illusion. Focas is vacant within, insubstantial, and he is unaware of the fact. Calderón fears that the social order, the hierarchies built around the monarch, supported and reinforced by the parapets and buttresses of the *comedia* and the social images it engendered, may be made of the same stuff as dreams. His greatest hope and confidence in authority is rooted in a deep trust in the ability to balance illusion and reality: he hopes that a ruler will emerge able to secure the social structure on the basis of his healthy skepticism and self-control.

Calderón offers three distinct appraisals of the fantastic palace, each a different estimation of illusion: that of naive confidence (Focas), that of doubt overcome by sheer power (Leonido), and that of doubt guided by self-restraint (Heraclio). These are three alternative evaluations of sensory experience, each one determined by a different capacity for self-control. Calderón sees that the richest possibilities for man in this world lie where he exercises authority over his own situation, even if it should be illusory. His characters who, like

Focas, trust appearances, reap no satisfaction from their power in this world; their rule is hollow. Leonido sees a superficial value in the world of appearances, he holds it to be of worth in and of itself; only Heraclio, the self-controlled skeptic, achieves the proper balance of worldliness and spirituality, self-control and public power, illusion and authority. He learns through illusions to evaluate himself in terms of a larger, ultimately transcendent, order. Calderón probes various possible postures toward the world of illusion through the metaphor of representation itself. Even where the representation is the product of his own imagination, he knows that it must be put to civic use, that the value of the temporal world, like that of the theatre, is false and hollow if not subjected to restraints.

Mira de Amescua draws flatly didactic conclusions in his version of the play. *La rueda de la fortuna* was written under the sign of asceticism prominent in Counter-Reformation Spain. For Mira, the lessons of the illusion of earthly life go no deeper than the unilateral doubt of all surface appearances. He derives no critical self-appraisal from this asceticism. The play is designed to instruct, to set forth a thesis. Its poetry is intended to impress the audience, to shake their habitual self-confidence and false evaluation of earthly life. The poetic metaphors are dynamic throughout: vivid, spiritually searing, but destructive of their own sensory appeal.

> Gusano de seda fuiste,
> Que en tus entrañas trujiste
> Tu muerte y tu sepultura[6]

(You were a silk worm, for in your bowels you carried your own death and your own tomb.)

One thinks of Mira's play in terms of Zárate's pulpit fire, of El Greco's vision of Toledo's tormented sky. Like Calderón, Mira is concerned with the domain and limits of human power, with the need for restraint in human action, and with the illusory quality of temporal existence. But he fails to apprehend the paradoxical role of the theatre in the formation of these critiques. His play is a lesson in skepticism, not belief; it fails to criticize itself. The solitude of Mira's Focas is pitiful: "¿Qué pretendo haber de un miserable / Que en el mundo no cabe su desdicha?" ("What can I expect from a miserable man whose misfortune is larger than the world?") (16b). He is neither a convincing tyrant nor a hollow man. He is exemplary in a negative way. He turns desperate and contemplates suicide. He is a model for living – a warning: "Tú lazo estrecho, aprieta mi garganta; / Ciega el órgano ya por donde espera / El pulgón deste cuerpo desdichado" ("Tight noose, squeeze my neck; blind the organ through which this wretched body takes its breath") (16b). At Mauricio's death, we are given a model for dying as well. Mira's implicit response to the skeptic is stoic:

> Nunca tengas olvidada
> La muerte y eterno abismo,
> Pues tu principio es nada,
> Y has de volver a ese mismo
> En el fin de la jornada
> . . .
> Toma siempre buen consejo,
> Honra al clérigo y al viejo,
> Reparte a pobres tus bienes,
> Y por si soberbia tienes,
> Pobre y humilde te dejo.   (19b,c)

(Never forget death and the eternal abyss. For your beginning is nothing and you will return to that very beginning at the end of your journey . . . Always take good advice, honor the priest and respect the aged, share your goods with the poor, and should you be proud, I leave you poor and humble.)

Corneille's *Héraclius* is, on balance, also a minor work. Yet, as always in Corneille, the stage is charged with the attributes of physical, personal space. The characters communicate in ponderous alexandrines, unfolding passionate selves as their egos press against one another. Their diction is the expression of *personal* desire and limitation. The characters have a sense of identity that is inviolable because it is contained in the very physical stuff of their bodies. Corneille's theatre is grist for Merleau-Ponty's mill, very much a theatre of "incarnation." The phantom existence which some of Calderón's theatrical selves lead is alien to it. From the same events of which Calderón built a critique of authority and illusion, and Mira de Amescua a lesson in disbelief, Corneille fashions a sheath for the personal *grandeur d'âme* of his characters. *Héraclius* is built around precarious and complex personal relationships. The identities of Héraclius and his twin (Martain) are not merely in doubt, the two are actually confused. Thus the problem is not only royal succession and social authority, but incest and parricide, passionate and bodily transgressions both. Corneille suggests the violent bickering and family bloodshed proper to Greek tragedy. Phocas would have Héraclius marry Pulchérie – hence the threat of incest. And

Pulchérie, who takes her brother Martain for Héraclius, begs him to avenge the death of her father. She exhorts her lover "Léonce" (actually Martain) to avenge the emperor Maurice. Thus Martain, unknowingly, plots to kill Phocas. Incest is more than the flicker of passion that it was in *La dama duende*; parricide also looms as a threat.

In Corneille's play, Phocas' *crise d'identité* stems from a tangible defect of birth, a flaw in the bloodline. Because of the conditions of his birth, he is neither noble nor great. There is little that might compensate for such faults. They are real, not illusions. In stark contrast to Calderón's straw man, Corneille's Phocas is hardened, tough, real. But since his rise was by force, not by right, he never ceases to look for self-assurance. He takes Héraclius as his personal prize: "Je tiens Héraclius, et n'ai plus rien à craindre" ("I have Héraclius, and no longer have anything to fear") (v. 999).[7] On the contrary: he fears the people, the gravely silent public mass. He fears for his life, and for his claims to the throne. He is not so much afraid of dying as he is anxious about his self-perpetuation; the issue is not his mortality but his continuity after death. He is a pathetic figure because, endowed with so strong a presence, he is incapable of imagining a *future* context into which he will fit. He finds no continuation to the story he imagines for himself:

> Hélas! je ne puis voir qui des deux est mon fils;
> Et je vois que tous deux ils sont mes ennemis.
> En ce piteux état quel conseil dois-je suivre?
> . . .
> O malheureux Phocas! ô trop heureux Maurice!
> Tu recouvres deux fils pour mourir après toi
> Et je n'en puis trouver pour régner après moi!
>
> (v. 1361–3, 1384–6)

(Alas! I cannot tell which of the two is my son; and I see that they are both my enemies. In such a pitiable state, what advice should I heed? . . . Oh unhappy Phocas! Oh too happy Maurice! You recover two sons to die after you and I can find none to reign after me!)

Corneille's hero suffers a crisis of "self-fashioning" at least as severe as Calderón's. Both Corneille and Calderón see the unsettling paradoxes of a potentate whose public authority rests on no strong mandate. But where Corneille understands the problem through an essentially linear and narrative mode – Phocas' inability to finish his own story – Calderón understands the matter in theatrical terms: he sees that an illusion of authority is fostered by the national theatre, and he offers the muted hope that a theatrical critique of illusion might reroot the faltering monarch. More typical of his court plays than of *La vida es sueño*, to which its poetic conventions nonetheless owe large debts, *En la vida* is a play which alludes to the tangles of contemporary politics. Even where the characters intone the commonplaces which Calderón perfected as poetic statements of the delicate balance between reality and illusion, *En la vida* sets in motion a field of political and social concerns which lend the touch of pertinence to otherwise abstract beliefs. Calderón intuits the crucial fact that the causes and resolutions of the Spanish political quandary lie in the very culture of which his own *comedia* forms a part. Through the failures of Focas as a theatrical creature, he shows us the flaws built into the culture; and through the felicitous resolution of the plot, he offers hope for the future of the nation. The work points to a central paradox of human culture, which Calderón interprets for his time: that the ways of self-imagining which give a people definition are those which limit them most. No people can do without its own culture, yet it must also strive to overcome the self-limitations thereby imposed. Calderón sees both the source and the solution as bound up in the theatre; in this play, at least, he finds a place for the theatre in the service of its own critique. It is, for that reason, a remarkable achievement among his later works.

11

The use of myth: *Eco y Narciso*

In the Palace of the Buen Retiro, in the Coliseum, a play was performed in May for the birthday of the Queen. The author was Calderón. The play used the most extraordinarily elaborate costumes, scenery, and effects ever seen in the theatre. The set changed seven times! There were lights for illumination! The production lasted a full seven hours! First, the Monarchs saw it, then the second day the Councils of Government, then the third the people of Madrid. And it ran for 37 days more, the longest run ever in Madrid.[1]

Such was one journalist's account, in the *Anales de Madrid* for 1652, of Calderón's *La fiera, el rayo, y la piedra*, a mythological extravaganza. It could have been any of Calderón's mythological showpieces. The exuberance, the massive attention to detail, the sheer weight of theatrical effect are remarkable. Only Broadway, Hollywood, or the Lido can provide any points of comparison. Indeed, Valbuena Prat said that Calderón's mythological plays were the genre "most akin to current tastes and sensibilities."[2] They are artificial, and shamelessly so, "the merest and purest artifice," the elevation of artifice itself to its own subject matter, as one critic put it.[3] They are virtuoso pieces of artificiality. Conventional in every way, they are brilliant crystallizations of Calderón's theatrical showmanship. They sustain an illusion that is so elaborate that it becomes, necessarily, self-conscious. Indeed, they are so artificial that even when they falter they come crashing down awash with brilliance.

Looked at from the point of view of action, motivation, or characterization, these plays are anomalous. For all their outward energy and exuberance, they are static. Because there are no deep motives for the action of these plays, it would be a mistake to consider them as truly dramatic. Their only dynamism is that of the self-contained, motionless lyric; their beauty is crystallized in still ornament. Calderón gave up plotting at the deep level, and took to the invention of infinite arabesques, superficial complications that were themselves either familiar because they were mythical or entirely predictable because they were shaped like conventional romances. Philosophically, they are meditations on the themes we know from earlier works: identity and its vicissitudes, the need for self-control, the demands of integrity, the deceit of the senses, the seductions of the material world, and a dozen more, all trivial by comparison to the sheer artifice of their theatricality. They are superficial in literal ways: visually, sonorously, spatially.

Looked at poetically, which is the only way to see them, these plays have a distinctively delicate and sumptuous lyricism, unique within Calderón's *oeuvre*. For Menéndez y Pelayo, this was their undoing. To a Neo-Classical aesthetic sensibility, they were the culmination of an epoch of poor taste: "Calderón partook of all the bad customs that at the time pervaded lyric poetry and theatre; and as he was the last of our great dramatists, he was also the most uneven in matters of style, the one who paid greatest tribute to redundance, to hyperbole, to the bad and muddy rhetoric that has been plaguing us since Góngora."[4] Menéndez y Pelayo disparaged their pageantry: "In these mythological plays, the poet always remains inferior to the engineer and the set designer" (*Calderón y su teatro*, p. 381). He disapproved of their tone, thinking it ridiculous for courtiers to masquerade as ancient gods: "taken out of their natural conditions, the fables of antiquity cannot in any way produce the effect they do in the works of the ancients" (*ibid.*, p. 32). But these plays must be seen as belonging to the theatrical traditions of royal celebrations, pageant entries, court masques, tourneys and parades. "Serious" primarily in their own artistry, they have more to do with the work of Monteverdi or Alexandre Hardy than with classical tragedy. To be sure, it is precisely comparison with classical drama that we must avoid in reading these plays.

Menéndez y Pelayo's rejection of Calderón's mythological plays is reminiscent of Hazlitt's censure of *A Midsummer Night's Dream*. Hazlitt saw in that play an attempt to create "real" supernatural occurrences, when Shakespeare's audience expected nothing of the sort. Unwittingly, Hazlitt hits the mark when he recommends the "poetry" over the "representation":

All that is finest in the play is lost in the representation. The spectacle is grand; but the spirit was evaporated, the genius was fled. Poetry and the stage do not agree well together . . . Where all is left to the imagination (as is the case in reading) every circumstance, near or remote, has an equal chance of being kept in mind and tells according to the mixed impression of all that has been suggested. But the imagination cannot sufficiently qualify the actual impressions of the senses. Any offense given to the eye is not to be got rid of by explanation. Thus Bottom's head in the play is a fantastic illusion, produced by magic spells; on the stage it is an ass's head, and nothing more; certainly a very strange costume for a gentleman to appear in. Fancy cannot be embodied any more than a simile can be painted; and it is as idle to attempt it as to personate *Wall* or *Moonshine*. Fairies are not incredible, but Fairies six feet high are so.[5]

C. L. Barber saw through this censure in a way that should guide us through the thicket of criticisms to which Calderón's mythological plays are vulnerable: "excluding all awareness that 'the play' [within *A Midsummer Night's Dream*] is a play, misses its most important humor."[6] Similarly, if the characters and the audience are deprived of the awareness that Calderón's ancient gods and demiurges are but characters in a play, the self-conscious impersonation loses its attraction; the effect seems cloying, if not effete.

Eco y Narciso is to my reading one of the finer specimens of this group of plays. Calderón's strength lies not in saturnalian comedy, which was Shakespeare's forte in the way of court entertainment, but in a delicate fusion of comic and serious shadings. He uses the *gracioso* as always, but in novel ways for treatment of a myth. He very nearly captures Ovid's sense of guileless wonder at the natural world, even if this Narcissus play is Ovid at one or two removes. Calderón could only be self-conscious in a work like this: his courtly audience was sated with theatre and with the classics of mythology. As was obligatory for the court dramatist, Calderón drew on Renaissance sources; he used Baltasar de la Vitoria's *Teatro de los teatros* and Pérez de Moya's *Philosophia Secreta*. But mere transmission of the Narcissus myth through these works will not account for Calderón's adaptations. He diminishes the pagan force of the myth, but he does not allegorize as in the mythological *autos*. He does not interpret "a lo divino," but attempts something more subtle. Drawing on the latent literary suggestions of the myth, his Arcadian setting refers more to the aesthetic possibilities of that tradition than to its mythological roots. His theatrical conception shifts emphasis from problems of fate and foreknowledge to the nature of action in a world of illusion. The theatrical artifice thus serves to reconcile the pagan foundations of the myth with Calderón's Christian outlook: the problem for his mythological characters is not simply to overcome prophecies but, as for Segismundo in *La vida es sueño*, to recognize illusion and then to find appropriate modes of action.

To be sure, the characters of this play, and Narciso in particular, are not as successful as Segismundo, but there is a notable poignancy in their failure that stems from the fact that Calderón was himself now exploring more elaborate forms of theatrical illusion, with public success. *Eco y Narciso* for instance is one of the early examples of that uniquely Spanish form of mixed-media entertainment, the *zarzuela.* We do not know exactly why the full-fledged, Italian-style opera never took deep root in Spanish soil; *Celos aun del aire matan* and *La púrpura de la rosa* were the only two full operas produced at the seventeenth-century Spanish Court.[7] To be sure, opera requires large infusions of cash, and the economics were unfavorable, but that did not halt the sheer profligacy which went into the making of Calderón's pageant plays and operettas. Nonetheless the use of music in *Eco y Narciso* and other works like it, and the inclusion of dance in some (a special "Baile de las flores" was presented between Acts II and III of Calderón's last secular play, *Hado y divisa de Leonido y Marfisa*), show that these plays fit into the tradition of French opera, German *Singspiel* and, more remotely, the nineteenth-century *Gesamtkunstwerk*. Some Spanish *zarzuelas*, in Calderón's time much as today, are frivolous confections of unalloyed fluff, yet the music in *Eco y Narciso* has a special thematic function in the poetry of the play. The musical motifs allude, in large measure, to the pastoral setting of the Narcissus myth and recall its Ovidian roots. The sounds of the birds, the soft murmurings of the streams, the harsh hill and woodland echoes, draw out the longstanding alliances between the pastoral and musical worlds: pastoral leisure is particularly pleasing for the purely aesthetic enjoyment offered by such proximity to the sounds of nature.

By convention, the music of the pastoral is only imagined to be like that of nature. But if the conventions are understood, the music can be seen as central to the pastoral's suggestive contrast of life in the city or at Court to rustic life. The "musical" sounds of nature at the performance of Calderón's *zarzuelas* would have been played by a modest orchestra; as Thomas Rosenmeyer wryly observed of the music which might have accompanied the "melodious murmurs" in

Milton's *Paradise Lost*, such sounds would have puzzled a herdsman, "if they did not shatter his ears";[8] but they would have been no source of dismay for Calderón or Milton, who were accustomed to such conventional overlay. Throughout the Renaissance and even more so in the Baroque period, the pastoral fed on courtly convention. Indeed, a certain culturedness was only to be expected from this cross-breed of city sophistication and country life. Theocritus, the first writer of pastoral whose name has come down to us, was himself a city man. Even in his first *Idyll* we find a finely carved work of art, a supremely artificial object set within the rustic frame. As if this contrast was not itself paradigmatic, Theocritus describes a coquet-tish woman figure on the carved cup; we can imagine her in full plumage ("she wore a cloak and headdress"). Two lovers vie for her attention, "But these things do not touch her heart. / For now she turns to him and smiles, and now / to him, while they, both hollow-eyed with love, still waste themselves away in vain."[9] For all its name seems to say, the pastoral is a hothouse growth, cultured and sophisticated in important ways.

For these very reasons, the pastoral was easily adapted to the tenor of seventeenth-century courtliness. As became increasingly common in Calderón's career, the pastoral was placed in service of the self-reflective imaginings of the Court, but this too was well within the traditional uses of the genre. Milton's *Arcades*, a masque, is a good precedent to keep in mind. The aristocrats here were intended to represent different parts in the performance, and the fountains and groves were supposed to mirror the court by recognized convention. Some critics have speculated that the key to a work like Cervantes' *Galatea* is concealed in the roster of some court, or that, like Montemayor's *Diana*, it was a courtly *roman à clef*. The practice was absolutely appropriate to the pastoral, which blended naturally with courtly masques, or simply masquerades.

Certain conventional compromises are made between courtly and natural settings, and of these the music is one. Because of this tension between natural and cultured environments, the pastoral has a special dynamism, if not a "dramatism" (Kenneth Burke's word) built into it. The critique of one environment in and through the next is natural for the pastoral. The genre is dialectical by birthright, and often in construction as well. The amoeban song modeled by Theocritus and made traditional by Virgil, the alternating voices in Garcilaso's and in Lope's eclogues, the discourses that Spenser so subtly worked out in *The Shepheardes Calender*, are well served by the representation of actual voices in contest. When Garcilaso spoke of *imitating* the complaints of his two shepherds at the opening of his so-called first eclogue ("sus quejas *imitando*"), he was thinking of vocal mimesis. In the representation of voices, especially, the pastoral displays a theatrical bent.

And yet the pastoral resists becoming successful drama in the full sense. It may well be that the value of *otium* weighs too heavily against the kind of successful conflict that would make for strongly motivated dramatic drive. One cannot make leisure the engine of a good plot. The pastoral is broad enough to include violence (think of Garcilaso's second eclogue) but its favored images conjure up a languorous world, a landscape of repose. Tasso, for one, ran up against this problem. *Aminta* has, from the start, been criticized as an unsuccessful play. Principal objections have been to infractions of the Aristotelian unities, and to the artificial resolution, but the play suffers more from built-in, pastoral stasis. The pull toward repose saps strength from the action. The piece is a wonder of spoken poetry, but is not altogether viable as representation. Garcilaso faced related problems in his early second eclogue. Finely structured as the poem may be, it is too long even to be read aloud, and unless represented it is too digressive to sustain interest.

Calderón was confronted by some of these same barriers when composing *Eco y Narciso*. The stasis which seems endemic to the pastoral also infects this play; there is no deep motivation or appreciable action worth sustained analysis. The play must be conceived as an eclogue, relished for its fine lyricism. To be sure, the infinite symmetries of plot and diction that can be uncovered in it are an artificial delight. There are no real conflicts among the characters, at least none that are driven by the strong inner needs and convictions we see, for example, in Angela of *La dama duende* or in Gutierre of *El médico*. The dialogue is like the variable song of an eclogue: neatly patterned, symmetrical, richly lyric.

The parallels and contrasting symmetries seem superfluous, frivolous artifice bound to no deep content. Calderón was not interested in the usual form of moral critique available to writers of pastoral. He conceived *Eco y Narciso* as a play to be *represented*. The staging is built into the poetry, and the visual spectacle, the artifice of the form, is itself made thematic. This is where *Eco y Narciso* is unique in the pastoral canon: the play is a critique of courtly convention and vanity, yet in transgressing that very critique it is itself sustained by artifice. If the form of the work is taken into account, the play is richly ambiguous; it works against itself. Calderón is able to speak to us about the vanity of earthly life, about the false confidences and illusions of this world. He is capable of intoning a litany of praise for the heavenly life or of preaching the need to accept our transient roles. But so were Mira de Amescua, Tirso de Molina, Fray Hernando de Zárate, and a hundred homilists in Counter-Reformation Spain. Calderón went beyond moralization if only because, as an artist, he found himself caught up in a celebration of the same values he denounced. Only through theatre could he have transmitted the poignantly ambiguous options. He would have us reject neither the artifice and spectacle, nor the heavenly life beyond.

In the *Metamorphoses* (339–519), Tiresias foretold that Narcissus would live to a ripe old age "si se non noverit," "if he does not know himself." In *Eco y Narciso*, the prophecy is itself a precious lyrical flower. It refers to the sensory world:

> Una voz y una hermosura
> solicitarán su fin
> amando y aborreciendo.
> Guárdale de ver y oír.   (I, 1914b)

(A voice and a beauty will seek his end in love and in hate. Protect him from seeing and hearing.)

The ambiguity seems more complicated than it is. The trick of meaning hinges on *guardar*, which indicates both "prevent," in the sense of "keep from," but also "take care," in the sense of "teach."[10] Superficially, the verses tempt fate by commanding Liríope to keep Narciso apart from the world about him. So isolated, he could only be a brute like Segismundo, or a captive of his own unfulfilled desires. Calderón accepts the literary workings of prophecies, themselves wholly conventional: they lend themselves to nuanced ambiguities, and they are fulfilled in unexpected ways. In Calderón's hands, their uncanny predictability is less threatening than in the ancient world. The fate which they invoke is part of a self-enclosed, circumscribed world. This was Walter Benjamin's basic perception with regard to the Baroque *Schicksalsdrama*. A play like *Eco y Narciso* may or may not be a *Trauerspiel*, in the German distinction, but the emphasis undisputedly falls on the "play" – in both senses – more than on the sadness or mourning.

The ostensible instruments of the prophecy are Tiresias and Liríope. Tiresias was not only a seer, but a magician as well, reminiscent of Basilio the astrologer–king of *La vida es sueño*, ". . . el sutil / mágico que tantas veces / . . . / asombraba con su ciencia / a los dioses " ("the keen magician who so often astounded the gods with his knowledge") (I, 1914a). By what irony is it that the seer has no sight? Liríope followed him, and met her punishment:

> Porque [Tiresias] se quiso igualar
> a Júpiter, él allí
> ciego y preso le tenía.
> Consideradme ahora a mí
> presa allí y ciega también.   (I, 1914a)

(Because he [Tiresias] wanted to equate himself with Jupiter, he was held there blind and a prisoner. Now consider me, a prisoner, and blind as well.)

It is no real surprise that Liríope misunderstands the prophecy. She was ill-advised to follow Tiresias: she is bold and defiant. "Desclavaré de su epiciclo los astros" ("I will unhinge the stars from their sphere") (I, 1931a) are her words in the third act.

Calderón was meticulous in his actual formulation of the prophecy. Any slight variation from the Ovidian version is significant. He specifies that *sight* and *sound* will be Narciso's undoing. Narciso dies deceived by appearances, closed to the surrounding world, save for its most superficial aspects. The deeper inevitability of the prophecy consists in the fact that Narciso could not help being exposed to visual and verbal beauty, least of all on Calderón's sumptuous stage.

Arcadia, the setting of the play, is splendidly beautiful, but vicious. It is a mirror of courtly society – finely polished on the surface, hollow within. The landscape is dominated by a vain nymph. (It is but a small leap of the spirit from Calderón's Eco to Cocteau's Jocasta, smearing coldcream on her face.) Calderón's Arcadian shepherds are consumed in amorous rivalries and jealous love affairs. Is this all really – Calderón asks – any better than the wilds where Narciso was reared? Calderón knew only too well that the cultured and courtly beauty of the pastoral was deeply ambiguous. Unlike Ovid, who was concerned with self-knowledge, Calderón had the virtual experience of the whole of Renaissance courtly self-imagining behind him. The pastoral in *Eco y Narciso* is part of an implicit self-indictment, a strain that runs deep in Calderón's best work.

The paradox of the first segment of Tiresias' dual prophecy suffuses the setting of the play. Silvio, the first to speak, points to the physical vault of the mountain: "Alto monte de Arcadia, que eminente / al cielo empinas la elevada frente . . ." ("Towering mountain of Arcadia, you who raise the peak of your lofty brow to heaven") (I, 1906a). Liríope, cosmically bold, is the characteristic inhabitant of the region. The verdant splendor of the Arcadian lowlands predominates in Febo's verses. He praises the "Bella selva de Arcadia, que florida / siempre estás de matices guarnecida" ("Beautiful forest of Arcadia, who are always green and adorned with nuanced hues") (I, 1906a). He hails the timeless beauty of the setting.

This setting, heavy with the pleasures of the senses, is spiritually suffocating for Narciso. He cries out to a mute landscape. He might well be Segismundo in his complaint: "aves, repetid mis quejas; / montañas, dadme salida; troncos, decidme la senda" ("birds, repeat my cries; mountains, give me leave; trees, tell me the way") (I, 1911a). He never finds his way out of nature. As he seeks, he becomes entranced by its superficial splendor. And as he dies deceived by his own image, he is transformed into a flower and is wedded to the stillness of the natural world. Where Calderón differs notably in temper from Ovid is in the frozen permanence of this final transformation. There is no real sense of natural renewal through transformation in Calderón's mythological plays. Shakespeare could achieve that sense in some of his comedies. *The Tempest* and, especially, *A Midsummer Night's Dream*, are moved by the energies of metamorphosis. In Calderón's mythological plays, that energy is usurped by the sheer *presence* of the theatrical effect, by the brilliance of the stage itself.

Calderón's insistence on time, change, and ruins, standard Baroque poetic currency, contrasts with his intuition of the ultimate stasis of nature. This intuition lends an exquisitely lyrical quality to the play. The quintessentially Baroque concerns which are set in motion – permanence and decay, endurance and age, temporal and celestial beauty – culminate in Febo's sonnet:

> Todo vive sujeto a la mudanza.
> De un día a otro día los engaños
> cumplen un año, y este al otro alcanza.
> Con esperanza sufre desengaños
> un monte, que a faltarle la esperanza,
> ya se rindiera al peso de los años.   (I, 1920b)

(Everything lives subject to change. From one day to the next, deception itself ages a year, and this year leads to the next. A mountain withstands deceptions by means of hope, for without hope it would crumble under the weight of the years.)

Calderón seems only too aware of the transience of his own medium. In a landscape that seems timeless, Eco the nymph considers herself ageless. She is blithely ignorant of her mortality, and is vain and self-assured in her irresistible sonority. Indeed, she is the very embodiment of superficiality, the incarnation of nothing less ephemeral than a voice. Eco is the crucial second element of Tiresias' prophecy. Her words are a fair summation of the *flatus vocis* which⟫ characterizes courtly conversation. Act I opens at her birthday. Silvio, an admirer, plans to join in the celebration. Depending on one's taste or ideology, this image of courtly festival is the wondrous quintessence of artifice or the odious abuse of theatrical form. Some, no doubt, would see in it the first large bloom born of the divorce of true civilization from "culture." All that can be said in Calderón's defense is that his taste in artifice is impeccable and that he is not uncritical of his own efforts.

As a flower, Narciso is consigned to the silence of the inanimate world. There is a certain just repose in the rest he is given. Throughout the play we see (or, rather, we hear) the disappearance of the vocal world. Sounds and music, the vanishing essence of Eco's world, are Narciso's temptation. However ephemeral, Eco's voice is entrancing and seductive. Her vocal doubling parallels Narciso's visual reflection in the pool. (The echo effect is reminiscent of Monteverdi's *Orfeo*.) Ironically enough, Liríope has taught Narciso one human virtue: speech. To compound the irony, Eco tells of Narciso's fate by repeating the final words of his phrases. Her insubstantial voice is in the end prophetic. Narciso's words are feckless. But Eco also gets her due: she is exiled to the silence of the caves. By contrast to the long and muscular harangues of Liríope, Eco's voice is feminine. In the contrast, in Eco's fate, Calderón seems to have been driving at what Shakespeare meant at Coriolanus' greeting of Virgilia: "My gracious silence, hail!" (*Coriolanus*, II. i. 165). Beneath the codified, institutional laconism, he is well aware of female banter and talk.

In *Eco y Narciso*, words are exactly, literally, what they say; they are emblematic, much as Narciso becomes a floral icon. This does not mean that the characters always understand one another. They remain unaware from a hardness of hearing, a poetic deafness written into the lines they speak. At the moment of Narciso's second speech, for instance (I, 1910–11a), Líríope does not overhear or listen in. He sees her on the stage, but we do not share her perspective. She and her son inhabit separate aural registers. The audience receives these speeches stereophonically, like the alternating voices of an eclogue.

In *Eco y Narciso*, Calderón revises the theatrical convention of "verbal scenery" which Shakespeare and Lope used for simple lack of visual effects. Whereas on an Elizabethan stage, or in the open-air *corrales*, the characters would carry their scenery in their poetic lines, Calderón was working with elaborate stage effects. The characters in this play move about the stage and point to their surroundings: "trees," "forest," "mountain." Because those are plain to see, the characters themselves become object-like. If they seem flat, one-sided, incapable of dialogue, it is because they, like their poetry, are part of the scenery we see.

Much as we might wish to psychoanalyze these characters, they resist clinical diagnosis. They have no "other sides" to hide, no "hidden selves" to reveal, and without those covert aspects, psycho-analysis is of little use. Calderón has taken care of all the analysis he wants to allow. We *already* have the psychic symbols parading about on the stage before our eyes. We can push no further into the characters, who will yield no more than their voices. As they verbalize their actions – as in Narciso's first complaint – they are their own poetic essences, and nothing more.

The "dialogue" of the play (one would hesitate to use the term at all) is utterly depersonalized. As Benjamin said of Sigmund von Birken, this is essentially ballet, a musical drama where the dis-position of the images and visual movements prevail: "The spoken word makes no pretense to be dialogue; it is only commentary on the images, spoken by the images themselves."[11] This is dance with talking pictures; the characters are props who speak their own captions. Language is poetry, not dialogue, and poetry is hardened into diamantine shape, or made to dissolve in silence. The conven-tions of parallel speeches (Laura's and Nise's, for instance) resolve the complexities of communication into a stylized and lyric scene. Calderón is interested in Eco because she is the paradoxical *embodiment* of a voice; he found the idea itself irresistible. He is concerned with the shape of that voice, not with a character. The tensions and conflicts of the play are worked out in planned and patterned ways, in symmetrical kaleidoscopy. At their most emo-tional moments, the characters simply cry out in vocal anguish to the scenery and the audience. Nothing could be more distant from the "contienda literaria" (Castro's phrase) of Rojas' *Celestina*. The conflicts of Calderón's play are plastic: they are vocal and visual.

Calderón will always stand out as a man of the theatre more than as mythographer, philosopher, or social critic. But he is sensitive to the anomalies of his own work. His plays register subtle changes in self-perception. He "thinks" theatrically, but he also questions his own efforts to do so. In *Eco y Narciso* he seems aware that any attempt to engage the moral life in theatrical and sensory ways must necessarily be paradoxical – if not blatantly hypocritical. As we share in the theatrical display, we also learn that it can deceive by its own consummate artifice. At the end of *Eco y Narciso*, Bato the *gracioso* underlines the enigmatic nature of the theatrical illusion. After Narciso's transformation, Bato undercuts the illusion and challenges the audience: "¡Y habrá bobos que lo crean!" ("And some fools may believe it!") (1, 1940b). This is a final ironic distancing from the illusion, the final moment of moral suasion, the last intimation of hope that there may be *more* to the world than artifice and gilt. It is a disconcerting disengagement from the spectacle. The plot of the play, conventional as it is, the schematic staging, the over-elaborate scenery, all serve a theme that is derived from the Narcissus myth. But, as Bato's words stress, the play will not submit to the orthodox limits of the myth's moral statement. Bato will not let us forget that Calderón has dramatized the myth, and that he himself could be indicted for overindulgence in illusion. A play like *Eco y Narciso* depends largely on the willing suspension of disbelief of a courtly audience. Yet Calderón finally punctures the artificial veil. The play exposes the artist who has made it: he wrenches himself free from its seductions. However humorous, Bato's final comment rings with the sobriety of Calderón the self-conscious artist. It is the laughing echo of a man whom no one thinks of as laughing; but better to laugh than to confuse the poet with God.

12

Prometheus and the theatre of the mind

Is it any easier to resist the seductions of the mind than those of the senses? Or does the intellect itself not threaten to enclose us in the illusory world of its order with even more guile than that with which nature solicits our confidence? Are not the sins of the mind in fact graver than those of the flesh? Aquinas thought so (see the *Summa*, I^{a}II^{ae}, 73, 5). What happens, then, after Calderón finds a final, ironic way of escape in a play like *Eco y Narciso*, disengaging himself and us from the beautiful object of his own fashioning, giving us over, instead, to an unbroken, closed surface for intellectual contemplation? Thematically, *La estatua de Prometeo* is the complement to *Eco y Narciso*, and in some ways the problem it poses is far more deeply rooted in Calderón's total *oeuvre*. If the mind is powerful enough to subvert physical nature, how may it overcome its own overweening tendencies? And how are the attractions of beauty not to sway us from moral goods? In the Scholastic tradition, in the *Summa* and in the commentaries on the *De divinis nominibus*, beauty is defined in terms of radiant form and intellectual brilliance, as consisting of "a certain clarity and due proportion," each "firmly rooted in the reason [whose function it is] to shine the light in which beauty is seen and to set things in proportion" (*Summa*, II^{a}II^{ae}, 180, 2). Formally and stylistically, Calderón displays a will to order and clarity of expression derived from this Scholastic tradition. Dante shared this sensibility. But how can we be sure that the intellect touched by splendrous light, as at the close of the *Divina Commedia*, will not degenerate into a Spinozistic search for the "intellectual love of God" which, in the end, leaves us with only nature? These questions are familiar from our discussion of *El gran teatro del mundo*.

Like Calderón, the mythological hero of *La estatua de Prometeo* is intelligent, rational man, maker of forms and seeker of knowledge. The theme of the play revolves around the aesthetic and literally *scientific* functions of the intellect, its relations to the bodily passions, and the limits of the human capacity for thought and invention. Formally, the play is every bit as uncompromising in its pursuit of beauteous order as is *Eco y Narciso*. The parallels and the contrasts, the symmetries, are perfectly drawn. Calderón meets little resistance from his materials. The achievement of the play is that which Kenneth Burke attributes to form in general: it summons up appetites in the mind of the audience, and sees to their fulfillment.[1] Ideologically, this constant renewal and fulfillment of formal appeal indicates a sated public, a collective body in spiritual atrophy, incapable of empathy with the sufferings of a character on the stage. Indeed, Prometeo is not a character in any real sense of the word at all. He is a self-aware symbol, a key vertebra in the formal spine of the play.

In other plays, Calderón exploits theatrical form and illusion to help him think – *La vida es sueño* is a good example; he deploys illusion as part of the audience's response to his characters, as in *La dama duende*; in plays like *El médico de su honra* and *El mayor monstruo del mundo*, the representational space lends moral or metaphysical texture to the action, and to the motives and judgments of the characters. But in *La estatua de Prometeo*, the subject is form itself; in it, Calderón takes what Burke calls "eloquence" as the matter of the play. To the world of the stage, which is already highly conventional, are now added the artist's meditations on his art of form-building. As a result, the play is eloquently conventional and conventionally eloquent. The play is abstractly neat and schematized in contour. Calderón attempts to think reasonably about the seductions of the mind, but there is not enough friction between the play's form and the dramatist's thought. The effects are achieved too easily. There is no violent irony as at the close of *Eco y Narciso*. In many respects, the play would work better in some undramatized, poetic rendering, as a work of purely "mental" theatre. What is interesting about the play in the end is Calderón's inability to forsake interest in the physical world, the world of the passions and of war, associated with Prometeo's brother Epimeteo.

The myth of Prometheus as man-making artist was current in the Middle Ages – in Augustine, in Tertullian, in Lactantius – primarily in negative versions, as a pagan travesty of the Creation myth. The Christian medieval tradition naturally tried to reassert the primacy of the Biblical story, but not until Boccaccio's *De genealogia deorum* did the Prometheus myth take on its hybrid Renaissance cast. Boccaccio distinguishes two creations – the one a mere calling into existence, the other a conferring of intellectual content on that life. Through the first, man is given physical substance; through the second, he acquires intelligent form. Through the gifts of culture, the products of the intellect, Prometheus literally "reforms" man, impressing on him a new form and a new essential character. Ernst Cassirer sees a broad individualizing tendency in Renaissance versions of the myth; the Renaissance Prometheus is a hero of human culture, the bringer of wisdom and of moral order.[2]

Earlier, in Bovillus' *De sapiente* (1509), the Prometheus myth was a bridge between natural philosophy and metaphysics. This vein of the myth has implications for Calderón's treatment. As Cassirer said,

Bovillus uses the Prometheus motif as the connecting link joining his philosophy of nature with his philosophy of mind. When he makes the heavenly out of the earthly man, the actual out of the potential man, intellect out of nature, the wise man is imitating Prometheus, who rises to the heavens to take from the gods the all-animating fire. The wise man becomes his own creator and master; he acquires and possesses himself, where the merely "natural" man always belongs to a foreign power and remains its eternal debtor.[3]

Calderón is deeply aware of the need for self-mastery, particularly where the powers of intellectual animation are as formidable as those of Prometheus. Drawing on the collective figure that emerges from Hesiod, from Aeschylus, from Ovid, from medieval and Renaissance texts, his Prometeo is a light-bearing creature. But since he strives for self-criticism and control, the light he bears is that of skeptical reason; in fact, the will to self-governing order diminishes the heroic grandeur which follows on the Renaissance drive for individual excellence. Calderón's Prometheus play looks forward from Bovillus to the monumental act of knowledge of Sor Juana's *Sueño*. Prometeo doubts with as much perseverance as a Descartes, convinced that the world is bedeviled by a *malin génie*.

Like Sor Juana in her nocturnal flight, Prometeo fails. He is the intellectual who leads a solitary existence, living alone in a cave because of intellectual (not, like Segismundo, because of paternal or political) repression:

> a vivir conmigo en esta
> melancólica espelunca
> me reduje: que no hay
> compañía más segura
> que la soledad, a quien
> no encuentra con lo que gusta.   (I, 2069a)

(I reduced myself to living alone in this melancholy cave: for he who finds no pleasing company finds no surer company than solitude.)

Prometeo wants light as a form of science, "que quien da luz a las gentes / es quien da a las gentes ciencia" ("for he who gives man light is he who gives man science") (I, 2076b). One senses that Calderón is "feeling forward" to the central Enlightenment myth, that of Faust.

> Yo, dada mi inclinación
> a la paz de la lectura,
>
> . . .
>
> me di a la especulación
> de causas y efectos, suma
> dificultad en que toda
> filosofía se funda   (I, 2068a–b)

(Given my inclination to the peace of reading, . . . I dedicated myself to speculating on causes and effects, the greatest difficulty on which all philosophy is based.)

Prometeo's error lies in overstepping the limits of his mental powers, in exceeding his domain. With the aid of knowledge, he wishes to turn art into life. The dangers of intellectual illusion, in fact, compound those of the senses. Prometeo confuses art and life and values them equally. Unlike most of the characters in Calderón's repertoire, who are punished for excessive self-interest, for overweening pride, or for overstepping the bounds of personal freedom, Prometeo is punished for excessive dedication to Minerva, a statue, for his desire to turn art into life by dint of his mental powers.

The division between mind and body, sense and passion – recognized as early in the Renaissance as Petrarch's *De remediis* – is acutely modeled in the geminate traits of Prometeo and Epimeteo. The two were born twins ("de un parto nacimos yo / y Epimeteo") (I, 2068a). If Prometeo is the intelligent faculty, Epimeteo is the body. The two are in contention:

> *Prom.* de un parto nacimos yo
> y Epimeteo, sin duda
> para ejemplar de que puede
> haber estrella que influya
> en un punto tan distantes
> afectos, que sea una cuna,
> en vez de primero abrigo,
> campaña de primer lucha.
> Opuestos crecimos.   (I, 2068a)

(Epimeteo and I were born together, no doubt as proof that a single star can at one moment control passions so different that our cradle was our first field of battle, rather than our first shelter. We grew up in opposition.)

Calderón apportions the traits of mind and body equally. Prometeo is given to solitary study and reflective meditation; Epimeteo is forceful and rebellious; he is the tireless and fearless master of the wilds.

Calderón is not able to deny either of the two human facets. He blames exclusively neither the mind nor the body but rather seeks reconciliation. Both brothers favor construction of the temple of Minerva, and Calderón arranges parallel scenes between Prometeo and Minerva, Epimeteo and Palas. Palas, the goddess of war, invokes Discordia, in her campaign against Minerva. Calderón calls on the god Apolo to judge, but Apolo is neutral to the outcome of the battle; he wants an integration of mind and body and a reunion with nature. Neither claim can be satisfied, neither rejected. A price must be paid for the division, and Prometeo suffers at the hands of Epimeteo. But because Calderón, as artist, is himself closer to Prometeo than to Epimeteo, he gives us a more subtle critique of mental, rational images, and of the dangers of overlooking the limits of the imagination, as we have already seen in the case of Gutierre, the "surgeon of his honor." What is unique about *La estatua de Prometeo* is that the intellectual man suffers, not the passionate man, as is more usual in Calderón.

In educated debate over dramatic theory, the poet laid claims and responded to demands analogous to the character traits of Calderón's two heroes. The poet's allegiances were often dual. Boileau's *Art poétique* registers the tension neatly. On the one hand, the poet had formally to "aimer . . . la raison" ("love reason"), yet in response to the pragmatic demands and desires of an audience, and in light of the understanding of the function of rhetoric in swaying their passions, he had also "to seek the heart, stir and move it" (I, 37; III, 16). To be sure, the *comedia* was born and raised in *corrales* where the *gusto del vulgo* necessarily prevailed over the claims of reason; in the *Arte nuevo* (c. 1609), Lope ostensibly pleaded for the supremacy of the passions of the mob over the authority of reason, "porque a vezes lo que es contra lo justo / por la misma razón deleyta el gusto" ("because what offends reason / is often pleasing for the same reason") (v. 375–6). But the *Arte nuevo* is shrewdly ironic. It was written for a Madrid Academy at the very moment when the *comedia* was being taken into public theatres. As Lope hints by playing on the rhyming pair *gusto – justo* – here as in

Fuenteovejuna – the poet should ideally seek to reconcile the two, or at least to keep them in balance.[4] This is possible under the aegis of love (as in a play like *Fuenteovejuna*), or in the play of irony (as in the *Arte nuevo*). In Calderón's hands, the *comedia* became more deeply enmeshed in a classicism which, both in England and elsewhere on the Continent, flourished from roughly 1500 until 1750. As official court dramatist, Calderón was writing for an elite and well-educated public. Tastes had changed; he could see things through more cultured eyes. As far as we can tell from his plays, he tried to meet the double demands of reason and pleasure.

Outside of Spain, in England and France, sixteenth- and seventeenth-century dramatic theory anticipated the Enlightenment concerns toward which *La estatua de Prometeo* looks ahead thematically. Even before Descartes, Malherbe declared that "l'art est objet de science."[5] The Abbé d'Aubignac said that the "rules of the stage . . . are not founded upon Authority, but upon Reason; they are not so much settled by Example, as by the natural judgement of Mankind."[6] For Boileau, the ideal was to please by the use of reason; the poet "plaît par la raison seule" (*L'Art poétique*, III, 423). Pope founded arts and sciences alike on reason; Le Bossu said that "in both we are to be guided by the light of nature."[7] Calderón's split allegiance – on the one hand to the demands of his audience and to the satisfaction of the passions, and on the other to the art of rational form-building and, more important, to the intellectual contemplation of beauty in the Scholastic manner – is mirrored thematically in Prometeo and Epimeteo. His final posture is that of Apolo, traditional god of poetry, who refuses to favor either of the two brothers.

In fact, Baroque poetics in general and those of the Spanish Baroque in particular underline the Promethean intellectual engagement between the mind and the object of its contemplation. The "self-consuming artifact" (Stanley Fish) relies on a mental participation, a kinetic relationship between the mind of the reader and the object of his thought. The latinate syntax of Góngora's poetry, the elaborate wordplay and recondite allusions of Sor Juana's *Sueño*, Quevedo's conceits, are dependent on a vigorous mental action. The appeal to the senses is only half of Baroque poetics; the other half concerns the intellect. The reader implied in a poem like *Paradise Lost* or in Bacon's *Essays* is a player in a drama of the mind.

In Spanish poetic theory of the seventeenth century, there was a shift toward the kind of intellectualization which weighs heavily against the passionate needs of Epimeteo. In comparison to Sánchez de Lima's *Arte poético en romance castellano* (1580), El Pinciano's neo-Aristotelian *Philosophia antigua poética* (1596), and Cascales' *Tablas poéticas* (1617), all of which are poetics of the artistic *object*, Gracián's *Agudeza y arte de ingenio* (1642, 1648) is grounded in the *concepto*, an intellectual act of perception. For El Pinciano and Cascales, the Aristotelian questions of verisimilitude, of the appropriateness of subject matter to form, of poetic versus historical truth, are motivated by an understanding of poetic creation as imitation, as mimesis of content and form. For Sánchez de Lima, the fixed forms of Spanish verse are themselves objects of theoretical interest. Gracián's Baroque poetics, by contrast, derive from the manifold workings of the artist's intellect and the potential for mental engagement yielded by the *concepto*. The *concepto*, defined as "an act of the intellect which expresses the correspondence that is found between different objects,"[8] is the early ancestor of the late Symbolist and then Imagist, Creationist, and finally Surrealist *image*. For Gracián, the tropes and figures of speech are the intellectual pathways which guide the wit (*agudeza*). They are "like the material and like a foundation so that on them the wit can construct its beauties, and what is for rhetoric formality, is for our art the very substance on which it coats the enamel of artifice" (*Agudeza y arte de ingenio*, p. 133). The superficial crafting of the Baroque style may, in other words, reveal a surprising intellectual depth.

The Jesuits as an order helped sustain the duality of intellectual and sensory appeal that characterized the Baroque. Saint Ignatius' *Ejercicios espirituales* rely heavily on visual, sensory images produced in the mind (the *entendimiento* or intellect) to affect the "spirit" (will) of the practitioner as he exercises his memory and recalls his sins. The Jesuits placed the world of the senses, including the theatre itself, in the service of religious instruction. Their *colegios* provided basic schooling for Lope, Calderón, and countless others, and theatrical representations were important in their educational programs.[9] Fueled at the outset by the Counter-Reformation, the Jesuit appeal went beyond the senses to a deeper intellectuality. Jesuit meditational methods look to memory and the conscience as much as to the vivid images that guide the practitioner. They hinge on the active workings of the *intellectus*.

The Loyolan meditational methods were spread in translations, in summary form, in adapted formats, well after the Counter-

Reformation. The sacred oratory of a Paravicino, Lope's *Soliloquios amorosos de un alma a Dios*, Gracián's *Comulgatorio*, Calderón's *Psalle et Sile*, all have meditational roots. Whether specifically directed to the contemplative intellect and, ultimately, to the will, or whether latent beneath a surface of sensory appeal, the intellectual tenor of the Baroque style determines the crucial matter of the response of the audience or reader. The Loyolan influence on the tradition of lyric poetry, as in Fray Luis' ode on the Ascension and Lope's "romancero espiritual" – in the colloquial tone, the brief monologues, the solitary cues – is widely known.

The transformation of action and passion (the latter in two senses, both as suffering and as the opposite of action, viz. passivity) through meditation is central to the theatrical adaptability of the Loyolan practice. At the same time, meditation makes apparent the non-rational powers of the mind, and brings forth its capacity for *immediate*, visionary insight, which may be free from the intervention of reason. This is made possible by the emphasis of meditation on visual images of an almost scenic character. Consider the preliminary Loyolan exercise, the "composición de lugar" ("composition of place"), which probably had more direct influence on seventeenth-century theatre than any other single component of the spiritual regime. Preceding any of the colloquies between the soul and God, which may include an intimate dialogue within the meditational scene, the practitioner or performer was instructed to concentrate his thought and imagination, to train his mind's eye on a specific locus or spot and to construct a locus in which the meditation would unfold dramatically: "in contemplation on visible matters, such as the contemplation of Christ our Lord, Who is visible, the composition will be to see with the eyes of the imagination the corporeal place where the thing I contemplate is found."[10] Characteristically, the meditation would focus on a scene of suffering, and the practitioner would alternately witness the scene reflectively (i.e. passively) and involve himself in it actively through the silent dialogue of prayer. Meditation thus provided a way to summon up and yet to contain vivid images of suffering, much as one would witness and vicariously participate in the action on the stage of a theatre.

The contemplative aspect of Calderón's theatre, in which his work resembles a "theatre of the mind," certainly relies on these Loyolan precedents, but at the same time Calderón's language, in the service of this "mental theatre," shows affinities with a rhetorical tradition that reaches back at least to Cicero. In Cicero, the all-important capacity for verbal "invention" was bound to the commonplaces (*topica*) of discourse, and all were subsumed under the broader conception of the "locus," a classical antecedent of Loyola's "composition of *place*." These rhetorical categories of language were not susceptible to the objections, the defenses, or the rules of reason. "Place" rather than "reason" is for Cicero the basis of rhetorical argument: "Just as of those things that are concealed, the proof and the discovery are easy if the place is noted and indicated, so if we examine a theme, we must know its place; thus they are called by Aristotle places, as it were, from which the arguments stem, and so one can say that the place is the seat of arguments."[11] According to Cicero, the *topica* have roots in Aristotle, but the Aristotelian *Rhetoric* was generally overshadowed in the sixteenth and seventeenth centuries by the *Poetics*, and Aristotle was considered by some to have rationalized the topics. Cicero and the Humanists who admired him attempted to reintegrate philosophy and rhetoric by founding ways of thought themselves, and not just patterns of argument as Aristotle indicated, on the "topical" nature of discourse. This program was not wholly rational, just as the cornerstones of Baroque poetics, "invention" and the *ingenium*, are not fully accountable under the umbrella of reason. The most important features of Baroque poetics cannot of course be reduced to the function of the topics in the classical sense, but they can nonetheless be seen as late developments of certain non-rational qualities of rhetorical speech. The primacy of the *ingenium* and the *agudeza* – particularly in Pellegrini, in Tesauro, and in Gracián – underlines the special nature of insight, literally the "vision within," made possible through a rhetorical conception of human language. Looking to Aristotle as a model, Tesauro claimed that "seeing relationships [*convenienza*] between the most distant things is proper to acuteness and *ingenium*." For this reason, ingenious activity provides "a theatre full of wonders":[12] one marvels and cannot always explain. In the *Agudeza y arte de ingenio* Gracián directed his attention to the *concepto*, which gives us not only the rational component of the image but also a glimpse of the unmediated phenomenon, a sense of numinous perception free from rational intervention. We move from Gracián's *concepto* to Vico, where the topics and the *ingenio* are fully absorbed into the conception of a certain type or branch of human intellect which "finds and collects" (*ritruova ed ammassa*); the topical mind may be less exact than the "critical" (i.e. rational) mind, but it is richer and less "dry."[13]

Like the Baroque theorists, Calderón began to discover the connections between the reasoned principles of style and pre-rational artistic insights: he saw that even in Prometheus – rational, intelligent man – there are persistently non-rational strains. Just as the gyrating and asymmetrical lines of Baroque sculpture – in Bernini, for example – leave surface traces of an indomitable and passionate irrationality in the most planned and meditated of forms, Calderón finds that his own stylistic exuberance and poetic perspicacity lead him to an un-tempered encounter with pre-rational human capacity. In *La estatua de Prometeo*, Calderón tries to resolve the problems of artistic insight and rational control through the balanced judgment of Apolo. Yet the godly judgment is less convincing than Prometeo's final victory. Calderón was driving toward a severe critique of reason, but he finds that the exercise of the intellect perforce leads to irrational con-sequences, that the life of the mind overflows with non-rational effects. Calderón works hard to temper irrationality; in his play, the amorous rivalries among Prometeo, Minerva, Palas, and Pandora are brought to felicitous resolution.

Calderón does not punish Prometeo, but allows him to marry Pandora. Unlike Aeschylus and Hesiod, Calderón makes marriage part of a conventional happy ending, but this ending in turn imposes limits on his self-critique. Calderón can be unyielding with his characters, but in this play he is clement. Like Apolo, he refuses – or is unable – to indict. His critique of human rationality, his intuition of the intricate checks and balances between the mind and the irrational passions, is a limited exercise in self-restraint and warning, not a radical self-questioning.

The play offers an awkward positive skepticism. Calderón's loyalties are divided. Much as he would like to believe, with a Malherbe, that "l'art est objet de science," he is aware of the precarious status of reason itself. His own style, his own technical mastery, which show up in the stylistic exuberance of a play like this, contribute to the ambiguities. The scientific, reasoned drives rep-resented in Prometeo do prevail over Apolo's balanced judgment, but they offer constant reminders of their irrational foundations, as the Baroque language shows. Style and theme create unresolved tensions. In his final play, *Hado y divisa de Leonido y Marfisa*, reason and control become hinges in the transformation (some would say the reduction) of art into technical display.

Calderón's last play: the *comedia* as technology and romance

Esa es la ignorancia:
a la vista de las ciencias,
no saber aprovecharlas.

(That is ignorance:
in view of the sciences,
not knowing how to use them.)

El mágico prodigioso

Throughout Calderón's career, the function of theatre in the service of self-imagination and critique is adjusted to a variety of specific needs, with greater or lesser success, depending on the dramatist's ability to incorporate the forms of the theatrical illusion critically within those same forms. As a result, Calderón's most successful plays show an understanding of human nature that incorporates but ultimately surpasses the rigid conception of man in terms of fixed essences. To be sure, there are strong reasons for recognizing this facet of Calderón's work: on the one hand, Calderón inherited peculiarly Spanish values from the earlier epic and *comedia* traditions which celebrated heroic integrity (*entereza*) and unvacillating identity (e.g. in the formulaic phrase, "soy quien soy"); on the other, Calderón's language and thought show a distinctively Scholastic bent, a thorough assimilation of the idea of Being as that which is determined as singular and as true ("omne ens verum est" would be the Scholastic slogan). But we have seen that Calderón's theatre, like the earlier Humanist model to which it is indebted for its central, self-conscious conceit of the *theatrum mundi*, incorporates a vision of man in which human nature is seen in situational terms and in which essences are redefined along the more rhetorical lines of *use* (meaning "custom," rather than "utility") and *convention*; these refer to the products of human culture – and theatre foremost among them for Calderón – as significant *orderings* of nature. As I want now to argue for Calderón's final play, *Hado y divisa de Leonido y Marfisa*, this conception of the value of human culture as appropriate (i.e. convenient, fitting, or conventional) ordering can legitimately be expected to extend to the stylistic and representational aspects of the dramatist's art; but we find that in this play the failure to go beyond the static conception of human nature as a fixed and essential identity is in fact fostered by the representational artifice.

Throughout his work, Calderón stresses that intellectual mastery and control are by themselves insufficient; any human ordering must be appropriate to its material. Indeed, in a play like *El mágico prodigioso* the devil himself is not wrong, and so evil is not simply an intellectual flaw; if Aquinas could not deny the devil's intelligence (see *Summa*, 1, 63, 1 ad 4), surely Calderón could not. The devil chooses, but does not see the appropriate use of his resources. *La vida es sueño* turns on the same principle: it is not wrong to try to interpret the natural signs we see; what matters is the *use* we make of what is written in the stars. As Segismundo says,

> Lo que está determinado
> del Cielo, y en azul tabla
> Dios con el dedo escribió,
> de quien son cifras y estampas
> tantos papeles azules
> que adornan letras doradas;
> nunca engañan, nunca mienten,
> porque quien miente y engaña
> es quien, para usar mal de ellas,
> las penetra y las alcanza. (1, 532a–b)

(What is determined by the heavens has been written on that blue slate by God; all those blue sheets adorned with golden letters are His ciphers and marks; these never deceive, never lie; he who deceives and lies is he who reaches and penetrates them to use them for ill.)

Calderón recognizes the possible dissonance between nature and art, as between body and mind, passion and intellect. If we consider the action of the play, we see that reconciliation must be sought, and freedom from determination by the body and its passions or the mind and its artifices must be won, by the fitting use of both mind and body. By the same token, Calderón's own theatre invites evaluation according to what use it makes of its resources, and it is here that his final play is open to severe criticism.

One way of formulating this critique would be to say that in Calderón's last play poetry (or *poiesis*) degenerates into technology (ancient *techne*). One need not be Martin Heidegger, and postulate a moment outside the principal arc of Western metaphysics when poetry and *techne* were one, in order to see in seventeenth-century thought and practice their increasing separation.[1] Most notably in Galileo and Descartes the concept of method, itself originally bound to *techne*, took on an independent life.[2] This provided a tempting way to resolve the discords of nature and art, body and mind, passion and intellect, mentioned above, but also entailed the isolation and effective abstraction of each of those terms. Galileo for instance established the concept of inertia in a way that could not be realized in actuality. He did not submit to the "irreducible and stubborn facts" of the world but instead imagined a perfectly smooth and frictionless, directionless plane, setting the ordering capacity of human reason over and against the brute facts of nature. Bacon's understanding of the advancement of learning was founded on similar premises. Indeed, the "Copernican revolution" was not on the whole achieved through new observations or information but by the subjection of nature to rational controls. The study of nature along these lines, however, presupposed that the mind itself was like a stainless mirror of the universe with mathematical properties, a frame bounding space for purely rational consideration, of the same order of abstraction as the Cartesian plane and providing for a similar geometrization of space.[3] In a world so conceived, the kind of dialectical self-imagining which we saw in Vives' *Fabula de homine* was no longer possible and, if it had been, would have been abjured in the interests of reason and method that lay at the base of the new "technology."

Seen from one angle, Calderón's career is an object-lesson in the shift of balance from nature to art and of the misapprehension of the function of art as a form of technology. Here I shall largely be discussing the stage effects and plot-structure of *Hado y divisa de Leonido y Marfisa*, but it is worth keeping in mind that the same shift can be seen in the more explicit philosophical content of some of Calderón's later plays. His Prometheus, for instance, whom we have already seen, stands on the verge of a Faustian conception of man which would not have been possible without the Copernican–Galilean revolution and the ensuing birth of Newtonian physics. Strangely enough, however, Calderón has often been considered a naive or mediocre philosopher, or a thinker oddly out of step with his age. But the same has been said of Ramus, whose development of a "method" at the expense of dialogue and dialectics parallels Calderón's theatre in many ways.

Calderón's pageant plays, of which *Hado y divisa* is one of the most remarkable, draw on technical effects which, as we can glean from contemporary accounts, were utterly convincing in the creation of illusion. Given his pervasive understanding of the need to embrace, and thereby to limit, the use of illusion, Calderón would naturally be concerned that the world of the representation might compete with and even efface the natural world. In large part because the technical proficiency of his stage designers, painters, craftsmen, and musicians had become so formidable toward the end of his career, this was a real worry, and ultimately the Achilles' heel of his final play. Working with promethean technical means, a play like *Hado y divisa de Leonido y Marfisa* differs fundamentally from a play like *La dama duende* because the technical backing is so much more in evidence. Purely theatrical resources affect the dramatic conception of the play and its viability as a critical vehicle of personal and social values.

The play is accompanied by several lengthy marginal passages of stage directions which, to my knowledge, are unique in Calderón. We do not know for certain if these passages were indeed penned by Calderón, but Hartzenbusch thought they were and Angel Valbuena Prat and Bruce Wardropper have since followed him.[4] They describe the performance given for Charles II and María Luisa of Orleans on March 3, 1680, apparently for that year's carnival celebration. Act I opens in a forest, "in places leafy and dark, imitating nature [*imitando la naturaleza*]"; to one side "there was an enormous rocky mountain, not artificially made on scaffolds, but actually brought out onto the stage, which made it seem like a lofty summit" (II, 2098a).[5] In Act II, a cave is concealed among rocks adorned with jewel-like stones (artificial emeralds, rubies, amethysts, and turquoises are specified) and arranged to create the impression of depth: "The rocks were very large in size; but due to the distance they were proportioned in such a way that all the arches appeared strewn with jewels, the said design making them all appear of equal size . . . Discourse cannot find among the variety of its tropes the phrases which could imitate the least part of such magnificence" (II, 2115a).[6] Calderón is not concerned about the legitimacy of the artistic representation here. The superiority of art over nature is an issue which had in a sense already been decided by Paravicino in his sonnet to El Greco: "Divino Griego de tu obrar no admira, / que en la imagen exceda al ser el arte" ("Divine Greek, do not be surprised at your work, for in images art surpasses life").[7] For Gracián, writing a few decades later, "art is the complement of nature and *a second self* which beautifies it extremely and even pretends to surpass it in its works"; without art, without this crucial "assistance of artifice," nature would remain crude and uncultured.[8] Calderón's descriptive passages reveal that his technological resources had grown so great that the created image could well be viable in its own right. The comparisons by which the staged representation is said to rival the natural world suggest that the artist's powers as a maker of illusion, given conditions such as those Calderón had available to him, may not be subject to restraint. As I shall argue, this kind of unrestraint may have made for wonderfully exciting theatre and amazing spectacle, but it made for bad drama; more important, it was of no benefit to a nation in the midst of serious political and cultural decline.[9] At a moment when Spain was falling precipitously from power, when her culture was drying up, not for want of invention but for lack of self-scrutiny, Calderón owed his audience something more than unadulterated spectacle, three acts of constant marvel. His final play is not so much conventional in its artifice, as might have been said of his early plays, as pure theatrical extravaganza.

To be sure, the theatricality of *Hado y divisa* holds interest, even today; the ingenuity of some of the stage effects is remarkable. In Act II, for instance, the audience is treated to Mount Etna belching smoke and sparks; apparently the volcano-machine broke down later in the act, and could not spit fire as it was supposed to, but still Calderón says that the audience was startled and amazed at the spectacle of a volcano hurling rocks across the stage. In Act III we move rapidly from the opening forest scene to the setting of an exquisite garden, adorned with pots of flowers hanging from balustrades and a mechanical peacock strutting about the stage, as if "courting the flowers with the showy pomp of its feathers, and stretching out its many-colored mantle, with its bright eyelets" (II, 2131b–2a).[10] Among the audience, the Monarchs enjoyed a privileged place for this spectacle and, as we can tell from further description of the production, it was conceived with them foremost in mind. The ceiling of the Coliseo at the Buen Retiro, where the play was first staged, was repainted for the occasion to represent the newly joined coats-of-arms of Charles and his bride; they themselves were seated on a raised dais in the center of the theatre. In the prelude to the play (the *Loa*, which celebrates their union) portraits of the King and Queen were displayed so that the Monarchs could sit facing themselves. Bruce Wardropper described the idea as Calderón's highest achievement in the staging of *Hado y divisa*, largely because it captures the exuberant narcissism which suffuses the entire play. In the middle of the front wall was a throne and canopy, and beneath it the royal portraits, "so lifelike that, as they were placed opposite their originals, they seemed to be a mirror into which were transferred their wonderful perfections."[11] Theatres like those at the Buen Retiro were of course intended to display and magnify the royal image, and Calderón's play is directed toward this end, which is no less than one would expect of a court dramatist. With regard to the royal portraits, Calderón's description goes on to say that "because of the desire to see the monarchs everywhere, we would have liked to see their images repeated more often."[12] A theatre which celebrated heroic virtue, such as we find in *Hado y divisa*, was designed as a guise for royal flattery.

Hado y divisa enshrines the rigid invulnerability that had been the mark of Spanish heroes since the *Cantar de mío Cid*. But in late seventeenth-century Spain those monolithic values were not supple enough to respond to the actual political and cultural disasters that had penetrated deep beneath the artifice and show. Structurally, the heroic virtues celebrated in this play are arranged according to the shape of romance, so that the play is not simply a late avatar of the Spanish epic tradition but a throwback to the books of chivalry that Don Quixote read. Leonido, the hero of the play, is the quintessence of epic integrity. His struggles involve trials of role and identity, but he ensures that he will suffer only superficial wounds. He is utterly unlike Angela of *La dama duende*, who uses shifting roles to discover a personal authenticity, or Pedro of *El médico de su honra*, who plays a double role as king and intrigant, or even Focas of *En la vida*, whose vacuous identity is pregnant with political implications. Leonido disguises himself chameleon-like, but he never allows himself to alter his essential nature. His changes are cosmetic, and he remains steely and inflexible at heart. His principal action consists in the recovery of an identity which has not been lost through any flaw or defect on his part, but merely threatened by circumstance. His lack of deep vulnerability is the reason why he is uninteresting as a character, despite his exemplarity. Even as he takes the role of the *caballero alemán* his role-playing is a ploy, a strategy in the service of the dramatist's plotting, not an outward mirror of inward development. His seemingly protean heroism and inventiveness point to an underlying inviolability. The most dangerous threats, his conflicts with Polidoro, are prearranged. There is no personal tension, no disjunction between interior and exterior person in him.

Leonido blazons his personal valor about on the *escudo* he carries: "con el nombre de Leonido, / y un león de oro por empresa" ("with the name of Leonido and a golden lion for an emblem") (II, 2101a). He carries a *lámina* with his personal insignia, which reinforces his identity and intrinsic worth. Here, we find the same root forms of self-imagination as Castro saw to be peculiarly Castilian in the epic, ballad, and theatrical traditions. The integral value of a person is lodged in outward signs. A society ruled for centuries by social opinion, where the inner self was subservient to exteriorized *honra*, had grown accustomed to purely outward displays of self-worth. In Calderón's final play, such a matrix of value is evident in the static structures which buttress a surface of great movement and excitement. The vicissitudes of Leonido's fortune bring threats to his personal *entereza* that highlight an unchangeable personality. His *escudo* and *lámina* are ready-mades, systems which he uses in order to operate in the world, much as the *comedia* itself is a system for the nation to deal with the problems of its own conflictive history. In autistic gesture, his shield says exactly what the *comedia* had proclaimed from the start: "soy quien soy." This phrase is the pedal-point of the whole genre. We know modulations in different tessituras and keys (e.g. "padre soy, hago mi oficio," in Mira de Amescua's famous phrase), all of them *reprises* of the national *cantar de gesta*.

Calderón's final play gives the impression of a nation in good health, gifted with boundless energy, with stores of untapped spiritual resources and limitless self-confidence. But in fact it is symptomatic of a genre nearing exhaustion for want of change. In certain ways, the *comedia* had not altered since its invention by Lope de Vega. The genre was born to fill a public need for affirmation, and Calderón was as aware as Lope of what his public wanted. As much as Lope, Calderón came to specialize in wish-fulfillment. In earlier plays, he had tempered the showman's drive with a deep vein of self-criticism. But in *Hado y divisa* he allowed his audience to ignore the politically, economically, and socially troubled world in which they lived and to take refuge in the heroic, nearly mythical, visually stimulating, and ultimately stabilizing, world of the heroes Leonido and Marfisa.

Exciting and extravagant as a play like this might be, it offered no serious line of defense against the charge that it was theatrical flummery, artistic pap. Calderón's last play was a long nod of acknowledgment to his sated audience. He offered his public all they could want to satisfy their appetites, but he did not challenge them. There is not a *comedia* worth remembering after this one, and this one only because it is Calderón's last.

Considered solely on the basis of its plot, the play is a bizarre, complex, and byzantine romance. Leonido the hero is put through the paces of a difficult quest. He is separated from Arminda, the lady he loves, and from his sister Marfisa. At the end of the play, he is reunited with his sister and his beloved, and is returned to his rightful place at home in Sicily. As is not infrequent in romance, the hero is a pawn, and he here serves the dramatist's virtuoso show of plotting. The conflicts in which he engages are depersonalized; he is open to no real threats. It is his friend Polidoro who as "Leonido" does battle with the *caballero alemán*.

Northrop Frye thought that romance was itself a form of wish-fulfillment.[13] Recent critics have identified affinities between the *comedia* as a genre and the plot-structure of romance. Donald Larson saw the structures of romance at work in a number of Lope's plays.[14] Marcos A. Morínigo suspected that the *comedia* as a whole took the place of the romances of chivalry which declined in popularity roughly simultaneously with the *comedia*'s rise:

The desire to escape from reality into a world of fantasy, that previously had been satisfied in the novel [*i.e.* the romances], now finds a wide path in the theatre. The public rushes to the theatre, gives it life and stimulates it, but at the same time imposes conditions on it. And so the theatre will also be as the novel was, an unreal world exempt from criticism: poetic and anachronous. The Spanish theatre will not create characters, it will not make of the particular a universal symbol, it will not discover man's intimacy. The Spanish theatre, and above all the theatre of Lope and his first disciples, does not belong to the literature of the modern world. Its world is still the colorful and fantastic, beautiful and unreal world of Amadís, Orlando, and Don Tristán.[15]

At least since the publication of the first part of the *Quixote*, critics and readers alike have, at least tacitly, related the *comedia* with the romances of chivalry popular in the first half of the sixteenth century; Santa Teresa's enthusiasm for the tales of knights errant in her *Vida* is reminiscent of a period before the Lopean *comedia* was born. In the eyes of Cervantes' Curate at the beginning of the seventeenth century, the *comedia* and the books of chivalry are guilty of the same infractions of the Aristotelian–Horatian and Ciceronian norms:

Señor Canon, said the curate, by touching on this subject you have awakened an old grudge of mine against the comedies [*i.e. comedias*] of today, one that is equal to that which I hold against the books of chivalry. For, according to Tully, a comedy should be a mirror of human life, an example of manners, and an image of the truth; yet those that we see now are mirrors of nonsense, examples of foolishness, and images of lasciviousness.[16]

Yet as Cervantes knew, despite the ironist's voice, the essence of romance lay in intricate action. How could the author keep the events sufficiently entangled and yet not be faulted for digressing? How could he maintain the unity of his work while still sustaining interest through variety of incident? Gracián stated the principle of complication, which is the heart of the whole matter: it is the art of deft entanglement

which makes epics, fictions, novels, comedies, and tragedies so pleasurable and entertaining: the events keep piling up, and chance occurrences keep getting so close, that at times there seems to be no way out . . . But here is the beauty of the art and skill of invention's greatest feat: in finding an extravagant, yet verisimilar, way to get out of the tangled labyrinth, with great pleasure and fruition for the reader and listener.[17]

The art of the romancer is the daredevil art of narrative plotting; he must show virtuoso skill. Gracián's description is a fair appraisal of the plot of *Hado y divisa*, which is a showpiece in itself, a wonder of organization and manipulation that would outrage Cervantes' Curate.

The astounding reversals and marvelous transformations which characterize romance have their origin in the vulgar sense of "paradox," of that which goes against reason. ("An astonishing reversal of fortune, an event contrary to expectation, a recognition or discovery that evoked strong emotions like joy and fear – these were all 'paradoxes.'")[18] The romances themselves speak time and again of situations being "strange and new," "against reason," "unthought of," and so on. But Arthur Heiserman is among the few to recognize that paradox is one of the cardinal points of the genre. The early Greek romances apparently have connections with ancient paradoxography.[19] More subtly, the paradoxical peripeties of romance could be used to convey a sense that the universe itself was a cohesive network of contraries. Heiserman argues plausibly that "When art made a paradoxical peripety or recognition seem probable, the reader might also enjoy a wonderful reconciliation of opposite opinions – that fortune is mindless and that there is a design in life after all; and this latter, sublime inference could be an aesthetic equivalent of the speculation that resolved contraries within a philosophical system." He hastens to add, however, that "since the main job of poets was thought to be the arousal and consummation of powerful emotions, the dramatic paradox, the marvels generated by the plot, naturally became the stock-in-trade of narrative art" (p. 78).

To be sure, the conventions of entangled plotting and marvelous reversals as used by Calderón are drawn from a conventional stock; they are "invented" only in the literal sense, that of "found." The sense that the antinomies of a contradictory world can be resolved through these reversals is achieved at the expense of his hero. There is something so rigid and inflexible about the values which Leonido flaunts that, despite his transformations, he is an almost mechanized set of responses to the world, a "system" in the pejorative sense. He is far less supple than Calderón's early Proteus, Angela the phantom lady, and he is less a source of insight into contradictory circumstances than she. In a play like *Hado y divisa de Leonido y Marfisa*, the characters uphold their avowed values so staunchly in the face of adverse circumstances that there is an energy of repulsion at the centre of their world. This is the same energy which generates the tension in Calderón's metaphors and poetic similes. It rises from deep within his work.

Historically, romance was, with paradoxography, a mode of narrative self-imagining closely allied to historiography. There is a therapeutic purpose inherent in the mode. When Shakespeare drew on Holinshed and Hall and Polydore Vergil for his history plays, he was tapping the resources of romance for its uses in public healing. The history plays that Shakespeare derived from the chronicles promulgated a Tudor myth just at a moment when the legitimacy of the Tudor line was open to serious question. While vastly different from Lope's historical plays in the perceived interrelationships of past and present, Shakespeare's histories differ less from the Spanish history plays than is commonly supposed. Some of the affinities derive from the common romance shape.

But since romance is a form which is most successfully used in non-historical works, it was only too easy for the writer of *comedias* to look past the moral and social responsibilities which history placed on him and attend only to his duties as romancer. It was tempting for him to

be consumed with interest in his own performance as arranger of
extraordinary events. Pursued on a massive scale, the healing powers
of romance could prove harmful. Once, the *comedia* could uplift the
public spirit without sacrificing the social and moral obligations
incumbent upon it; it could provide healing and support for the
values of caste as they were being eroded; but eventually the *comedia*
relinquished its critical functions. If Calderón is guilty of the overuse
or misappropriation of romance, this is because the form impeded the
formation of critical self-images and became instead a placebo for the
national psyche.

The objections to romance registered by its Horatian detractors are
no mere formulae; they express a legitimate demand, perhaps the
essential demand, to which any art pursued on a national scale must
respond. In the case of the *comedia*, its tendency toward romance
facilitated its eventual moral collapse. Perhaps the most simple and
telling fact of Calderón's use of romance in his final work is that the
marvels of plot-construction sap historical relevance from the play. As
the *comedia* lost its historical pertinence, and as writers like Calderón
lost sight of the historical needs to which Lope's *comedias* had
responded, the genre exhausted its social role.

In Lope's plays – in *Fuenteovejuna*, in *Peribáñez*, in the early *Los
comendadores de Córdoba* – the strong tendency of romance toward
harmonious resolution, toward the transcendence of all obstacles and
the stabilization of all ironies, still left room for critical self-evaluation.
The villains of those plays, monsters, embody real threats. They are
incarnations of specific social or moral ills; they underline the decay of
social institutions (e.g. the orders of chivalry); they expose the moral
gap between present and past ages, the irresponsibility of military
leaders, or the inflation (and concomitant devaluation) of honors.
Calderón himself saw the advantages of this use of romance in, for
example, *El alcalde de Zalamea*. But in the later plays, as in *Hado y divisa*,
we find Evil as an abstract and impertinent threat. And in the end
Evil is a far less convincing and powerful force than some specific evil,
some evil which is a menace to us or the audience of the day.

Because the *comedia* seeks so hard to mirror and affirm the society in
which it is rooted, its images of evil are often weak. The affirmative
energies of the *comedia*, the fact that it was rooted in a strong collective
mode of identification, left little room for dealing with the dark
underside of society's identity. The key phrase of the *comedia*, "soy
quien soy," which has Biblical resonances, is a slogan of positive and

affirmative identification. Where Calderón's plots tend most strongly toward romance, though, his capacity for negative identification is weakest. Tirso's Don Juan, or even Calderón's own Angela, are negative and daemonic mirrors of the dominant social ideology, but they are exceptional characters within the genre. Fredric Jameson explains the antinomies of romance in this way:

Romance in its original strong form may . . . be understood as an imaginary "solution" . . . a symbolic answer to the perplexing question of how my enemy can be thought of as being *evil* (that is, as other than myself and marked by some absolute difference), when what is responsible for his being so characterized is quite simply the identity of his own conduct with mine, the which – points of honor, challenges, tests of strength – he reflects as in a mirror image.[20]

What this means in application to romance-like *comedias* such as *Hado y divisa* is that identity cannot ever fully be subverted; it can be tested and tried, but even the trials – themselves a formal ingredient of romance – act to confirm the hero's identity. The forces to which he is exposed may be uncommonly strong, but they are conquered because they are essentially *conquerable* by a like force. In generic terms, what the pull of romance toward identification means is that it is the exact obverse of satire; seen in this light, the failure of a play like Cervantes' *El retablo de las maravillas* is easily accountable. Satire brings a nervous or discontented awareness that man is captive in the world, not its master, that human consciousness is inadequate to understand the world fully.

Where satire brings division, romance yields redemption. The romancer looks through, beyond, above, the conflicts. Hayden White's description of romance may help explain its propensity toward identification and away from satire: "The Romance is fundamentally a drama of self-identification symbolized by the hero's transcendence of the world of experience, his final victory over it, and his final liberation from it."[21] This "transcendence" need not be literal (although it certainly is in a play like *El mágico prodigioso*). Often it is simply symbolic, "a drama of the triumph of good over evil, of virtue over vice, of light over darkness, of the ultimate transcendence of man over the world in which he was imprisoned by the Fall" (p. 9); consider the quest for the Holy Grail, or the story of the Christian Resurrection. Hayden White saw the shape as the basis of Michelet's *History of the French Revolution*. For the vision of history it offers, one which looks from the past to a transcendent future, it is worth comparing that work to the *comedia*. Michelet foresaw a moment when the rivalries of "cities, countries, and corporations" – obstacles and ramparts, as he called them – might "crumble and fall in a day." At that time, there would be nothing but "what breathes the pure love of unity."[22]

As a romance, the *comedia* gives this same illusion of unity and transcendence. It celebrates reconciliation made possible and harmony achieved. It strives to reaffirm the identity of the hero and, through him, of society. Consider *Fuenteovejuna* in this regard. The collective identity asserted in the phrase "Fuenteovejuna lo hizo," a direct response to the question of identity posed by the Inquisitors, also seals the supremacy of the group over the monstrous evil, the menacing Comendador, who has threatened it. Lope looks forward to a moment of unity marked by the transcendence of such obstacles. He dispenses an enormous sense of hope, of the human capacity for social unity; he is profligate with good will. In Lope's world, the binding force of love is simply stronger than the divisiveness of evil. This is the root of the feeling of harmony which Leo Spitzer found amidst the platonizing language in Lope's play.[23]

In the tradition which followed on Lope's work, there is no full-scale attempt to subvert the romance, to deploy it in its negative or ironic modes; Cervantes' satires are overt and were recognized as such. Certainly a play like Calderón's *Hado y divisa* is no exception; the shape of the plot, the motives behind the action, the purpose of characterization, conform to the expected patterns. Indeed, it seems at first difficult to conceive of negative or subversive instances of romance. In England, whose imperial circumstances parallel those of Spain, there is the example of Conrad. *Lord Jim* (1900) and *Heart of Darkness* (1899) in particular show that even though the romance is assertive of positive self-images, it can nonetheless be used in the service of social criticism. The point is worth remarking because while the Spanish theatre ceased with the decline of the imperial mission, English literature was able to continue at a comparable moment in history; the capacity for self-critique seems to be essential. In the case of Conrad, his relatively peripheral perspective as a Pole may have given him the necessary vision. In his hands, romance is an adventure into an unknown world of evil; it is the obverse of what we see in the *comedia* with its happy endings and neatly sealed reconciliations. Conrad was critical of the illusions of transcendence fostered by romance, but he expressed that critique from within the form. For his project he marshaled images from the very seat of imperial power. Martin Green, writing on the alliances between the "dreams of adventure" (romance) and the "deeds of empire," remarks on Conrad's assumptions:

One must accept the illusion, including the illusion of adventure, one must live in it, interact with it, in order to keep afloat. England represented that method in action . . . So this is an endorsement of adventure. The adventure idea may seem to us [men of letters] to have betrayed Jim, because it incited him to a heroism which he could not achieve, and then to savage self-punishment. But Conrad meant rather that Jim betrayed it.[24]

In all these ways, Calderón is Conrad's opposite. In *Hado y divisa*, for example, the adventure is upheld, the adventurer does not fail the ideal, and he is duly rewarded. The contrast with Conrad extends as far as their respective styles. Conrad is averse to the totalizing organization and unification of experience under any governing "point of view." He opposes the purveyance of any single "I" or ideology; even in description, he gives us images liberated from any point of view.[25] Calderón's theatricalization of romance, by contrast, is a consecration of stable ideologies through the enforcement of a unifying "point of view," in terms of character and plot. The heroes of *Hado y divisa* have monolithic personalities; the author attempts to demonstrate his astonishing ability to tie together the many diverse strands of a plot which appears to pull in all directions at once. He acts as ultimate controller of a complex world. But he turns away from his earlier, more subtle, intuitions: that love is potentially dangerous, yet still not strong enough to unify man and the world about him, or that the cost of reconciliation is so high that it leaves never-healing scars. Instead, he satisfies a will to unity and a need for affirmative identification by attacking the illusively complex, chimerical problems of plot.

In the work of Fredric Jameson and Martin Green to which I have referred, there are implications of some deep connections between romance and ideology. Although the political interpretation of narrative forms is very large terrain, much of which is still unexplored, there are reasons which strongly support the view of the *comedia* as an instrument of national ideology. The dreams of adventure of the English are of a piece with their "deeds of empire," and the same holds true for Spain. It was through an expansion of its caste system that the British Empire was able to expand; in Spain, the period of the *comedia*'s rise was marked by an upsurge in the ideals of the dominant caste at home and an expansion to the Americas. The British tales of adventure – the literature of Defoe, Scott, Kipling, in particular – were often in fact modeled on earlier Spanish adventure tales. The conquest of Mexico, which Prescott found so stimulating, was taken as paradigmatic and exemplary.

Why was Calderón's last *comedia*, then, a failure by any reasonable standard? We may explain it (which would also be to explain the *comedia*'s decline as a genre) in a number of ways. It failed partly because Calderón faced the problems which confront all writers who come at the end of an age. When the received traditions and accumulated weight of convention become as dense and thick as they had by 1680, there are natural tropisms toward artistic complacency. After Calderón there is only Sor Juana to close the Hispanic Golden Age, and her work was accomplished within the matrix of the newly forming Mexican culture. She was, however, able to tap the parodic possibilities offered by the amassed conventions of the Peninsular Baroque (witness her wonderfully coy and playful sonnets). In the best of Calderón's late work, in *Eco y Narciso* for instance, there is a sense of communion gained from the conventions shared by players and audience; this is one of the advantages possible only because of the preceding tradition; it is important because it shows that convention does not necessarily work against the artist and that in Calderón's case it could be theatrically effective. But in Calderón's final play, his talent for artifice and his mastery of the conventions of the genre produced a dull and leaden play. The technology which went into the making of the 1680 performance of *Hado y divisa* is in fact more interesting than the action of the play itself. As a romance, however, the play is representative of the *comedia* as a genre which gave ideological expression to the imperial moment in Spanish history. Calderón could not conceal the fact that the heroic adventures of this play were conceived for a nation of intrepid posture and grand achievement; but by 1680 the politics of empire were turning in a direction unfavorable to Spain, and the great arc of the Spanish expansion had begun to shrink. It is this deep inappropriateness, more than any abuse of convention, that plagues Calderón's last secular play. During the seventeenth century, Spain was wrenched from its position as the very pivot of history; Calderón wrote his final *comedia* in the darkness of the Spanish decline. For all its exuberance, the work is shot through with the signs of collapse.

Notes

Introduction

1 My translation is freely adapted from that of Nancy Lenkeith, in *The Renaissance Philosophy of Man*, ed. Ernst Cassirer, Paul Oskar Kristeller, and John Herman Randall, Jr (Chicago: University of Chicago Press, 1945), pp. 387–93, following the Latin text of Joannis Ludovici Vivis Valentini, *Opera omnia* (Valencia, 1783), IV, 3–8.

2 Ernesto Grassi, *Rhetoric as Philosophy: The Humanist Tradition* (University Park: Pennsylvania State University Press, 1980), p 11.

3 For the date of this *auto*, see William A. Hunter, "Toward a More Authentic Text of Calderón's *El gran teatro del mundo*," *Hispanic Review*, 29 (1961), 240–4.

4 Citations refer to the *Obras completas* of Calderón de la Barca, I, *Dramas*, ed. Angel Valbuena Briones, 5th edn (1966: repr. Madrid: Aguilar, 1969); II, *Comedias*, ed. Angel Valbuena Briones, 2nd edn (1960; repr. Madrid: Aguilar, 1973); III, *Autos sacramentales*, ed. Angel Valbuena Prat, 2nd edn (Madrid: Aguilar, 1967); references are to volume, page, and column. Unless otherwise noted, translations are my own. Citations have been checked against the facsimile editions by D. W. Cruickshank and J. E. Varey (Farnborough, Hants: Gregg International Publishers Ltd, in association with Tamesis Books, 1973), 19 vols.

5 Kenneth Burke, *A Grammar of Motives* (1945; repr. Berkeley: University of California Press, 1968), p. 137.

6 Benedict de Spinoza, *Ethics (Ethica Ordine Geometrico Demonstrata)*, trans. R. H. M. Elwes (New York: Dover Publications, 1955), Book II, Prop. xl, note 1 (p. 112).

7 Kenneth Burke, "*Coriolanus* – and the Delights of Faction," originally in *Hudson Review*, 19 (1966), 185–202; repr. in *Language as Symbolic Action* (Berkeley: University of California Press, 1966), p. 84. For an expanded reading of Calderón (the *comedia Darlo todo y no dar nada)* in terms of Burke's "situational" and "dramatistic" conceptions, see my "Calderón: The Enduring Monument," *Revista canadiense de estudios hispánicos*, 7 (1983), 213–29.

8 Giordano Bruno, *The Heroic Frenzies*, trans. Paul E. Memmo, Jr, University of North Carolina Studies in Romance Languages and Literature, 50 (Chapel Hill: University of North Carolina Press, 1964), pp. 128–9. It is worth noting that Spain remained in touch with at least the "theatrical" facet of certain occultist trends, in part because of Philip II and Juan Herrera, the architect of the Escorial. Philip, for example, owned a manuscript of Giulio Camillo's *L'Idea del Theatro*. See Frances A. Yates, *Theatre of the World* (Chicago: University of Chicago Press, 1969), p. 38.

1 *La vida es sueño*: Calderón's idea of a theatre

1 *The Idea of a Theatre* (1949; repr. Princeton: Princeton University Press, 1972).
2 Antonin Artaud, "The Theatre of Cruelty *(First Manifesto)*," in *The Theatre and its Double*, trans. Mary Caroline Richards (New York: Grove Press, 1958), p. 84.
3 For an extensive study, see Jonas Barish, *The Anti-Theatrical Prejudice* (Berkeley: University of California Press, 1981).
4 I have discussed this aspect of Calderón's work at greater length in "Calderón's Encyclopaedic Rhetoric," *Neophilologus*, 66 (1982), 56–65.
5 Giordano Bruno, *Opere italiane*, ed. Paul de Lagarde (Göttingen, 1888), pp. 439ff.
6 René Descartes, "Meditation 1," in *The Philosophical Works of Descartes*, trans. E. S. Haldane and G. R. T. Ross (Cambridge: Cambridge University Press, 1967), I, 149.
7 Søren Kierkegaard, *Concluding Unscientific Postscript*, trans. David F. Swenson and Walter Lowrie (1941; repr. Princeton: Princeton University Press, 1974), p. 302.
8 Lawrence Manley, *Convention 1500–1700* (Cambridge, Mass.: Harvard University Press, 1980), p. 278.
9 Descartes, *The Passions of the Soul*, in *The Philosophical Works of Descartes*, I, 398; my italics.
10 Benedict de Spinoza, *The Ethics (Ethica Ordine Geometrico Demonstrata)*, trans. R. H. M. Elwes (New York: Dover Publications, 1955), Book III, Prop. vi, vii; Book IV, Prop. iv, xxvi.

2 *La dama duende*

1 In "Calderón's Encyclopaedic Rhetoric," *Neophilologus*, 66 (1982), 56–65.
2 *The Idea of a Theatre* (1949; repr. Princeton: Princeton University Press, 1972). See especially pp. 4–6.
3 "The 'Terrible Mother' Image in Calderón's *Eco y Narciso*," *Romance Notes*, I (1960), 133–6.
4 The date was established by Cotarelo y Mori, *Ensayo sobre la vida y obras de D. Pedro Calderón de la Barca* (Madrid: Tipografía de la Revista de Archivos, Bibliotecas y Museos, 1924), and subsequently accepted by Harry W. Hilborn, *A Chronology of the Plays of D. Pedro Calderón de la Barca* (Toronto: University of Toronto Press, 1938).
5 Gaston Bachelard, *The Poetics of Space*, trans. Maria Jolas (New York: Orion Press, 1964).
6 *Calderón and the Seizures of Honor* (Cambridge, Mass.: Harvard University Press, 1972), p. 130.

3 Calderón and Tirso: *El galán fantasma*

1 Pedro Salinas, "El nacimiento de Don Juan," in his *Ensayos de literatura hispánica: Del 'Cantar de mío Cid' a García Lorca*, ed. Juan Marichal (Madrid: Aguilar, 1967), pp. 158–67; José Ortega y Gasset, "Las dos ironías, o Sócrates y Don Juan," in *El tema de nuestro tiempo* (1923), in his *Obras completas*, III, 5th edn (Madrid: Revista de Occidente, 1962), pp. 174–8.
2 Salvador de Madariaga brings this out in his biography of Cortés, *Hernán Cortés, Conqueror of Mexico* (New York: The Macmillan Co., 1941). See also the review of Madariaga by Ramón Iglesia in *Columbus, Cortés, and Other Essays*, trans. and ed. Lesley Byrd Simpson (Berkeley: University of California Press, 1969), pp. 257–61.

3 Stephen Greenblatt, *Renaissance Self-Fashioning; From More to Shakespeare* (Chicago: University of Chicago Press, 1980), pp. 222–54; see p. 226 for the reference to Peter Martyr, *De orbe novo*, Seventeenth Decade.

4 See also Daniel Lerner, *The Passing of Traditional Society: Modernizing the Middle East* (New York: Free Press, 1958; rev. edn 1964). I owe this reference to Greenblatt, *Renaissance Self-Fashioning.*

5 I follow the editions of Blanca de los Ríos, in the *Obras completas*, 3 vols. (Madrid: Aguilar, 1968–9), citing volume, page, and column.

4 *El secreto a voces*: language and social illusion

1 See *The Art of "La Celestina"* (Madison: University of Wisconsin Press, 1956).

2 *Die Literarisierung des Lebens in Lope's "Dorotea,"* Kölner Romanische Arbeiten (Bonn and Cologne: Rohrscheid, 1932).

3 This is evident in the work of Juan Eugenio Hartzenbusch, who was influential through the editions in the Biblioteca de Autores Españoles (BAE).

4 Suárez de Figueroa, *El pasajero* (Madrid: Sociedad de Bibliófilos Españoles, 1914), p. 124.

5 The literature on the topic is vast. See in particular Jerrold Siegel, *Rhetoric and Philosophy in Renaissance Humanism* (Princeton: Princeton University Press, 1968), and Nancy Streuver, *The Language of History in the Renaissance* (Princeton: Princeton University Press, 1970).

6 Ion Agheana, *The Situational Drama of Tirso de Molina* (New York: Plaza Mayor Ediciones, 1972), p. 72.

7 Roland Barthes, *The Pleasure of the Text*, trans. Richard Miller (New York: Hill and Wang, 1975), pp. 4–5.

8 The acrostic is virtually impossible to render. The sense of the passage is as follows: *Federico* (to Flérida): "My lady, it is impossible to obtain my happiness; suffering is my soul, and dying is my life." *Laura* interprets (*aside*): "My love, my lady, my soul and life." *Federico* (to Flérida): "My love is such a tyrant, my feelings so cruel, my hope so fierce, my death so unhappy . . ." *Laura*: "This cruel, unhappy beast . . ." *Federico* (to Flérida): "Today, at the price of my life, it has driven me insane; but my fear stops me from speaking to you about this." *Laura*: "Today I am tired of speaking to you." *Federico*: "Don't blame me or become tired of me; for that would be my death, and the garden then an unworthy tomb." *Laura* (summing up the sense of Federico's message to her): "My love, my lady, my soul and life, this cruel, unhappy beast keeps me from speaking to you today: therefore don't go to the garden [i.e. as we had planned]."

9 "Lope's *La dama boba* and Baroque Comedy," *Bulletin of the Comediantes*, 13 (1961), 1–3.

5 Toward tragedy

1 James E. Maraniss, *On Calderón* (Columbia: University of Missouri Press, 1978); see for example p. 40 in connection with *La vida es sueño.*

2 *A Rhetoric of Irony* (Chicago: University of Chicago Press, 1974), p. 151.

3 See for example Bruce W. Wardropper, "Calderón's Comedy and His Serious Sense of Life," in *Hispanic Studies in Honor of Nicholson Adams*, ed. J. E. Keller and K.-L. Selig, North Carolina Studies in Romance Languages and Literature, 59 (Chapel Hill: University of North Carolina Press, 1966), pp. 179–93.

4 On this relationship, see Milton A. Buchanan, "Partinuples de Bles: An Episode in *Amar por señas*, Lope's *La viuda valenciana*," *MLN*, 21 (1906), 3–8, and Frederick

A. de Armas, *The Invisible Mistress: Aspects of Feminism and Fantasy in the Golden Age* (Charlottesville: Biblioteca Siglo de Oro, 1976).

5 See Larry S. Champion, *The Evolution of Shakespeare's Comedy* (1970; repr. Cambridge, Mass.: Harvard University Press, 1973), pp. 9–11.

6 George Lyman Kittredge, ed., *Sixteen Plays of Shakespeare* (1939; repr. Boston, Mass.: Ginn and Company, 1946), "Introduction" to *As You Like It*.

7 Champion, *The Evolution of Shakespeare's Comedy*, p. 66.

8 *Ibid.*, p. 67.

9 C. L. Barber, *Shakespeare's Festive Comedy* (1959; repr. Princeton: Princeton University Press, 1972), p. 223.

10 Norman Rabkin borrows the term from Niels Bohr. See *Shakespeare and the Common Understanding* (New York: Free Press, 1967).

6 *El médico de su honra*

1 The phrase is Lope de Vega's, from the *Arte nuevo de hacer comedias*, v. 328.

2 Marcelino Menéndez y Pelayo, *Calderón y su teatro*, 4th edn (Madrid: Revista de Archivos, 1910), p. 299.

3 *The Literature of the Spanish People* (Cambridge: Cambridge University Press, 1953), p. 284. Cf. Edward M. Wilson, "Gerald Brenan's Calderón," *Bulletin of the Comediantes*, 4 (1953), 6–8.

4 A. A. Parker, "The Approach to the Spanish Drama of the Golden Age," *Tulane Drama Review*, 4 (1959), 42–59, first published in booklet form (London: Diamante, 1957); A. E. Sloman, *The Dramatic Craftsmanship of Calderón* (Oxford: Dolphin Book Company, 1969), especially p. 42.

5 "Peter the Cruel or Peter the Just?" *Romanistisches Jahrbuch*, 14 (1963), 346. Contrast D. W. Cruickshank, "Calderón's King Pedro: Just or Unjust?" in *Spanische Forschungen der Görresgesellschaft, Erste Reihe – Gesammelte Aufsätze zur Kulturgeschichte Spaniens*, 25 (1970), 113–32. In Cruickshank's view, we see Pedro degenerate "from a well-meaning but incomplete 'justiciero' to a king who for reasons of state and convenience deliberately perverts justice" (130). I find the views of Frank P. Casa, "Crime and Moral Responsibility in 'El médico de su honra,'" in *Homenaje a William L. Fichter* (Madrid: Castalia, 1971), pp. 127–37, more subtle and convincing.

6 "The Dramatization of Figurative Language in the Spanish Comedia," *Yale French Studies*, 47 (1972), 189–98.

7 A royal decree to the President of the Council of the Indies (Feb. 18, 1622), for example, orders a window to be cut into the wall of his council chamber. See Jonathan Brown and J. H. Elliott, *A Palace for a King: The Buen Retiro and the Court of Philip IV* (New Haven: Yale University Press, 1980), pp. 41, 260 (n. 19).

8 Leonor calls Pedro the "planeta soberano de Castilla, / a cuya luz se alumbra este hemisferio" ("sovereign planet of Castile, by whose light this hemisphere is illumined") (i, 323b), thus reinforcing the possible allusion. Philip was known as "el rey planeta"; Juan de Caramuel y Lobkowitz wrote that the sun was a symbol of Spain and also of "His Catholic Majesty, who illuminates distant hemispheres: 'he shines and warms' [*illuminat et fovet*], his escutcheon reads" (*Declaración mystica de las armas de España invictamente belicosas*, Brussels, 1636; cited in Brown and Elliott, *A Palace for a King*, p. 40).

9 In *Curiosidades bibliográficas*, ed. Alfonso de Castro, BAE, 36 (Madrid, 1855), p. 317. I owe this reference to Dian Fox (my translation).

10 *The King's Two Bodies* (Princeton: Princeton University Press, 1957).

11 But cf. Dian Fox, "*El médico de su honra*: Political Considerations," *Hispania*, 65 (1982), 28–38, who argues otherwise.
12 H. D. F. Kitto, *Form and Meaning in Drama*, 2nd edn (London: Methuen, 1964).
13 By the etymology *porro videns*.
14 "El personaje singular: un aspecto del teatro del Siglo de Oro," *Nueva revista de filología hispánica*, 26 (1977), 480–98.
15 Ricardo J. Quinones, *The Renaissance Discovery of Time* (Cambridge, Mass.: Harvard University Press, 1972), p. 500.
16 Otis H. Green, *Spain and the Western Tradition* (Madison: University of Wisconsin Press, 1966), IV, 9.

7 Herod and Hercules: theatrical space and the body

1 The other version is entitled *El mayor monstruo, los celos*. The differences are minor. See the edition by Everett Hesse (Madison: University of Wisconsin Press, 1955).
2 See his study of *Bérénice*, in *The Idea of a Theatre* (1949; repr. Princeton: Princeton University Press, 1972), pp. 42–67.
3 I follow the edition of C. L. Walton (London: Oxford University Press, 1965).
4 *Sur Racine* (Paris: Seuil, 1963).
5 Stephen Greenblatt, *Renaissance Self-Fashioning: From More to Shakespeare* (Chicago: University of Chicago Press, 1980), p. 200.
6 As cited by Harry Levin, *The Overreacher: A Study of Christopher Marlowe* (1952; repr. Gloucester, Mass.: Peter Smith, 1964), p. 3.
7 *Opera* (Basle, 1563), p. 758. The translation is given in Jackson Cope, *The Theatre and the Dream: From Metaphor to Form in Renaissance Drama* (Baltimore: Johns Hopkins University Press, 1973), p. 43.
8 *Opera*, p. 633; the translation is in Cope, *The Theatre and the Dream*, p. 44.

8 *El mágico prodigioso* and the theatre of alchemy

1 Jacques Derrida, "The Theatre of Cruelty and the Closure of Representation," in *Writing and Difference*, trans. Alan Bass (Chicago: University of Chicago Press, 1978), p. 250.
2 Antonin Artaud, "The Theatre of Cruelty (*First Manifesto*)" in *The Theatre and its Double*, trans. Mary Caroline Richards (New York: Grove Press, 1958), p. 96.
3 See his "No More Masterpieces," in *The Theatre and Its Double*, p. 81.
4 Walter Benjamin spoke of the miniaturization characteristic of the *Trauerspiel* in this way. See *The Origin of German Tragic Drama*, trans. John Osborne (London: NLB, 1977), p. 81, regarding *La vida es sueño*.
5 Stephen Greenblatt, *Renaissance Self-Fashioning: From More to Shakespeare* (Chicago: University of Chicago Press, 1980), p. 220.
6 Harry Levin, *The Overreacher: A Study of Christopher Marlowe* (1952; repr. Gloucester, Mass.: Peter Smith, 1964), p. 121.
7 Antonin Artaud, "The Alchemical Theatre," in *The Theatre and Its Double*, p.49.
8 Harry Levin, *The Overreacher*, p. 111.

9 The illusions of history

1 See Jonathan Brown and J. H. Elliott, *A Palace for a King: The Buen Retiro and the Court of Philip IV* (New Haven: Yale University Press, 1980), p. viii.
2 Olivares to the Archbishop of Granada, Sept. 18, 1632, in J. H. Elliott and J. F.

de la Peña, *Memoriales y Cartas del Conde Duque de Olivares*, II (Madrid: Alfaguara, 1980), Doc. XIIa, as translated in Brown and Elliott, *A Palace for a King*, pp. 40–1.

3 Brown and Elliott, *A Palace for a King*, p. 31.

4 *Ibid.*, pp. 96–104 ("Paying for the Palace"), and especially p. 102.

5 See J. Vicens Vives, *Manual de historia económica* (Barcelona: Editorial Teide, 1959), and John Lynch, *Spain Under the Habsburgs, II: Spain and America, 1598–1700* (New York: Oxford University Press, 1969).

6 See J. H. Elliott, "Self-Perception and Decline in Early Seventeenth-Century Spain," *Past and Present*, 74 (1977), 59.

7 See Ramón Carande, "La expansión ultramarina," in *Siete estudios de historia de España* (Barcelona: Ediciones Ariel, 1969), pp. 50–1.

8 J. H. Elliott, *Imperial Spain, 1469–1716* (1963; repr. Harmondsworth: Penguin, 1975), p. 317.

9 See Elliott, "Self-Perception and Decline," 41.

10 *Ibid.*, 58–60.

11 *Restauración política de España*, ed. Jean Vilar (Madrid: Instituto de Estudios Fiscales, Ministerio de Hacienda, 1974), Discurso I (cap. 12), p. 110.

12 See Willard King, "Cervantes' *La Numancia* and Imperial Spain," *MLN*, 94 (1979), 200–21, and Carroll Johnson, "*La Numancia* and the Structure of Cervantine Ambiguity," *Ideologies and Literature*, 2 (1980), 75–94.

13 In John Lynch, *Spain Under the Hapsburgs, II: Spain and America, 1598–1700* (New York: Oxford University Press, 1969), p. 74.

14 In his *Obras completas*, ed. E. Correa Calderón (Madrid: Aguilar, 1944), p. 28.

15 "Gracián y los separatismos españoles," in *Teresa la santa y otros ensayos* (Madrid: Ediciones Alfaguara, 1972), pp. 264–5. The Testament is discussed in greater detail in the Introduction to *La realidad histórica de España*, 5th edn (Mexico: Editorial Porrúa, 1973), p. [11] (of the Introduction).

16 *The Spanish Temper* (1954; repr. New York: Harper and Row, 1965), p. 61.

17 Cited in Pritchett, *The Spanish Temper*, p. 62.

18 *Imperial Spain*, pp. 300–1.

19 Stanley G. Payne, *A History of Spain and Portugal* (1973; repr. Madison: University of Wisconsin Press, 1976), I, 318.

20 In Henry Kamen, *Spain in the Later Seventeenth Century, 1665–1700* (London: Longman, 1980), p. 21.

21 *Imperial Spain*, p. 361.

22 I follow the edition of Madrid, 1876 (p. 298).

23 See José Antonio Maravall, *La cultura del Barroco* (Barcelona: Editorial Ariel, 1975), p. 296.

24 Francisco Xarque, *Declamación panegírica en el dichoso nacimiento del Serenísimo Príncipe Don Felipe el Próspero* (Zaragoza, n.d., dedication signed Jan., 1658), cited in Maravall, *La cultura del Barroco*, p. 298.

25 *Conservación de monarquías y discursos políticos sobre la gran consulta que al Consejo hizo el señor rey Felipe Tercero* (Madrid, 1626), pp. 149–50.

26 José Antonio Maravall, *Estado moderno y mentalidad social: Siglos XV a XVII* (Madrid: Revista de Occidente, 1972).

27 Jerónimo de Barrionuevo, *Avisos (1654–1658)*, ed. A. Paz y Melía, Colección de Escritores Castellanos: Historiadores (Madrid, 1892), I, 53, 193.

28 Miguel Herrero García, "La monarquía teórica de Lope de Vega," *Fénix*, 2–3 (1935), 196–7.

29 In *Obras completas*, ed. Luis Astrana Marín (Madrid: Aguilar, 1941), pp. 698–700.

30 See N. D. Shergold and J. E. Varey, "A Problem in the Staging of the *Autos Sacramentales* in Madrid, 1647–1648," *Hispanic Review*, 32 (1964), 12–34, and A.

A. Parker, "The Chronology of Calderón's Autos Sacramentales From 1647," *Hispanic Review*, 37 (1969), 164–88.

31 *Avisos*, I, 368–89. See Shergold's comments on this play in *A History of the Spanish Stage* (Oxford: Clarendon Press, 1967), pp. 312–13.

10 Authority and illusion: *En la vida todo es verdad y todo mentira*

1 *Les Ombres collectives: Sociologie du théâtre*, 2nd edn, (Paris: Presses Universitaires de France, 1973), pp. 279–80.
2 *Ibid.*, p. 287.
3 *Renaissance Self-Fashioning: From More to Shakespeare* (Chicago: University of Chicago Press, 1980).
4 D. W. Cruickshank, in his edition of the play (London: Tamesis Books, 1971), pp. civ, cv. I have used this edition to verify quotations from this play.
5 *Authority* (New York: Vintage Books, 1981), p. 195.
6 I cite from the Biblioteca de Autores Españoles edition, *Dramáticos contemporáneos a Lope de Vega*, II (Madrid, 1858), p. 8c. All references to this play henceforth indicate page and column.
7 I follow the *Oeuvres de Pierre Corneille*, V, ed. M. Ch. Marty-Laveaux (Paris, 1862).

11 The use of myth: *Eco y Narciso*

1 Antonio León Pinelo, *Anales de Madrid*, ed. Pedro Fernández Martín (Madrid: Instituto de Estudios Madrileños, 1971), p. 438.
2 *Calderón, su personalidad, su arte dramático, su estilo y sus obras* (Barcelona: Editorial Juventud, 1941).
3 James Maraniss, *On Calderón* (Columbia: University of Missouri Press, 1978), p. 87.
4 *Calderón y su teatro*, 4th edn (Madrid: Revista de Archivos, 1910), p. 409.
5 *Characters of Shakespeare's Plays* (1817), in *The Complete Works*, ed. P. P. Howe (London: J. M. Dent and Sons, 1930), pp. 247–8.
6 C. L. Barber, *Shakespeare's Festive Comedy* (1959; repr. Princeton: Princeton University Press, 1972), p. 141.
7 See Jack Sage, "Nouvelles lumières sur la genèse de l'opéra et la zarzuela en Espagne," *Baroque*, 5 (1972), 107–14, and "Texto y realización de *La estatua de Prometeo* y otros dramas musicales de Calderón," in *Hacia Calderón, coloquio anglogermano*, ed. Hans Flasche (Berlin: Walter de Gruyter, 1970), pp. 37–52.
8 *The Green Cabinet* (Berkeley: University of California Press, 1969), p. 145.
9 The translation is that of Anthony Holden, in *Greek Pastoral Poetry* (Harmondsworth: Penguin, 1973), p. 46.
10 Covarrubius gives its meaning as "conseruar, defender, amparar," and also as "guardarse, vale recatarse de lo que se le puede acarrear a vn hombre daño, como guardarse de su enemigo, guardarse del Sol, de el frío &c." *Tesoro de la lengva castellana, o española* (1611; repr. Madrid, 1674), s.v. *guardar*.
11 *The Origin of German Tragic Drama*, trans. John Osborne (London: NLB, 1977), p. 195, citing Julius Tittmann, *Die Nürnberger Dichterschule. Harsdörfer, Klaj, Birken. Beitrag zur deutschen Literatur- und Kulturgeschichte des siebzehnten Jahrhunderts*, Kleine Schriften zur deutschen Literatur- und Kulturgeschichte, 1 (Göttingen, 1847), p. 148. For a more lengthy comparison of Benjamin and Calderón, see my "*Comedia* and *Trauerspiel*: On Benjamin and Calderón," *Comparative Drama*, 16 (1982), 1–11.

12 Prometheus and the theatre of the mind

1 "Psychology and Form," in *Counter Statement* (1931; repr. Berkeley: University of California Press, 1968), p. 31.

2 *The Individual and the Cosmos in Renaissance Philosophy*, trans. Mario Domandi (1963; repr. Philadelphia: University of Pennsylvania Press, 1972).

3 *Ibid.*, pp. 96–7.

4 See Bruce W. Wardropper, "*Fuente Ovejuna*: *El gusto* and *lo justo*," *Studies in Philology*, 53 (1956), 159–71.

5 "Art is an object of science." See Lawrence Manley, *Convention 1500–1700* (Cambridge, Mass.: Harvard University Press, 1980), p. 269.

6 François Hédelin, Abbé d'Aubignac, *The Whole Art of the Stage* (London, 1684), pp. 22–3, cited in Manley, *Convention*, p. 269.

7 *Treatise of the Epic Poem* (London, 1695), p. 1.

8 *Agudeza y arte de ingenio*, ed. E. Correa Calderón, in *Obras completas* (Madrid: Aguilar, 1944), p. 64.

9 See J. García Soriano, *El teatro universitario y humanístico en España* (Toledo: R. Gómez, 1945); J. Millé y Giménez, "Lope, alumno de los jesuitas," *Revue hispanique*, 72 (1928), 247–55; R. M. Hornedo, "Lope y los jesuitas," *Razón y fe*, 106 (1963), 405–22. Calderón studied in the Jesuit Colegio Imperial from 1609 until 1614, before moving to Alcalá and then to Salamanca.

10 *The Text of the Spiritual Exercises of Saint Ignatius*, trans. John Morris, 4th edn (Westminster, Md: Newman Bookshop, 1943), p. 20.

11 Cicero, *Topica*, II, 7.

12 Emmanuele Tesauro, *Il Cannochiale Aristotelico* (Venice, 1670), pp. 47, 70.

13 Giambattista Vico, "Polemiche relative al *De Antiquissima Italorum Sapientia*," in *Opere*, I, ed. Giovanni Gentile and Fausto Nicolini (Bari: G. Laterza, 1914), p. 271. For the connections between Vico and the reevaluation of classical rhetoric, see Ernesto Grassi, *Rhetoric as Philosophy: The Humanist Tradition* (University Park: Pennsylvania State University Press, 1980), ch. 3 ("Historical and Theoretical Premises of the Humanist Conception of Rhetoric"), and especially pp. 35–47.

13 Calderón's last play: the *comedia* as technology and romance

1 See for instance "Die Frage nach der Technik," trans. William Lovitt, in *The Question Concerning Technology and Other Essays* (New York: Harper and Row, 1977), pp. 3–35.

2 See Justus Buchler, *The Concept of Method* (New York: Columbia University Press, 1961).

3 See Nancy L. Maull, "Cartesian Optics and the Geometrization of Nature," *The Review of Metaphysics*, 32 (1978), 253–73, and the classic study by Alexandre Koyré, *From the Closed World to the Infinite Universe* (1957; repr. Baltimore: Johns Hopkins University Press, 1974), especially ch. 4. ("Galileo and Descartes").

4 Juan Eugenio Hartzenbusch, ed., *Comedias de Pedro Calderón de la Barca*, IV, Biblioteca de Autores Españoles, 14 (Madrid, 1850), pp. 355n. and 356n. Valbuena tacitly follows Hartzenbusch in the *Obras completas*; my references to the *Loa*, which is not in Valbuena's edition, follow Hartzenbusch. Bruce Wardropper concurs with Hartzenbusch in "Calderón de la Barca and Late Seventeenth-Century Theatre," in *Painting in Spain 1650–1700: A Symposium, Record of the Art Museum of Princeton University*, 14, no. 2 (1982), 38.

5 "A un lado había un peñasco, no fingido en los bastidores, sino sacado al teatro, cuyo artificio dispuso que se le mirara como muy altiva eminencia."

6 "Era el tamaño de las piedras grande; pero al beneficio de la distancia se proporcionaban de suerte que parecían estar todos los arcos sembrados de joyas, haciendo dicha labor igual todas ellas . . . No puede la retórica hallar, entre la variedad de sus tropos, frases que imiten la menor parte del lucimiento que allí hubo."

7 See Juan López Rey, "Idea de la imitación barroca," *Hispanic Review*, 11 (1943), 253–7.

8 Baltasar Gracián, *El criticón*, 1, ed. M. Romera Navarro (Philadelphia: University of Pennsylvania Press, 1938), p. 243.

9 The period 1665–1700, which includes roughly the second half of Calderón's career, was not one of absolute economic and cultural decline, and now some scholars have pointed to a revival of learning in this period; but still the situation was bleak. See for example Henry Kamen, *Spain in the Later Seventeenth Century, 1665–1700* (London: Longman, 1980). My claim, which I think Calderón's last secular play supports, is that this period saw the collapse of collective national values; epic posturing and royal theatrics became plainly inadequate in the face of contemporary circumstances.

10 "Dispuso el artífice un pavón que anduvo paseando sus cuadros y galanteando sus flores con la pompa vistosa de sus plumas, y entendiendo su variado manto con los lucientes ojos de que se componía."

11 I follow Hartzenbusch, p. 358, here: "En la frente del salón, ocupando el medio de la perspectiva, se hizo un trono cubierto de un suntuoso dosel, debajo del cual había dos retratos de nuestros felicísimos monarcas, imitados tan al vivo, que como estaban frente de sus originales pareció ser un espejo en que trasladaban sus peregrinas perfecciones" (accents modernized). See also Sebastian Neumeister, "Los retratos de los reyes en la última comedia de Calderón (*Hado y divisa de Leónido y Marfisa*, Loa)," in *Hacia Calderón: cuarto coloquio anglogermano, Wolfenbüttel 1975*, ed. Hans Flasche, Hermann Körner, and Hans Mattauch (Berlin: Walter de Gruyter, 1979), pp. 83–91.

12 "El ansia que desea verlos en todas partes, quisiera hallar más repetidas sus copias" (ed. Hartzenbusch, p. 358).

13 See *Anatomy of Criticism* (Princeton: Princeton University Press, 1957).

14 *The Honor Plays of Lope de Vega* (Cambridge, Mass.: Harvard University Press, 1977).

15 "El teatro como sustituto de la novela en el Siglo de Oro," *Revista de la Universidad de Buenos Aires*, 5ª Epoca, 2 (1957), 57.

16 Trans. Samuel Putnam, 1949 (repr. New York: Random House, Modern Library, n.d.), p. 430 (ch. 48).

17 *Agudeza y arte de ingenio*, ed. E. Correa Calderón, in *Obras completas* (Madrid: Aguilar, 1944), p. 277.

18 Arthur Heiserman, *The Novel Before the Novel* (Chicago: University of Chicago Press, 1977), p. 77.

19 See A. Giannini, "Studi sulla paradossografia greca: 1. Da Omero a Callimaco: motivi e forma del meraviglioso; 2. Da Callimaco all'ete' imperiale: la letteratura paradossografica," in *Paradoxographorum Graecorum Reliquiae*, Classici Greci e Latini, Sezione Testi e Commenti, (Milan: Istituto Editoriale Milano, 1965), and Christian Jacob, "The Greek Traveler's Areas of Knowledge: Myths and Other Discourses in Pausanias' *Description of Greece*," trans. Anne Mullen-Holl, *Yale French Studies*, 59 (1980), 65–85, and especially 66–7.

20 Fredric Jameson, "Magical Narratives: On the Dialectical Use of Genre Criticism," *The Political Unconscious* (Ithaca: Cornell University Press, 1981), p. 118.

21 Hayden White, *Metahistory* (Baltimore: Johns Hopkins University Press, 1973), p. 8.

22 *History of the French Revolution*, trans. George Cocks, ed. Gordon Wright (Chicago: University of Chicago Press, 1967), pp. 444–5.

23 Leo Spitzer, "A Central Theme and Its Structural Equivalent in *Fuenteovejuna*," *Hispanic Review*, 23 (1955), 274–92.

24 Martin Green, *Dreams of Adventure, Deeds of Empire* (New York: Basic Books, 1979), p. 314.

25 Cf. Jameson, "Romance and Reification: Plot Construction and Ideological Closure in Joseph Conrad," *The Political Unconscious*, pp. 231–2: "theatrical terms like 'scene,' 'spectacle,' and 'tableau,' which urge in the reader a theatre-goer's position with respect to the content of the narrative . . . are . . . abundant in Conrad, yet they are reappropriated by the perceptual vocation of his style, which undermines the unity of the theatrical metaphor just as surely as would the attention of a deaf or foreign schizophrenic visitor who had eyes only for the color combinations of this or that theatrical production. Conrad displaces the theatrical metaphor by transforming it into a matter of sense perception, into a virtually filmic experience." An example from *Lord Jim* is revealing: "There was, as I walked along, the clear sunshine, a brilliance too passionate to be consoling, the streets full of jumbled bits of color like a damaged kaleidoscope: yellow, green, blue, dazzling white, the brown nudity of an undraped shoulder, the bullock-cart with a red canopy, a company of native infantry in a drab body with dark heads marching in dusty laced boots, a native policeman in a sombre uniform of scanty cut and belted leather" (New York: Norton, 1968, p. 96).

Index